Queer Defamiliarisation

New Materialisms
Series editors: Iris van der Tuin and Rosi Braidotti

New Materialisms asks how materiality permits representation, actualises ethical subjectivities and innovates the political. The series will provide a discursive hub and an institutional home to this vibrant emerging field and open it up to a wider readership.

Editorial Advisory board
Marie-Luise Angerer, Karen Barad, Corinna Bath, Barbara Bolt, Felicity Colman, Manuel DeLanda, Richard Grusin, Vicki Kirby, Gregg Lambert, Nina Lykke, Brian Massumi, Henk Oosterling, Arun Saldanha

Books available
What if Culture was Nature all Along?
Edited by Vicki Kirby
Critical and Clinical Cartographies: Architecture, Robotics, Medicine, Philosophy
Edited by Andrej Radman and Heidi Sohn
Architectural Materialisms: Non-Human Creativity
Edited by Maria Voyatzaki
Placemaking: A New Materialist Theory of Pedagogy
Tara Page
Queer Defamiliarisation: Writing, Mattering, Making Strange
Helen Palmer
Biopolitics, Materiality and Meaning in Modern European Drama
Hedwig Fraunhofer

Books forthcoming
How Literature Comes to Matter: Post-Anthropocentric Approaches to Fiction
Edited by Sten Pultz Moslund, Marlene Karlsson Marcussen and Martin Karlsson Pedersen

Visit the series web page at: edinburghuniversitypress.com/series/nmat

Queer Defamiliarisation

Writing, Mattering, Making Strange

Helen Palmer

EDINBURGH
University Press

Edinburgh University Press is one of the leading university presses in the UK. We publish academic books and journals in our selected subject areas across the humanities and social sciences, combining cutting-edge scholarship with high editorial and production values to produce academic works of lasting importance. For more information visit our website: edinburghuniversitypress.com

© Helen Palmer, 2020

Edinburgh University Press Ltd
The Tun – Holyrood Road, 12(2f) Jackson's Entry, Edinburgh EH8 8PJ

Typeset in 11/13 Adobe Sabon by
IDSUK (DataConnection) Ltd

A CIP record for this book is available from the British Library

ISBN 978 1 4744 3414 0 (hardback)
ISBN 978 1 4744 3416 4 (webready PDF)
ISBN 978 1 4744 3417 1 (epub)

The right of Helen Palmer to be identified as the author of this work has been asserted in accordance with the Copyright, Designs and Patents Act 1988, and the Copyright and Related Rights Regulations 2003 (SI No. 2498).

Contents

Acknowledgements	viii
Introductions	1
Introduction 1: Defamiliarising	1
Introduction 2: Queering	13
Introduction 3: Mattering	21
Chapter summaries	32
1 Synvariance	35
Horizontal/vertical	36
By any other name a rose is a rose by any other name	39
Stasis/flow	44
Repetition/difference	45
Every term must be supplanted by another term	47
Variance/invariance	49
Zombie signs/metanoia	52
Axis/assemblage	55
Intra-acting/intra-secting	58
Boycunt/logic of the 'as'	62
2 Mythorefleshings	65
Personae: conceptual, narrative, collective?	69
Paradoxical relationalities: intimacy and estrangement	87
Gendered perception: queer defamiliarisation	88
Conclusion: syntaxa/parataxa	89
3 A Field of Heteronyms and Homonyms: New Materialism, Speculative Fabulation and Wor(l)ding	91
Prologue: THE FIELD	91
Fictocriticism; or, flowers at the lip of the world	92
Worlding from Heidegger to Haraway	94
Agential realism and the material-discursive	98
Speculative topoi: Afrofuturism as uchronia	100
Wor(l)dings: speculative fabulation, hyperstition, fictioning, myth-science	106

vi QUEER DEFAMILIARISATION

    Wor(l)dings: heteronymy, homonymy, contingency   108
    Epilogue: THE FIELD   114

4 Sensorium   115
    Deforming the senses   116
    Deforming dimensions   120
    Deforming perception   125

    Interstitium 1: The Surface, or Alice and the Hermunculus   128

        Deforming touches: queer haptics   139

    Interstitium 2: Speculative Taxonomies   143

        Sirens and Organs, or, If These Whorls Could Talk   155

Concluding comments   168

Epilogue   171
A Hymn to Sol, or, She Rides the Tram in Different Voices, or A Heliochronic Tram Journey on Blackpool Promenade at Sunset, or, Radio Blackpool   171
- o We Pray to Gaia and Sol as the Sun Touches the Sea
- o Enheduanna Bellicosely Stalks the Promenade
- o Ghosha Rides the Tram Chariot
- o Some Unhomeric Sea-based Epithets
- o Julia Balbila Does Latinate Sunsplicing
- o Hypatia gets an Ice Cream and Teaches Conic Sections
- o Li Qingzhao Gathers Plastic Sea Ornaments
- o Marjery Kempe Paces the Windwhipped Sand in Trainers
- o Saint Teresa of Ávila Counsels the Seabound
- o Isabella Whitney Is a Contestant for Blackpool in Bloom
- o Aphra Behn Blurs Lines under the Pier
- o Phyllis Wheatley Sings the Satsuma Blues
- o George Eliot Envisions Young Saint Teresa Chewing Jelly Strawberries in Abingdon Street Market
- o Emily Dickinson Diffracts the Light and Blackens the Heart
- o Virginia Woolf Remembers Dropping a Mivvi on the Pavement
- o Gertrude Stein Does Yoga on the Pier next to Trev and Ann
- o H.D. Splices Sea and Sun
- o Mina Loy Worships Blackpool Tower

CONTENTS

o One or Several Alices Answer Back
o Charlize Kinbote Discovers New Fragment by
   Poet Joan Shade
o June Jordan Builds a Bridge Between Towers
o Gloria Anzaldúa Splices Language
o Audre Lorde Encourages A Humbled Mouthpiece
o Hélène Cixous, Luce Irigaray and Julia Kristeva
   Triangulate Desire and Conjugate Strangeness with
   Kathy Acker, and They All Get Topological Tattoos
o Eimear McBride Voices Those Not Given Voices Nat Raha
   Honours Kettling Hollie McNish Rides The Pepsi Max Big One
   Rupi Kaur Considers Openness Yrsa Daley-Ward Articulates
   Love Travis Alabanza Throws Colour Verity Spott Spots David
   Cameron on Easyjet Voiced Detritus Bloom (A Rose) Speaks
   Calyx and Corolla (App Design Creative Agency) Give Their
   Pitch to Some Students Circe Speaks to Afrekete from the
   Top of the Tower (Some Not-At All Targeted Facebook Ads)
   Penelope / A Fictional Character / Your Own Shorn
   Sharpenings / A Throb of Queer Desire

Bibliography   188
Index   210

Acknowledgements

I would like to thank Carol Macdonald and Kirsty Woods at Edinburgh University Press for their patience, encouragement and support while I completed this manuscript. Thanks to Rosi Braidotti and Iris van der Tuin, for their inspiration as feminist thinkers and also for including me in this series. I thank Iris along with Felicity Colman for their running of the COST Action IS1307 New Materialism: Networking European Scholarship on 'How Matter Comes to Matter', which I joined in 2015 and which opened up multiple new worlds. Thanks to Anna Hickey-Moody for feminist conversations and also for supporting a visiting scholarship position at the Department of Gender and Cultural Studies at the University of Sydney in 2017.

At Kingston University I was supported by the Race/Gender Matters research cluster, which has created space for discussions around gender, race, class, language and matter. Within Race/Gender Matters I am lucky to have the friendship and support of some amazing colleagues: thank you Éadaoin Agnew, Matthew Birchwood, Fred Botting, Martin Dines, Jane Jordan, Patricia Phillippy and Selene Scarsi. For multifarious inspiration and friendship during this project particular thanks also to Felicity Colman, Vikki Chalklin, Tina Chanter, Moira Gatens and Isabella van Elferen. Special thanks to Charlie Blake, toposophical comrade, for making it weird, always.

Thanks to the artists who inspired me into some of this thinking who are discussed in this book, and to the London queer scene, for being there and being strong, and supporting new performers with a genuine and heartfelt sense of community. May the Royal Vauxhall Tavern, the Glory and Wotever World flourish forever. This book is dedicated to my London queer family who show me time and time again that Sara Ahmed is right: queer family gatherings *do* make everything dance with renewed life.

Part of Chapter 2 appears as the following article: H. Palmer (2016), 'Rewritings/Refoldings/Refleshings: Fictive Publics and the Material Gesture of Defamiliarization', *Continuum*, 30 (5): 507–17. DOI: 10.1080/10304312.2016.1210724

Part of the Interstitium 1 in Chapter 4 appears as 'Beyond Surface Articulation: Alice and the Hermunculus', in M. Bolhmann and A. Hickey-Moody (eds) (2019), *Deleuze and Children*, Edinburgh: Edinburgh University Press, pp. 64–86.

Interstitium 2 in Chapter 4 is forthcoming in a Special Issue of *Philosophy Today* on New Materialist Concepts, ed. I. van der Tuin and Adam Nocek.

An excerpt from the Epilogue appears as 'Gertrude Stein Does Proteus at Sunset on Blackpool Promenade', *Minnesota Review*, 88, Special Focus: New Materialist Genealogies, p. 127.

Introductions

This book requires not one but three introductions. Defamiliarising, queering and mattering: these three verbs and the conceptual apparatus within and without each of them have not been explicitly interwoven before, but here I trace some of their various interweavings through a demonstration of some of the work they can do. I employ a material miscellany across the three introductions to help me demonstrate this: *substances*: margarine, gemstones, saliva; *gestures*: shifting, turning, transposing; *aspects of language*: sound, shape, sensory imprint; *concepts*: defamiliarisation, queer, matter.

Introduction 1: Defamiliarising

> The fragmentariness of life makes coherence suspect but to babble is a different kind of treachery.
> (Winterson 1997: 24)

> How can writing matter?
> (Acker 1997: 23)

Words matter. Complexly and wonderfully, language in its material strangeness has the power to advance feminist, queer and intersectional politics. This power exists because the operations we perform on language that manifest its materiality share their dynamic potential with movements of emancipatory politics. Such a unification of formal and material processes is at the heart of the argument underpinning this book, which charts three entangled processes. The first perspective outlined below is *defamiliarisation*: a making-strange; a shift in perception that I trace, back and forward, from its origin in Russian formalist thought into a contemporary theoretical understanding. The second perspective is *materialism* in multiple senses, but focused mainly on the realms of the material-discursive and the material-semiotic as discussed in new materialism: that is, how language is matter; how language matters. The third perspective informing and inspiring this book is *queer*, as the deliberate *un*straightening and *de*familiarisarion of bodies, desires and orientations. My aim is to demonstrate in this book that defamiliarisation can be queering can be mattering. I use that grammatical formulation deliberately: the threefold analogical function (A can be B can be C) does exist in colloquial speech, but perhaps takes us by surprise in academic writing. The syntactical repetition beyond the regular analogy of two (A can be B) takes us out of our automatic perception of 'transparent' words and reminds us of their thickness; their realness; their materiality. The power held in that moment of perceptual awakening through 'making language strange' is precisely what is investigated in this book. I sketch out these three perspectives and their entanglements below.

Perception and Sensation

I will begin with margarine. In her essay 'Uses of the Erotic: The Erotic as Power' Audre Lorde narrates a moment of sheer, queer, slippery and giddily epiphanic joy produced through the engagement with (and defamiliarisation of) a prosaic kitchen ingredient.

> During World War II, we bought sealed plastic packets of white, uncolored margarine, with a tiny, intense pellet of yellow coloring perched like a topaz just inside the clear skin of the bag. We would leave the margarine out for a while to soften, and then we would pinch the little pellet to break it inside the bag, releasing the rich yellowness into the soft pale mass of margarine. Then taking it carefully between our fingers, we would knead it gently back and forth, over and over, until the color had spread throughout the whole pound bag of margarine, thoroughly coloring it.
>
> I find the erotic such a kernel within myself. When released from its intense and constrained pellet, it flows through and colors my life with a kind of energy that heightens and sensitizes and strengthens all my experience. (Lorde 1984: 57)

This passage describes in intimate detail the way that the cheap and commonplace margarine is not only perceived but created anew, through a synthetic mixing and tinting process generated by haptic manipulation and chemical blending. The margarine is a *material* rendering of Lorde's *formal* analysis of the erotic as a mode; one might almost say as a device. To pay attention to the erotic for Lorde is a feminist stance; a shift in perception engendered through the heightening of sensation. 'For the erotic is not a question only of what we do; it is a question of how acutely and fully we can feel in the doing' (Lorde 1984: 54). It is feeling itself that operates as a device here, and as a device, it is feeling that empowers. As I will outline below, to defamiliarise is to perceive anew. Lorde's example here is one way that we might perceive defamiliarisation itself anew: in a queer, feminist, materialist *and* formalist sense.

> To re-encounter objects as strange things is hence not to lose sight of their history but to refuse to make them history by losing sight. Such wonder directed at the objects that we face, as well as those that are behind us, does not involve bracketing out the familiar but rather allows the familiar to dance again with life. (Ahmed 2006: 164)

Sara Ahmed's words above from *Queer Phenomenology* use the terms 'strange' and 'familiar' to think through different ways that we encounter subjects/objects; that we become close to and touch subjects/objects. The 'making-strange' that constitutes defamiliarisation is queered in Ahmed's work. In the process of queering, as in the process of defamiliarising, subjects, objects, things and structures are liberated from the strictures of their preconceived referents and permitted multiple potential reorientations. Queering is defamiliarising. It is not, however, my intention to valourise queer as more important than other categories of identity formation; neither is it my intention to further valorise those areas of avant-garde artistic experimentation which appear only created by and for those with multiple privileges: those of ability, economics, gender or race. Instead this book discusses writers such as Travis Alabanza, Quinn Eades, Nat Raha, Sofia Samatar, the Black Quantum Futurism Collective and many others, addressing the lacuna of representation and expression within avant-garde writing and performance for those who exist outside the white European male hegemony, through the critical exploration and creative expression of a 'making-strange'.

The genesis of defamiliarisation's revolutionary gesture in early twentieth-century Russia begins with a misspelling and ends with a supposed ideological retraction. Coined by Russian formalist Viktor Shklovsky in his infamous 1917 formalist manifesto 'Art as Technique' (or 'Art as Device', depending on the translation), the word *ostranenie* [остранение] was later quoted by Shklovsky as being spelt wrong. From *strannye* [странный] meaning 'strange' and therefore requiring a double *nn*, the word *ostranenie* was nevertheless repeated and disseminated throughout the world without the double *nn* which would link it to its root word, causing the term with its one amputated 'n' to 'roam the world like a dog with an ear cut off' (Shklovsky 1983: 73 in Shklovsky 2017: 56). This was later corrected by Shklovsky, but the original spelling persists, which seems fitting for a term which is by its very nature a turn away from the norm; a deliberate or necessary error.

Alternative English translations or synonyms of the term – 'estrangement' (with the added complications of its Marxist and Brechtian interpretations), 'making-strange' and even Benjamin Sher's neologistic 'enstrangement' – variously illuminate the dynamic gesture of the process, as an abstraction or moving-away from the correct path. Inspired by the explosion of the rules of representation that constituted the early Russian avant-garde, defamiliarisation is all about doing it wrong, on purpose. Cinematically, the gesture of *ostranenie* has been linked to Dzviga Vertov's 'Kino-Eye' (кино глаз) filming technique of the 1920s, one of which presents the scene of a Moscow street with the camera deliberately rotated sideways. (Latifić 2018). Interestingly, Shklovsky describes this shifting manoeuvre thus:

> In order to transform an object into a fact of art, it is necessary to detach it from the domain of life, to wrest it out from the web of familiar associations, to turn over the object as one would turn over a log in the fire. (Shklovsky 1990: 61)

The point of rotating, inverting or shifting the mode of perception causes the observer to see the object as if for the first time. Shklovsky himself is a figure known for sensational proclamations and also deviations, retractions and theoretical about-turns. Shklovsky's other famous gesture of the 'knight's move' describes an L-shaped manoeuvre, just as the knight moves on the chessboard, unable to openly move in one direction due to enforced ideological constraints. Shklovsky's book *Knight's Move* (1923) is titled thus because an L-shaped move is for him emblematic of the limited and contorted way he was forced to express himself in the wake of the Revolution. For Shklovsky, the knight moves in such a way because 'the knight is not free – it moves in an L-shaped manner because it is forbidden to take the straight road' (Shklovsky 1923: 3).

Shklovsky's perception of the difference between seeing and recognition is discussed in his formalist manifesto 'искусство как прием' (1917) ['Art as Technique' or 'Art as Device']. This begins with his belief that 'the artistic quality of something, its relationship to poetry, is a result of our mode of perception' (Shklovsky 1925: 2). Poetic thinking is the opposite of abstraction for Shklovsky: is embodied and laborious. As perception becomes habitual, it also becomes automatic and unconscious: it is mere 'recognition' as opposed to 'seeing'. Shklovsky describes this process as both abstract and algebraic.

> By means of this algebraic method of thinking, objects are grasped spatially, in the blink of an eye. We do not see them, we merely recognize them by their primary characteristics. The object passes before us, as if it were prepackaged. We

know that it exists because of its position in space, but we see only its surface. Gradually, under the influence of this generalizing perception, the object fades away. (Shklovsky 1925: 5)

This process is accompanied by an economy of mental effort. According to Shklovsky, it is the function of art to return sensation to perception: 'to make a stone feel stony' (чтобы делать камень каменным). One of the most interesting aspects of Russian formalism is the environment in which this crystallisation of strangeness was born; among the most radical avant-garde linguistic innovations of Russian futurism: *zaum* or 'transrational' language. I have discussed this in relation to Deleuze's thought elsewhere (Palmer 2014), and I discuss this in relation to the thought of another influential Russian futurist, formalist and structuralist, Roman Jakobson, in Chapter 1. Jakobson began his career as a radical linguistic innovator who assigned himself the pseudonym 'Aljgarov' in his younger years (Jakobson 1997: 22), and ended it as a technical structuralist linguist, and the co-constituence of the creative with the critical is precisely what links the three areas I am investigating in this book. Flawed and yet fundamental to modernist thought, defamiliarisation has become a philosophical statement in its own right as the 'formalisation' of linguistic deviance. Shklovsky's work has, however, been subjected to feminist critique in the past, among other angles. In relation to Shklovsky's 'to make a stone stony' remark, Eric Naiman asked in 1998 whether art exists 'to make a wife wifey', presenting Shklovsky's defamiliarising technique as a 'patriarchal device' (Naiman 1998: 345). Naiman here exposes streaks of misogyny in 'Art as Device', supposing that critics under the influence of this seminal text may have 'failed to recognize that the essence of the knight's move may be the capture of the queen'. Notwithstanding the self-evident masculinist conventions of much of early twentieth-century Russian thought, this book asks how might we move beyond this critique and map the affirmative gestures of new materialist thought and queer theory onto to the gesture of defamiliarisation, up to and including the pitfalls and paradoxes of normativity and historicisation.

Rosi Braidotti writes about defamiliarisation as a political strategy in her book on the posthuman. She says:

The post-anthropocentric shift away from the hierarchical relations that had privileged 'Man' requires a form of estrangement and a radical repositioning on the part of the subject. The best method to accomplish this is through the strategy of defamiliarization or critical distance from the dominant vision of the subject. (Braidotti 2013a: 88)

Braidotti's definition of defamiliarisation as 'a critical distance from the dominant vision of the subject' is useful here. The dominant vision of the subject, the *Anthropos* as Braidotti discusses using the figure of the Vitruvian man drawn by Leonardo da Vinci denoting Man as 'the measure of all things' (Braidotti 2013a: 13). Critical and creative defamiliarisation, then, can go beyond the linguistic and the aesthetic to critique the dominant mode of perception of the human subject, the *Anthropos*, and gesture towards what Rosi Braidotti calls *zoe*-inspired critical vitalism. In her materialist theory of the posthuman, Braidotti points out that vitalism is normally associated with the *Anthropos*, but she connects it to *zoe*, which she describes as 'the non-human, vital force of Life' (Braidotti 2013b: 60). The critical and creative *defamiliarisation* of this echoes Braidotti's earlier call in *Metamorphoses: A Materialist Theory of Becoming* (2002), for a creative critique of what Derrida called phallogocentrism (Derrida 1969), or phallocentrism and logocentrism combined, or indeed the ways in which logos (reason or language) is intimately tied up with the patriarchy. As Braidotti says, 'Feminism shares with poststructuralist philosophy not only the sense of a crisis of the Logos, but also need for renewed conceptual creativity and for politically informed cartographies of the present' (Braidotti 2002: 11).

Twenty-first-century interest in Shklovskian formalism developed by the Retroformalism research group is already concerned with the reinterpretation of 'error' in Shklovsky's famous text 'Monument to a Scientific Error' (1930) in which he retracts his earlier formalist beliefs, not as a sincere recantation but rather as a 'methodological axiom' (www.retroformalism.net). I believe that this position can be developed further in the manoeuvre of queering formalism, which rejects the straightforward literary-historical reading of both formalism and queer theory, instead looking ahead to a transversal, trans-historical, trans-disciplinary future plural of theory and creation, demonstrating that the affirmation of 'defamiliarised' or 'estranged' processes and modes of expression creates the necessary space for creative reconfigurations of the fundamental ways that we categorise our existence. Perception, as writes Vicki Kirby in *Quantum Anthropologies*, is an organ itself: an organ of conception and reconception. 'It is a desiring organ that seizes upon its own alienness, and in the wonder of the encounter, is reconceived' (Kirby 2011: 120). To seize upon one's alienness: a moment of defamiliarisation. It is precisely this process of defamiliarisation that is necessary to awaken us from automatic habits in our perception, creation, destruction and infinite reimagination of the categories of identity formation. It is *sensation* that is required for us to feel both ourselves and beyond ourselves. This is why I dedicate an entire chapter, Chapter 4, to the senses.

Estrangement and Aesthesis

While the criticisms of Russian formalism historically discern a wide chasm between Shklovskian 'enstrangement' and Bertolt Brecht's 'estrangement' effect, the conceptual link between these permutations of estrangement places them much closer together than they are generally conceived. The 'estrangement' or *Verfremdung* discussed and popularised by Brecht provides a link between Shklovskian estrangement or *ostranenie* and Marxist alienation or *Entfremdung*. While 'estrangement' is used by some translators for both Skhlovsky and Brecht, it is often described as an estrangement 'device' in Shklovsky and an estrangement 'effect' in Brecht. This of course highlights the agential and temporal opposition: a device is an active tool that seeks to estrange whereas an effect is something which happens *to* something or someone; it is passive. Despite these differences, it is clear that both Shklovsky and Brecht aim to problematise the process of perception and cognition in order to force the perceiver into new experiences. They may nevertheless differ in terms of the type of perception and the degree to which sensory experience figures in the process. Brecht's estrangement effect has also often been translated as an alienation effect, which aligns it much more closely with Karl Marx. Marx derives his theory of alienation from Ludwig Feuerbach, who in his *Essence of Christianity* (1841) discusses the alienation of men from God. Marx 'materialises' or renders-material this religious theory of alienation found within German Idealism, stating that the workers in a capitalist system are alienated from both themselves and from the means of production which is owned by the bourgeoisie (see Marx's *Economic and Philosophic Manuscripts of 1844*, 1932).

How then can we conceive of estrangement both as the negative alienation or detachment narrated by Marx *and* as a deliberate and affirmative movement of defiance? One moment in which this very co-constitutive double manoeuvre is seized upon is accelerationism. Marxist alienation finds a contemporary traction, augmentation and indeed acceleration in the accelerationist movement, through the celebration of technology in the manner of the Italian futurists' celebration of the machine, though mainly (with the exception of one or two) with opposite political orientations and goals. Alienation figures prominently in one feminist offshoot of accelerationism: the Xenofeminist (XF) Manifesto, titled 'A Politics for Alienation' (Cuboniks 2018). As one member of the Laboria Cuboniks collective, Diann Bauer, explains, 'When XF speaks it is not something one feels as an individual. It is not the estrangement of an individual subject from their community or society. It is instead the estrangement between our sapience and our sentience. Alienation is the capacity for abstraction that we have developed as a species' (Bauer 2019: 109). The separation between reason and feeling is what Bauer gestures towards in the description of estrangement between sapience and sentience. It is here that the different types of estrangement, from Shklovsky to Brecht, can perhaps be read through one another, or read diffractively perhaps (see van der Tuin 2014a, 2014b). Paradoxically it is the *connection* of reason and feeling that is brought about by the affirmation of estrangement. This leads us strangely back to Feuerbach, via George Eliot, as I will discuss below.

It is firstly worth taking a brief journey to Moscow, 1935, and retracing the steps of Brecht, famous for what Fredric Jameson describes as the 'V-effect' (Jameson 1998: 39), *Verfremdungseffekt*, alienation effect or estrangement effect. It is curious to note that Brecht's visit to Moscow in 1935 and his discovery of Shklovskian estrangement coincided with his witnessing of Beijing opera artist Mei Lanfang's performance. Mei was known for performing female lead roles or *dan* as they were known. While the practice of men performing *dan* was due to the commonly held belief at the time in China that women performing on-stage was immoral, it is nevertheless significant to note here that this influential theoretical phenomenon was in fact directly inspired and derived from a non-white non-Western cross-dressing performer. It is even more curious to note that Brecht's description of the defamiliarising performer as *beside himself* (Brecht and Bentley 1961: 132). 'Beside' is itself a curious preposition which again pre-empts some queer theorising on proximity, more of which will be discussed in Chapter 2. To be *beside oneself* conjures the sense of a geometrical impossibility, but not in the realm of the topological imagination. This will be discussed further in Chapter 4.

Fredric Jameson draws on both similarities and differences between Brechtian V-effect and Shklovskian defamiliarisaion. While both estrangements make things look strange in order to jerk us out of perceptual numbness or torpor, Jameson adds two further effects to Brecht's version. Firstly, the turning-off of empathetic reactions, and secondly, an unveiling wherein that which was presented as changeless and eternal is in fact revealed as historical and political (Jameson 1998: 40). The links between Brecht and Skhlovsky are deeper and more prolific than is generally accepted within the history of modern thought. There are links within German Romanticism as well as German Idealism. Indeed, as Douglas Robinson notes in his historical study of defamiliarisation, *Estrangement and the Somatics of Literature: Tolstoy, Shklovsky, Brecht* (2008), in 1966, decades later than the publication of his formalist manifesto and his subsequent enforced public retraction, Shklovsky actually acknowledges that the concept of *ostranenie* was derived from Romantic art, specifically Novalis. In his *Fragments* Novalis talks about making things pleasingly 'strange' and 'alien' and at the same time familiar and attractive. Robinson points out that Novalis' original term is *brefremden*, which is the verb that Brecht uses. While the combination of political twists and turns causing mistrust and downright interdiction of *ostranenie* as a term caused the proliferation of terms between Russian, German and English (defamiliarisation effect, estrangement effect and alienation effect are all used), Robinson nevertheless points out that this concept is common not only to Novalis but also to other thinkers in German and English Romanticism as well as German Idealism, namely Georg Wilhelm Friedrich Hegel's dialectical treatment of Jean-Jacques Rousseau's concept of alienation and Friedrich Schlegel's Romantic irony. 'The basic idea is that conventionalization is psychologically alienating, anesthetizing, and that the reader therefore stands in need of some sort of aesthetic shock to break him or her out of the anaesthesis (Robinson 2008: 80). It is important to note here that it is *anaesthesis* that is the automatised state, an absence of physical sensation. Hence the need for a reawakening, reorientation and reprioritisation of the senses. To be anaesthetised means to be estranged from sensory perception; the movement of 'estrangement' in fact restores sensory perception. *Ostranenie* is therefore a strange paradoxical process that requires both proximity and distance, that restores sensations to things through a distancing that is also a re-proximation, an approximation, a touching. Therefore it is both symptom and cure.

One of the aspects of the Brechtian estrangement with which my own version of queer defamiliarisation takes issue is the rejection of empathy or sympathy. I would argue that the foregrounding of a sensory, embodied reaction can in fact achieve the political reorientation, rerouting and rethinking that Brechtian estrangement ultimately aims to do, but precisely *with* an enfleshed and empathetic response. It is here that George Eliot, whose thinkings around sensibility through readings of Feuerbach, may help to unite the sensory with political commitment, through Eliot's and Feuerbach's shared connection between sympathy for fellow humans with the human sensorium (see Griffin 2017 for a comparative discussion of these thinkers and their relationship to collective feeling, sympathy and the senses). When we connect up reason and feeling we are able to feel as our fellow humans, we are able to feel sympathy. Sympathy is different to empathy: instead of feeling *as*, we are feeling *with* or *for* others. In her article in *Posthuman Ecologies* Elizabeth de Freitas connects sympathy with what Haraway calls 'sympoiesis' in *Staying with the Trouble* (Haraway 2016) in a process of what she describes as 'a process of *becoming other that does not erase the other*' (de Freitas 2019: 89). Sympoeisis for Haraway is a word for 'worlding-with, in company' (Haraway 2016: 58). It is relational and symbiotic, and connected to a particular type of embodied perception.

Two Spinozist feminist philosophers have considered the work of Victorian writer and philosophy George Eliot in the connections between reason and feeling. Both Moira Gatens and Rosi Braidotti highlight the importance of Eliot's Spinozism and her innovative connectivity between philosophy and literature: traditionally the realms of *reason* and *feeling* respectively (though this is of course an old-fashioned division). Braidotti is aware of the importance of Eliot's work in precisely the transversality of disciplines, particularly in the case of literature and philosophy. Along with Gatens, Braidotti also points out that Eliot was the first English translator of Spinoza's *Ethics*, asserting that she sees a 'vitalist materialism' everywhere in Eliot's work (Braidotti 2013: 55).

Moira Gatens believes that it is in Eliot's fiction where we find her philosophy, indeed that her novels 'should be understood as attempts to practice philosophy in an alternative key' (Gatens 2009: 74). Eliot's philosophical writing praxis as outlined by Gatens is significant it its aim, which Gatens describes as 'an interventionist practice that aim[s] to transform the ethical frame of human action through a forceful revisioning of reality' (Gatens 2013: 13). This makes absolute sense: in her Spinozist thinking, Eliot dismantles the division between not just reason and feeling but the other articulations and iterations of such a dualism: philosophy and literature, critical and creative, body and mind. Both Braidotti and Gatens read Eliot as a proto-transversal thinker: she crosses disciplines and produces philosophy through and within her realist fiction. One of the ways in which this book materialises its own conceptual trajactories is that it defamiliarises itself, shapes emerge and deform through the chapters through my own writing practice.

In thinking about Eliot and the connection between reason and feeling, Gatens draws on the two thinkers that Eliot herself read and translated: Ludwig Feuerbach and Benedict Spinoza. Religious experience in both thinkers necessitates that we think with others. As Gatens writes:

> Religious experience, Feuerbach argues, arises from our apprehension of ourselves as particulars belonging to a natural kind. In short, religion arises from the individual's awareness of his participation in a shared species [*Gattungswesen*]. In common with Spinoza's '*we think*' (*E*, II, Axiom 2), and in contradistinction to Descartes's solipsistic *I* think, Feuerbach asserts: *Man* thinks – that is, he converses with himself (EC, p. 2). Self-consciousness arises from an awareness of the nature that we share with others. (Gatens 2009: 77)

Gatens connects Feuerbach with Spinoza through the use of the imagination in order to produce sympathy through feeling with others. As she asserts, 'Spinoza's theory of the imitation of the affects resonates with Feuerbach's account of the distinctively human disposition to feel-with – an innate contagiousness of the emotions' (Gatens 2009: 79). Just as the erotic is a mode for Lorde, the imagination is a mode for these thinkers that Gatens draws together through the writing of Eliot. I believe both modes are productive for future work and aim to embody both in my own writing.

The way that Gatens perceives Eliot's own conception of art is important: 'Art, for Eliot, always involves revelation and vision: seeing anew what was taken to be ordinary, in order to make a new connection, or link the familiar past with the unknown future. Art is not discovered or found but vividly imagined, realised, materialised, through passion, memory and insight' (Gatens 2013: 11). This description is striking in its similarity to the descriptions of defamiliarisation that we have already discussed; the very word 'anew' appears again alongside the concept of a new mode of perception through art, and it will appear again anew throughout this book. An absence of feeling renders us unconscious; this is precisely what happens when we are unconsciously biased. Anaesthetic renders us unconscious so that horrific and gruesome things can be done to our bodies. This is why the past participle *woke* has become popularised as a term denoting awareness of social injustice and privilege. To stay woke means to actively combat unconscious bias. Woke (adjective; 'US informal'): 'Alert to injustice in society, especially racism' (*OED*). Most dictionaries cite the repeated lines 'I stay woke' in Erykah Badu's song 'Master Teacher' as a potential origin of the term, and explains how it became entwined with the Black Lives Matter movement after the shooting of Michael Brown in Ferguson, Missouri in 2014. The lines from Barry Beckham's play about Marcus Garvey, *Garvey Lives*, show an earlier usage of the term: 'I been sleeping all my life. And now that Mr Garvey done woke me up, I'm gon stay woke' (Beckham 1972).

The connection of 'reason' with 'feeling' within strategies of Russian formalist defamiliarisation extends beyond Viktor Shklovsky. It can also be perceived in Russian formalist and structuralist Roman Jakobson. I have already mentioned that Jakobson was a linguistic innovator as well as a formalist. He was simultaneously concerned with linguistic variance and linguistic invariants, invention and formalisation, movement and stasis. The clearest concretisation of this simultaneity in his linguistic investigations can be seen in his conflation of synchronic and diachronic linguistic perspectives. This is his move away from the synchronic structuralism of Ferdinand de Saussure: Jakobson injects dynamism into this system. Jakobson states that the primary goal of his career had been to seek for invariants *in the midst of variation*:

> Since my earliest report of 1927 to the newborn Prague Linguistic Circle I have pleaded for the removal of the alleged antinomy synchrony/diachrony and have propounded instead the idea of permanently dynamic synchrony, at the same time underscoring the presence of static invariants in the diachronic cut of language. (Jakobson 1985: 374)

I will discuss the particular combination of linguistic reason and poetic sensibility that makes up Jakobson's perspective in more detail in Chapter 1. For the current discussion, the spatiotemporal model of the synchrony/diachrony dualism which Jakobson effectively dismantles (or at least demonstrates mutual reciprocity) in the above quotation is useful here. It is useful because it shows that the reciprocity of movement and stasis – of the affordances of the horizontal and vertical cuts of linguistic study – to demonstrate the fact that the paradoxical structure of 'continuous variation' found in poststructuralist thinkers such as Gilles Deleuze and Félix Guattari is actually present within formalist thought even at the time of its origin. For Deleuze and Guattari's take on continuous variation, see *A Thousand Plateaus* (1980), for example, in terms of

> a fundamental heterogeneity: felt or patchwork rather than weaving, rhythmic values rather than harmony/melody, Riemannian space rather than Euclidean space – a continuous variation that exceeds any distribution of constants and variables, the freeing of a line that does not pass between two points, the formation of a plane that does not proceed by parallel and perpendicular lines. (Deleuze and Guattari 2004b: 539)

This goes some of the way towards explaining the following situation: not just in radical reworkings of Russian formalism but even in the minds of the original formalists, to a certain degree a preoccupation with form presupposes a creative rejection of it. This shows us how formalism is anything but static and very much 'open' for queering.

Introduction 2: Queering

> The production of 'queer' is violent, material, and excessive to the management of control and sociability . . . Queer might be felt as utopian or dystopian, quotidian, banal, speculative, public, private; yet, in each of its material operations on and through bodies, it carves out our relations temporally and spatially and proliferates connections through language.
>
> (Keeling 2019: 18)

Queer: a noun, a verb and an adjective. To queer is to estrange, and this is a dynamic, multivalent and material process. Contemporary queer theories have harnessed the creative potential of poststructuralist linguistic indeterminacy in order to celebrate and affirm infinite dimensions of sexuality and gender, creating space for all human beings to express themselves without the classification or judgement of prescriptive terminologies. Ineluctably linguistic at its source just like defamiliarisation, the liberating force of queer theory is derived from the removal of terminological boundaries. As Kara Keeling's description above outlines, queer is something that not only just relates to bodies and language but is produced by and through bodies and language.

What, then, does it mean to queer something? Perhaps to queer something means to estrange it. This links us lexically to estrangement as defamiliarisation, but perhaps there is more that we can discern intuitively about how these concepts might be entangled. When those existing outside the gender norm speak there is a palpable sense of terminological restlessness, an eternal rewriting, refolding and refleshing of the self that has no teleological goal. 'To be trans, black, and femme is to be a constant obstacle course // It is to be in continuous movement dictated from the track', writes performance artist and writer Travis Alabanza. Queer pop artist Ezra Furman writes in his biography of Lou Reed: 'I propose that for folks like me and Lou [Reed], the real meaning of queerness is defined by continual transformation . . .' (Furman 2018: 30). Furman's book is of course named after perhaps Reed's most famous album *Transformer*. What is useful and important for us here are the descriptions here of *continuous movement* and *continual transformation*, and will be returned to in the following chapters in a number of ways. The continuity of transformation (along with continual *deformation*, the state under which topological shapes retain their properties) is itself a paradoxical structure not unlike Deleuzo-Guattarian continuous variation. This, alongside the various historical interdependences of stasis and change, will be discussed in more detail in Chapter 1.

The multifarious and rapidly evolving disciplines of queer theory and gender studies seek to affirm the 'non-normative' in such a way that transcends unhelpful binaries and permits infinite variations and permutations of existence and experience, maintaining a necessarily paradoxical relationship between the resistance to and desire for categorisation. Radically new modes of perception are required to allow for these shifts in the thinking of one of the most fundamental divisions between human beings. As well as linguistic subjects and/or objects of defamiliarisation, however, we may also see bodies and matter. As thinking beings and bodies, how might we transcend the modes of perception available to us so that we become the subjects rather than the objects of defamiliarisation, moving from the passive 'recognition' of categorisation to the more active 'seeing'? Sara Ahmed talks about the political action of 'becoming conscious' of one's own position, one's implication in terms of gender and race:

> How can one be disturbed by one's own arrival? The familiar is that which receives to those who inhabit it. To become estranged from the familiar is thus to have it revealed to you. The familiar is disclosed in the revelation of your estrangement. (Ahmed 2010: 86)

Describing a scene in Andrea Levy's 1999 novel *Fruit of the Lemon*, this epiphanic moment takes place when Faith Jackson, a black British girl whose parents have migrated to England from Jamaica, realises her (dis)placement and her own version of 'defamiliarisation'. Faith witnesses a black woman being physically and violently attacked in London, and experiences a shift in perception in which she realises that unlike her friends, the woman 'was black like me' (Levy 1999: 156). As Ahmed states, 'The point of political identification rests on this recognition of another's hurt' (Ahmed 2010: 85). Faith is seized with a new sense of belonging, elsewhere and otherwise, and simultaneously a sense of estrangement from her peers. Though it is shocking and challenging, she nevertheless perceives herself anew.

Turning swiftly to Shklovsky's 1917 essay 'Art as Device', then, a vastly different yet analogous shift in perception is narrated:

> And so, in order to return sensation to our limbs, in order to make us feel objects, to make a stone feel stony, man has been given the tool of art. The purpose of art, then, is to lead us to a knowledge of a thing through the organ of sight instead of recognition. By 'enstranging' objects and complicating form, the device of art makes perception long and 'laborious'. (Shklovsky 1998 [1925]: 6; note that the neologism 'enstranging' is particular to Benjamin Sher's translation)

Shklovsky's use of 'laborious' is a positive one; he opposes a passive, non-differentiating 'recognition' to the more active 'seeing'. Recognition accepts without question preconceived categories of being, whereas seeing requires singular perception and therefore more labour. Defamiliarisation allows each individual subject or object to be experienced anew. How, then, do these two moments intersect or indeed intra-act? Ahmed's statement, written in London in 2010, and Shklovsky's statement, written in St Petersburg around 1917, do not appear to share much on the surface. Shklovskian formalism is generally viewed (and criticised) as a deliberate purification or distillation of linguistic and literary analysis, eliminating socio-economic concerns in favour of 'empty' internal structures. Ahmed's narrated moment above is a radically different, consciously politicised realisation, a manifestation of identity and a realisation or coming-into-being of a subject's race, class and gender. And yet there are important congruences. Shklovsky's theory anticipates phenomenological bracketing; Ahmed's work reads phenomenology retroactively (see particularly Ahmed 2006). These aspects are discussed further in Chapter 4. Both moments require and focus upon a shift in perception, and both thinkers are aware of the primacy of the shift itself. Artistic experimentation can be sourced within both revolutionary trajectories. Defamiliarisation is engendered within the aesthetic, and queer expression relies upon the aesthetic for its positive, playful and progressive movements. As a strategy, defamiliarisation estranges form, but requires it to do so. Defamiliarisation has been formalised as a methodological tool, but as a tool it leads to infinite variance. It is a lens or filter and works like a verb in the same way that queer does. When you queer something you defamiliarise it. This book is concerned with the ways that defamiliarisation can be taken up and used in multiple transdisciplinary ways: in a political sense, in a philosophical sense, in a linguistic sense, in an aesthetic sense, but really all of these senses at the same time.

How specifically do queering and defamiliarising operate analogically? Let us think of a word drawn from contemporary queer theory which narrates or accounts for the 'queer' version of the linguistic process of defamiliarisation. One word we could provisionally use is drawn from Sara Ahmed's important book *Queer Phenomenology*: she talks about disorientation. Agency is important when thinking about the disorientation of bodies, just as it is when talking about the defamiliarisation of language. Disorientation might be something imposed on us, something which we do not want to be subjected to and yet something which others presuppose of us. But it might also be something that we actively seek and promote, reordering the elements of existing structures and deliberately reconfiguring perceptions. Ahmed talks in the conclusion to *Queer Phenomenology* about a 'disorientation device' as way of experiencing the pleasure of deviation. To me this seems like the deliberate human enactment of defamiliarisation. The example she gives is of using the theme of the family within queer gatherings.

> For some queers, for instance, the very act of describing queer gatherings as family gatherings is to have joy in the uncanny effect of a familiar form becoming strange. The point of following is not to pledge allegiance to the familiar, but to make that 'familiar' strange, or even to allow that which has been overlooked – which has been treated as furniture – to dance with renewed life. (Ahmed 2006: 177)

The old forms are therefore not completely denatured, but rather the perception of them is shifted; the forms themselves are revitalised. As a device and similarly as a function, then, the adjectival 'queer' works. Mel Y. Chen has picked up on this more recently in *Animacies*, discussing queer as a function in a way that works analogously to Ahmed's description of the queer disorientation device: 'In linguistic terms, we might say that adjectival *queer*'s function is to modify an attached (implicit or explicit) noun concept . . . Adjectival *queer* therefore acts to shift meaning to the side of a normative interpretation, away from meanings associated with the notational center' (Chen 2012: 69). There is a comparable locative shift narrated here, a spatial shift 'to the side' of normativity, another deviation. What is interesting in Ahmed's knowing use of both Freudian and Shklovskian language: queerness is both uncanny *and* defamiliarised. What connects the Freudian *unheimlich* [uncanny] and the Shklovsian остранение [*ostranenie*, estrangement] here is the positioning of the normative part of the opposition within the word. This is a familiar phenomenon, as we know from deconstruction: to (de)construct (Derrida), to (de)familiarise (Shklovsky), to (dis)identify (Muñoz) and to (dis)orientate (Ahmed), to name a few, all require simultaneous affirmation and negation. The affirmative function of the negative prefix is crucial to queer defamiliarisation.

To queer something is to breathe new life into it. Shklovsky famously talks about making the stone feel stony, but queer goes further and makes the furniture dance. 'Queerness works by contiguity and displacement, knocking signifiers loose, ungrounding bodies, making them strange; it works in this way to provoke perceptual shifts and subsequent corporeal response in those touched' (Dinshaw 1995: 76). There is a lot to unpack in this statement from Carolyn Dinshaw. Firstly there is the deliberate use of Jakobsonian terminology, aligning once again Russian formalism with queer thought. Contiguity can be found in Jakobson's famous essay on the metaphoric and metonymic poles, in which it is defined as an external relation uniting external constituents of context and aligned with metonymy (as well as with the Freudian terms of displacement and condensation). Contiguity is opposed to similarity which is aligned with the metaphoric pole. The focus in Dinshaw's statement is on the fact that queerness works through grouped associations based on categorical differences rather than grouped similarities. The fact that queerness operates by contiguity in Dinshaw's statement underscores its inherent two-facedness; it cleaves through and between sameness and difference. The other notable aspects of the description are the operations of knocking signifiers loose and ungrounding bodies, both operations inherent to defamiliarisation. If the referent to which we refer is destabilised, if signifiers are transposed, altered, separated from their referents which are ungrounded, this is comparable to an ungrounding of bodies so the effect is that we must apprehend both bodies and signifiers anew. Perceptual shifts and corporeal responses are both reactions to this operation of queering-as-defamiliarising which materially en-gender newness.

There is a deliberate performative enactment of the process of defamiliarisation which occurs throughout this book. This means that the chapters become a little defamiliarised themselves in their style: their generic boundaries are troubled and the language is made strange through a foregrounding of its materiality. What this means is that there will be a shift in perception engendered in the reader through the shifting of formal boundaries. The aim is to remain simultaneously, in Braidotti's words, both *critical* and *creative*: that is, to demonstrate something through means other than regular exposition, but not at the expense of comprehensibility. There is, then, something about the (Cartesian) attributes of clarity and distinctness which are perhaps necessarily befuddled in a process of defamiliarisation, in the pursuit of an alternative type of perception: to perceive anew. 'Tell the truth but tell it slant –' (Dickinson 2009: 137), Emily Dickinson tells us, although her poem suggests that the slantwise movement is necessary because we must learn the truth slowly; it must 'dazzle gradually' or it will blind everyone. Ahmed similarly makes use of the slantwise motion in *Queer Phenomenology*, picking up on Maurice Merleau-Ponty's description in his *Phenomenology of Perception*. Merleau-Ponty describes a subject who sees the room in which he is only through a mirror which reflects it at an angle of 45 degrees and proclaims the general effect as 'queer' (Merleau-Ponty 2002: 289). Ahmed reads Merleau-Ponty in terms of the ways that bodies are 'lined up' with lines that are already given by the structures of compulsory heterosexuality, describing this, again with terminology reminiscent of formalism, as a 'straightening device' (Ahmed 2006: 23). These slantwise reorientations are immediately reminiscent of Vertov's Kino-Eye and Shklovsky's overall reorientation of perception already discussed. The difference between Dickinson's slant and the slant of queer defamiliarisation is that Dickinson tells us that the focus is on the truth to be accessed via the slant, whereas in queer defamiliarisation the focus is on the slant itself.

TRANS*: *We Do Not Yet Know What the Prefix Can Do*

The following matter-realisations of the trans- prefix are significant throughout this book in that they designate a shift without telos, the primacy of the shift itself. Through bodies and language thought together, both the affirmative gesture of the movement and the weight of socio-economic annexing and disenfranchisement are foregrounded in the following areas. Material conditions are relevant in all senses here: corporeally, economically, geographically and sensorially. Mel Y. Chen unites some trans-iterations together in terms of their resistance to regimes: transgender, transmogrification, translation, transubstantiation and transspecies, proposing the language of transubstantiation to understand the regulation and resistance of bodies to regimes. 'Each of these terms suggests a movement or dynamism, from one site to another, as in the sense of 'across' (Chen 2012: 154). Some of these movements are sketched out further below.

Trans: a shift, a change, a variance, a move across*

The 'trans-' prefix operates as a shifter in that it presupposes the movement of categories through its very enunciation, but it is important to stress that this movement is not necessary a movement from A to B, or M to F, or Q to Z or any other letter; it may designate an in-between. Performance artist Travis Alabanza asks: 'Why when I say I'm trans does someone ask "What will you have done? What is next?" As if trans can never be a destination. As if trans is synonym for broken body' (Alabanza 2018: 35). The addition of the asterisk to the prefix 'trans*' performs the solidification of fluidity: as an insoluble crystal, it defers finality. The asterisk shifts through its very being; it shifts as it affirms as it negates. It 'holds off the certainty of diagnosis; it keeps at bay any sense of knowing in advance what the meaning of this or that gender variant form may be, and perhaps most importantly, it makes trans* people the authors of their own categorisation' (Halberstam 2018: 4).

It is vital, however, as transfeminist poet and activist Nat Raha points out, not to disregard aspects of race and class in what Raha describes as 'trans liberalism', which aims for a fictitious state of 'equality' for trans people whereas 'the neoliberal states, in which these demands are made, reproduce socio-economic divisions along intersecting lines of race and class, gender, sexuality, dis/ability, nationality and immigration status' (Raha 2015). To counter this Raha presents radical transfeminism: 'a life praxis that understands the everyday of trans lives as struggles against transmisogyny and sexism, white supremacy and precarious work; that understands the herstory of trans and queer struggles as rooted in this' (Raha 2015). Raha here thinks through materialism in economic and class terms and how this relates to the materiality of the trans body. The reading-together or diffraction of trans and matter is something that has been theorised recently; Max van Midde, Ludovico Vick Virtù and Olga Cielemęcka define *transmateriality* as 'the material reality created by the oppressive structures built into the medical, psychiatric, legal and scientific regimes th their intersections with racism and history of colonialism that produce violence at control trans bodies; the binary normative system of sex/gender; as well as' (2018: 4). At the time of writing, here in the UK we are seemingly about to stumble out of the European Union and into a world of new harder borders and further checks and requirements for documentation that some simply do not have, at the same time as the continued dismantling of any remnants of the welfare state along with simultaneous sustained, increased (and ignored by many) crippling austerity measures. As Raha points out, as well as extra difficulties at border checks, capitalist restructuring and austerity policies have a disproportionate impact on LGBT people and people of colour:

> Manifestations of intermeshing forms of transphobia and transmisogyny, anti-blackness, racism, xenophobia, whorephobia, femmephobia, and ableism, working in concert to create conditions of slow death, social death, and actual death for poor trans women and trans femmes/of color and/or trans sex workers are inextricable from structural economic transformations and exacerbated by the fresh governance around immigration. (Raha 2017: 635)

Reece Simpkins argues that trans* materialities are part of a trans*feminist politics of becoming-intersectional. For Simpkins, this is directed at identification and subjectivity as well as, at its core, a dynamic understanding of matter's complexity which ultimately demonstrates that 'trans* materiality takes place at the ontogenetic level of materiality (Simpkins 2016: 228). Simpkins draws together trans* embodiment and feminist work on intersectionality because they both point to ways in which bodies extend beyond normative categorical frameworks. Simpkins uses Jasbir Puar's understanding of intersectionality as a dynamic event (Puar 2012) which I discuss in Chapter 1.

Transversality: a shift, a change, a variance, a move across

Transversality describes how spaces intersect. In the geometrical sense, a transversal line cuts across two or more usually parallel lines, as in the example of a garden gate consisting of several horizontal wooden planks with one diagonal one cutting across them. The diagonal plank of wood is a transversal line cutting across the horizontal ones and fortifying them. The transversal line cuts through the segregating lines, which could be identity categories or art forms or indeed academic disciplines. More complexly, transversality also occurs in differential topology wherein it formalises the idea of a generic intersection. Spaces can intersect transversally in different ways in a topological manifold.

Popularised by Félix Guattari as a radical clinical tool in the 1970s and more recently translated into new materialist terms (Palmer and Panayotov 2016), transversality has been described as a new materialist strategy in that it '*cuts across* or intersects dual oppositions in an immanent way' (Dolphijn and van der Tuin 2012: 100). It is a transversal movement that is required to cut across dualisms. It is transversality that permits a transposition, a shift or a leap in scale, or perhaps a shift from one order of dimensions or categories to another.

Transposition: a shift, a change, a variance, a move across

Indicating a shift in orientation or location, a transposition is discussed by Braidotti as

> an intertextual, cross-boundary or transversal transfer, in the sense of a leap from one code, field or axis into another, not merely in the quantitative mode of plural multiplications, but rather in the qualitative sense of complex multiplicities... As a term in music, transposition indicates variations and shifts of scale in a discontinuous but harmonious pattern. (Braidotti 2006: 5)

We might also use the term *transposition* to describe movements of scale-jumping, and this has been much discussed in aesthetico-epistemic circles (see Schwab 2018). 'Transposition transgresses ontological boundaries when, for instance in geometry, it jumps from the measure of land to the configuration of the stars, only to step from the empire of the senses into the realm of pure ideas, and from its graphic visualisation to its purely mathematical formalisation' (Malaspina 2018: 227).

The concept of 'creative transposition' is something that Roman Jakobson writes about in relation to language as a more radical, more creative alternative to translation. Translation is tricky when meaning is plural or unfixed, such as when neologisms have been coined. Creative transposition is Jakobson's suggested solution for the problem of non-equivalence between linguistic terms, and is more akin to a new creation altogether. I have discussed this in relation to Jakobson and the poetics of Deleuze and futurism elsewhere (Palmer 2014: 25). For now it is helpful to acknowledge this process as a specifically linguistic transpositional movement. There will be more discussion of Jakobson's unique take on the movements and axes of language in Chapter 1.

In another transpositional movement, Iris van der Tuin discusses transposition in terms of scale-jumping after Karen Barad and her discussion of geographer Neil Smith's theories of scale-jumping. Transposition enables van der Tuin to elucidate a meta-methodology of what she calls 'jumping generations' (van der Tuin 2015: 9) in her development of feminist politics. This is useful because it allows us to learn from all the different feminisms out there: 'black, radical, lesbian, queer, and trans feminisms . . . transgender and disability/crip perspectives'. Jumping generations 'enables *generative* thinking and acting and avoids dismissive discontentment with feminism as the result of stifling categorization' (van der Tuin 2015: 10). Transposition is also the term suggested by Eva Hayward to denote 'the spatial-sensual-temporal processes that mark such trans-sex transitions' (Hayward 2010: 237), with all of its musical, biological, etymological enfoldings and entwinings. 'Transpositions are poetic joins or trans-forms in which there is some transposing, some mixing at work that produces texture, not just bodies touching, but the provocation of those joins' (Hayward 2010: 238). I discuss Hayward's transpositions further in Chapter 4.

Introduction 3: Mattering

O body swayed to music, O brightening glance,
How can we tell the dancer from the dance?
(Yeats 1963: 130)

Yeats's question posed in 'Among Schoolchildren' highlights the inseparability of 'matter' and 'spirit' in a moment of consideration of the dancing body. When we consider the dancing body and the movements that make up the dance itself, there is another dance: the agential dance of subjectivity and objectivity. The distinction of subject and object is called into question under the remit of new materialist thought, which subjects not just bivalent oppositions but the very notion of separability, as well as the supposed neutrality of the observer and the apparatus in the classic scientific experiment, to a thorough and embodied critique. The primary figure to have thought this through in terms of both the sciences and the humanities in the early twenty-first century is Karen Barad, whose theory of intra-activity I discuss in terms of intersectional feminism in Chapter 1.

New materialism is defined variously by Rick Dolphijn and Iris van der Tuin in their *New Materialism: Interviews and Cartographies* (2012) as performing a number of functions related to the overturning of dualistic thought, particularly Cartesian substance dualism. The breaking through of dualisms is at the heart of new materialist endeavours for Dolphijn and van der Tuin. They also echo Karen Barad and others such as Isabelle Stengers, Brian Massumi and Manuel DeLanda in foregrounding the usefulness of the *topological* model as the most applicable mathematical model for new materialism. Karen Barad gestures towards non-Euclidean models when she states her aims as follows: '. . . to dislocate the Euclidean frame of reference by conceptualizing the notions of space, time and matter using an alternative framework that shakes loose the foundational character of notions such as location and opens up a space in which indeterminacies, contingencies, and ambiguities coexist with causality' (Barad 2001: 76). Topology relies on a concept of isomorphism (*isos* = equal; *morphe* = form) and/or homeomorphism (*homoios* = same; *morphē* = form): no matter how much a topological shape is deformed, it retains the same properties, the same form. Karen Barad and Michel Serres both highlight the significance of topology in their thought, and I discuss this further in Chapter 4.

New materialism emerges out of a vast conflation of humanities and science research, described as 'a paradigmatic shift' by Vera Bühlmann, Felicity Colman and Iris van der Tuin in their 'Introduction to New Materialist Genealogies' (2017: 47). As demonstrated by Rosi Braidotti's presentation of the 'enfleshed Deleuzian subject' (Braidotti 2006: 182), feminist new materialisms uphold *enfleshed* as a key term; the body is foregrounded as a threshold, 'the very axis around which all the binarisms (such as sameness/otherness, body-mind, nature-culture, the inside-the-outside, I-other) are falling apart' (Rogowska-Stangret 2017: 61). Corporeally speaking, the body in new materialist thought is just as subject to biological change as it is to social or discursive production (as in the thought of Michel Foucault or Judith Butler), flipping the constructivist paradigm. Elizabeth Wilson asserts this clearly in *Gut Feminism* (2015) when she states that 'biology is not a synonym for determinism and sociality is not a synonym for transformation' (Wilson 2015: 9). I think it is important to highlight that it is not that discursive production is rejected here; merely that language and bodies are mutually co-constituted and entangled, both produce and are produced by change. It is what Karen Barad calls 'the entanglement of matter and meaning' (Barad 2007) that is under investigation here. The feminist meaning of matter, or the feminist matter of meaning, is a complex territory mapped out in parts by thinkers such as Julia Kristeva, Hélène Cixous and more recently Vicki Kirby and Claire Colebrook, all of whom have inspired my thinking around this area. My own intervention is preoccupied with specific further entanglements within matter and meaning, concerning the ways in which queering and/or defamiliarising linguistic matter (or material language) can make a difference in the world.

Rosi Braidotti discusses 'neo-materialism' as 'a method, a conceptual frame and a political stand, which refuses the linguistic paradigm, stressing instead the concrete yet complex materiality of bodies immersed in social relations of power' (Braidotti, in Dolphijn and van der Tuin 2012: 21). It is vital to underscore here the feminist grounding of neo-materialism; Braidotti later echoes this in the etymological link to 'mater' in materialism when she states that 'the emancipation of mat(t)er is also by nature a feminist project (Braidotti, in Dolphijn and van der Tuin 2012: 93). Braidotti's refusal of the linguistic paradigm detailed here is voiced in Karen Barad's earlier article 'Posthumanist Performativity' when she states that 'Language has been granted too much power' (Barad 2003: 801). This first line from Barad is itself a powerful harbinger of the end of one supposed 'turn' and the beginning of another, the supposed end of language in favour of matter. One of the arguments of this book, however, is to demonstrate that language still matters, and it is through defamiliarising, queering and mattering that we can understand this.

The refusal to acknowledge the significance of language in discussions around new materialism therefore is something I wish to kick against in this book. I am in accord with Mel Y. Chen, who writes the following: 'I refute the recent moves to evacuate substance from language, for instance, the notion that language is simply dematerialized; one of the outcomes of this belief, it seems to me, is that language discussions seem to disappear in the theorizing of new materialisms' (Chen 2012: 51). Stacey Moran Nocek makes a similar argument when she points out the need to retain the significance of language within new materialist discussions: that within these discussions, 'language is not a thing we can simply throw out . . . Quite the contrary: it is the binary opposition between reality and language that needs to be redrawn' (Nocek 2016: 270). There is a danger in reading Barad's rhetorical statement about language above too literally. The poststructuralist landscape is assuredly linguistically contoured, but the neo-matter-realist landscapes currently being formulated are not empty of language – far from it. Language is material, but more specifically, it is material *in its political efficacy and agency*, for better or for worse. This is not a new argument, but it bears repeating. It is an argument drawn from avant-garde poetics (Lecercle and Riley 2005) multifariously known within queer theory (Butler 1997), and it can be seen in speech act theory (Austin 1962) and before that even in Ludwig Wittgenstein, who states that 'Words are deeds' [*Worte sind taten*] (Wittgenstein 1980: 50e). It was also considered by Mikhail Bakhtin, a Russian thinker with an interesting relationship to Russian formalism; consistently stifled from articulating himself fully due to political constraints, he nevertheless outlined a helpful schema for linguistic materiality in 1924:

> We can distinguish in the word as material the following moments or constituents: (1) the phonic side of the word, the musical constituent proper; (2) the referential meaning of the word (with all its nuances and variations); (3) the constituent of verbal connections (all the relationships and interrelations are purely verbal); (4) the intonational (on the psychological plane – the emotional-volitional) constituent of the word, the axiomatical directedness of the word that expresses the diversity of the speaker's axiological relations; (5) the feeling of verbal activeness, the feeling of the active generation of signifiying *sound* (included here are all motor elements – articulation, gesture, facial expression, etc. – and the whole inner directedness of my personality, which actively assumes through utterances a certain value-and-meaning position). (Bakhtin 1990 [1924]: 309)

This is a fairly comprehensive list of the ways in which the word can be deemed material. While those schooled in modernist or avant-garde poetics may take language's materiality as an obvious given, it may not be so obvious to those outside of that privileged position. I hope to demonstrate in this book some of the ways that language is matter, as matter, it matters. The fact is, however, that, as David Bleich comments in *The Materiality of Language* (2013), 'the university's approach to the study of language still involves the repression of the materiality of language' (Bleich 2013: 20). Again, while those schooled in continental philosophy or literary theory may also take language's materiality as an obvious given, Bleich's point still stands: generally, outside of literary/philosophical/artistic circles, language is understood and valued as a transparent medium without thickness. I would argue that an acceptance and augmentation of its colour, shape, texture and sound does not hinder but enhances comprehension. For some this argument is implicit; this book seeks to make it explicit.

Another important thinker of the materiality of language is Julia Kristeva, who outlines the ways language matters in *Language: The Unknown* as being firstly *concrete matter* and secondly *objective laws*. The concrete matter she refers to is 'the phonic, gestural, or graphic aspects that *la langue* assumes (there is no language without sounds, gestures, or writing)' and the objective laws are 'the laws that organize the different subsets of the linguistic whole, and that constitute phonetics, stylistics, semantics, etc.' (Kristeva 1989: 18). In the division of *langue* (the abstract system of language) and *parole* (its concrete enactment) derived from Ferdinand de Saussure, Kristeva posits both as material. She also describes the relation between language and the 'real', language and the world, as one of 'isomorphism' (Kristeva 1989: 36). These two gestures are important, firstly because they present language as material in its articulation and its signification, and also because they present language as inseparable from the world. Rather than viewing language's materiality as a step away from the political, Kristeva sees it as inherently political from every angle.

Inspired by both the deconstruction of Jacques Derrida and feminist politics, Vicki Kirby's *Telling Flesh: Substance of the Corporeal* (1997) is an explicit materialisation of linguistic theories through readings of figures such as Drucilla Cornell and Judith Butler. Kirby presents language as not merely enfleshed but as matter which escapes all attempts to contain it. 'The excessive identity of the sign swells like an illicit pregnancy that witnesses an improper breaching of borders ... Yet in the delirium of this copulation difference is not undone but rather invested with itself, fissured through with an involvement that transforms and complicates its original identity' (Kirby 1997: 51). Through reading both Butler and Derrida, Kirby's work operates as a new materialist stepping stone between Derridean deconstruction and Baradian entanglement; indeed this stepping stone later becomes explicit as we see in Kirby's later writing (see Kirby 2017: 19).

New materialist writings have often played upon the grammatical status of 'matter' as both noun and verb, particularly Barad whose

'Posthumanist Performativity' article explores 'how matter comes to matter' (Barad 2003: 801). Of course, grammar itself matters; the homonymy of matter as both noun and verb is one of several aspects linking it to queer, which is also both noun and verb. Using the form-matter distinction, however, might we just suggest the formulation 'form matters' to suggest that the concept of a materiality of form does in fact exist? We can perhaps find some justification in precisely this contested and moveable border of matter and form for the use of a strategy such as defamiliarisation for addressing what is often deemed as the very antithesis to formalist analysis: political use or drive. Form and matter are inseparable; they both matter, and this is of political importance across and between all intersecting (and inseparable themselves) categories of subjectivity. To pay attention to form means to pay attention to matter, and defamiliarisation is the process where this simultaneous paying-attention to matter and form takes place.

Importantly, Claire Colebrook discusses the concept of the materiality of the signifier through a discussion of some of Derrida's early thought in 'Matter Without Bodies' (2011). Particularly relevant here is Colebrook's re-presentation of Derrida as a materialist, but not as a materialist opposed to ontological presentations of language.

> Not only is conceptuality bound up with the material traces of language – such that our concepts would not be possible without phonematic and scriptural distinctions relying on the material forces of writing technologies and the human body (itself a technology and an apparatus) – all those forces that one attributes to matter already characterise what one might take to be mind, consciousness or ideality. (Colebrook 2011: 8)

What Colebrook is discussing and developing here is that materialism itself is a politics. The type of materiality Colebrook discusses here is a texual or rhetorical materiality which unites the Deleuzian and Derridean senses of materialism which she first distinguishes earlier in the essay. 'To consider textual worlds *materially* and to consider materiality *textually* is to admit that processes of language and meaning operate in the absence of human command, understanding and imagination' (Colebrook 2011: 18). She aligns textual materialism with Derridean undecidability. So similarly to saying there is no outside-text, she says that there is no way of knowing the proper sense of a text precisely because sense is material. Colebrook is very clear on the ways that linguistic materiality is a feminist matter, outlining the traditional schism between matter as feminine and form as masculine in her earlier essay in Alaimo and Hekman's *Material Feminisms* (2008) collection. Colebrook shows that literary language can demonstrate this through a discussion of its materiality: 'It is when language is *material* – or literary – that it resists relations and vibrates in itself' (Colebrook 2008: 59). Colebrook shows in this essay that it is precisely through defamiliarising the syntax and the grammar that language escapes the boundaries of the human.

I said above that the noun-and-verb homonymy is only one of several aspects linking *queer* to *matter*. What else links these? What is a queer matter; what is a queer form? Queer is material in the crudest sense because it deals with bodies. Perhaps this in fact leads us back to formalism. 'Why does queer = body?' This is the question that queer avant-garde writer Travis Jeppesen asks in his article on queer abstraction, which, in his words, 'posits that traditional figuration, as *representation of* the body, is less vital than possible/probable *writing of* the body: a shooting-off-into-space of the body-mind vehicle's inner substance' (Jeppesen 2019). It is the body that writes, and writing itself produces bodies. Writing, like fucking, is a praxis, as Jeppesen states:

> Fucking is praxis (creation). There's the old cliché that to fuck is to lose yourself in the other. This needs to be revised. To fuck is rather to mix one's selves (for one is always multiple) with the other's selves, to put all those selves into a blender and make a chunky cocktail that, when diluted, yields a post radial primordial mud: here comes a future when there's no such thing as names. (Jeppesen 2019)

In Chapter 4, I discuss the Stoics and their materialist theories of mixtures and blending through the lens of queer proximity and touch. There is something of a queering of Stoic materialism in Jeppesen's imagined scene narrated above. Bodies and their interpenetrations, bodily fluids and their intermingling – these are queer matters which are often presented in queer avant-garde expression in which the *form* of expression is manipulated and experimented with. There is something formalist about queer material, and there is something material about queer form.

Deformalism

> Aristotle says that the courage of a man lies in commanding, a woman's lies in obeying; that 'matter yearns for form, as the female for the male and the ugly for the beautiful' . . . that a female is an incomplete male or 'as it were, a deformity' . . .
>
> (Freeland 1994: 145–6)

> The deformed rules.
>
> (Cixous 1975: 390)

This book constitutes a thinking-together of what some might deem a traditional schism within philosophy between form: abstract, universal, invariant; and matter: concrete, particular, variant. Thinking back to ancient manifestations of this division, in Aristotle's *Physics* the doctrine of hylomorphism (Greek *hulê*, matter and *morphê*, form) perceives these as intertwined. This does not mean, however, that they are perceived as equal. They are also, as feminist philosophers such as Charlotte Witt and Cynthia Freeland have pointed out on reading Aristotle, assigned genders: matter is female and form is male. Matter is also inferior to form in the Aristotelian model; it yearns for form.

In her feminist reading of Aristotle's hylomorphism, Witt argues that we cannot 'cleanse' form of its gendered norms, nor can we perceive it as something outside of the cultural norms to which Aristotle ascribes it. Witt argues that Aristotelian form itself is normative; that it is 'a functional concept that operates in the context of a teleological metaphysics' (Witt 1998: 126). What she means by this is that form is a functional principle, and function for Aristotle is normative in that it carries expectations of how an organism *should* behave for its own good. Both the assumed superiority of form to matter and the functional nature of form constitute the inherent normativity of Aristotle's hylomorphism for Witt.

As the quotation beginning this section demonstrates, Freeland provides us with a catalogue of the ways that Aristotle's physics betray his misogyny. The inequality of the matter/form distinction renders the female as *deformed*. Much of the weight of this injurious description comes from the assumption of deformity as an unwanted deviation from a norm. It is worth considering the status of a norm and the conception of universality that the norm presupposes. Turning again to Audre Lorde, her concept of Lorde's concept of the *mythical norm*, which to her, speaking in 1980 in Amherst, was 'white, thin, male, young, heterosexual, Christian, and financially secure' (Lorde 1984: 116), is particularly resonant. Perhaps we would add a few more descriptors to the list nowadays – physically able and neurotypical, for example – but nevertheless, each item Lorde places there is still part of a mythical norm today. In theorising the disabled figure, Rosemarie Garland Thompson coins the neologism 'normate' to designate 'the social figure through which people can represent themselves as definitive human beings' (Thompson 2017: 8). Perhaps we need to think about the process of deformation in its agentially opposing senses: if something is deformed we think of it as deviating from a norm, but if something is deformed *on purpose* it is rendered differently for a specific reason. Much of this book orbits around the distinction between deformation as an existing unwanted state and deformation as an affirmative gesture. The complexities of this distinction are significant for the following discussion around the aesthetics of politics and the politics of aesthetics.

The complex entanglements of aesthetics and politics have historically produced multiple layers of interpretation and argument around the relationship between art and activism, layers which speak to one another in a range of complex iterations. As I have discussed elsewhere, the debate in 1920s Russia between Marxism (Leon Trotsky) and formalism (Viktor Shklovsky) came to represent political commitment versus Kantian autonomy (see Palmer 2014: 37). The concept of *autonomy* in aesthetics, traditionally seen within the significant strands of thinking derived from Immanuel Kant, is significant in the sense that 'fine art' (*schöne Kunst*) in Kant's *Critique of Judgement* is autonomous because it is defined as a 'mode of representation that is purposive on its own' (Kant 1987: 173). The focus is therefore on the mode of representation (and the experience or apprehension of it) rather than the thing being represented. Shklovsky's original provocations were diluted or utterly retracted due to Soviet pressures, but in their original articulation they are aligned with Kantian autonomy. They are also derived from the Russian avant-garde. Historically formalism is born out of the avant-garde and inseparable from it; nowhere more clearly do we see this than in Roman Jakobson's identification as both futurist *and* formalist.

To what degree does avant-garde and formalist experimentation *work* for those existing at the margins, for those physically, geographically, economically, sexually, racially disadvantaged? The conventional answer to this is the historically oversimplified autonomy-versus-commitment, Shklovsky-versus-Trotsky, or Formalism-versus-Marxism debate echoed in subsequent twentieth-century Anglo-American developments (Jameson 1972; Bennett 1989). Formalism outside of its Russian manifestation – formalism more transversally, which we might hesitantly define as a search for invariants within a system – might appear hopelessly archaic among those privileged enough to be schooled in Deleuzo-Guattarian continuous variation, and equally hopeless among those living the experiences of disempowerment or indeed alienation due to existing outside the parameters of the 'mythical norm', to use Lorde's words again. What could identity politics and formalism possibly have in common? Perhaps this question can be approached, *formally*, through a consideration of the function of invariants in a system and the ways that a system can be dynamic, the ways that it can shift or vary within itself. The dynamism of systems and the nature of invariance are both discussed in the following chapter. For now, let us retain the oversimplification of the autonomy/commitment debate a little longer and consider the division of 'form' and 'content', specifically from the perspective of literature, in order to think further about how these older debates fit into more recent discussions of new materialism.

To discover content *in* form and vice versa has become a modernist trope, as we can see from Samuel Beckett's claim in his essay on James Joyce which articulates this inseparability with bathos: 'The form that is an arbitrary and independent phenomenon can fulfil no higher function than that of a tertiary or quartary conditioned reflex of dribbling comprehension' (Beckett 2001 [1929]: 26). Dribble also strangely (or perhaps not so strangely) features in another discussion of form (or lack thereof) from the very same year, specifically in George Bataille's short paragraph 'Formless'. In a surrealist manner befitting its time of composition, Bataille writes in this paragraph that 'affirming that the universe resembles nothing and is only formless amounts to saying that the universe is something like a spider or spit' (Bataille 1985: 30).

How might we perceive these salivary matters anew? In a discussion around crude matter and formlessness, Kyla Wazana Tompkins asks whether crude materiality, in its relation to aesthetic form, presupposes *either* a rejection of form and gesture towards the material formlessness that Bataille talks about, *or* a *form-to-come*, which 'emerges into the social – which is to say, politico-aesthetic – legibility' (Tompkins 2017: 265). Tompkins uses Bataille's focus on spit (*crachat*) to think about 'the productive possibilities of thinking with the discarded and the deviant. Spit, the sticky. Kinaesthetic and synaesthetic reorderings' (Tompkins 2017: 267). The discarded, the deviant and the deformed. Here deformation is defiant. Tompkins talks about deformation as aligning with a project of *déclassement* – 'a queer, perverse, or non-normative aesthetic through which scholars and artists might access alternative organizations of the *sensus communis*' (Tompkins 2017: 267). Sensus Communis returns later in this book, an enfleshed and literary allegorical subject in a seventeenth-century play, in Chapter 4.

What Tompkins advocates here sounds like a radical detaxonomy or alternative taxonomy (or a speculative taxonomy, as I discuss later in this book): form perceived anew. The term that Tompkins ultimately suggests is 'deformalism'. This would presuppose the very opposite of formalism's historically pronounced apolitical nature, advocating instead 'a materialist aesthetics grounded in historical reading but uninterested in Kantian ideals of beauty, or in tracking consistency in the classically formalist sense . . . It begins in my understanding of the queer, but it seeks to answer to much, much more' (Tompkins 2017: 268). This is a programme at once both political and aesthetic, linked modernism and the avant-garde through a string of mucoid saliva. Spit, the sticky.

Where else might the spittlestring go? We might look to the work of sociologist Christina Hughes, who charts the complex Pavlovian salivation process of a jewellery designer and maker in Birmingham who salivates when she sees a particular gemstone that she wants to buy. The involuntary process of salivating as a reaction to the hunger-inducing stimulus of food is abstracted, commodified, made strange; the dollar signs are reflected not so much in this jeweller's eyes but in the watery substance secreted by the salivary glands in the mouth. The urge to consume remains. Seeing the right stone (called 'sweeties' in the business) produces an opioid effect, drawing attention to how the stones' very materiality 'is given a gloss of pleasure that is synonymous with the linkage of sweetness to pleasure given in neuroscience' (Hughes 2011). Spit, the sticky. Stickiness can of course also be culturally and affectively constituted. In *The Cultural Politics of Emotion* Sara Ahmed charts how not just objects but words, signs and relations can become 'sticky'; in a reading wherein it is impossible to disentangle the literal and the metaphorical (they are stuck to one another), Ahmed demonstrates to us how the property of stickiness can be perceived '*as an effect of the histories of contact between bodies, objects, and signs*' (Ahmed 2004: 90). A radical 'deformalism' might consider any or all of these various sticky strings of affective matter and their glistening trails through lived experience: aesthetic, political, socio-ecomic, felt, spat, stuck, dribbled and drooled.

Dribble or drool is generally one of the more abject of substances secreted from human and non-human animals, arguably differing from spit only in terms of the agency of its ejector. It might therefore work as an even stranger analogy for form, considering we stated in the previous paragraph that the crucial aspect of 'deformity' to be considered here is its agential bilateralism: to deform, to be deformed. Both deformity and saliva are subject to the active/passive distinction, and while their nature is changed according to this distinction, they both retain their affective halo of the abject whether the deformity is passively received or actively operated and whether the saliva leaves the oral cavity voluntarily or involuntarily. Defamiliarisation as a strategy seizes upon moments of historical assignation and sets them in motion; states of being are enlivened, animated. It therefore would take the grammatical forms I have just mentioned – to deform/to be deformed – and translate the distinction into something else entirely. The gerund or continuous present are grammatical forms that Deleuze is certainly sympathetic to, and something I have discussed elsewhere (Palmer 2014); rather than to deform/to be deformed we have something like *deformation*. It is not so much that the subject is removed from the equation; it is more that the subject is now ensconced within the action itself. It is its own subject, object, verb and declension. Form is deforming itself.

Chapter Summaries

In **Chapter 1**, 'Synvariance', I examine the spatiotemporal axes of language and how they have been reconstituted and mobilised by thinkers such as Roman Jakobson, constituting syntactical variation or what I call synvariance. Using Jakobson's theory of the poetic function I advance an argument powered by what I have called pareidoliac logic, tracing patterns in the texts consulted for this book and using a quotation from Gertrude Stein. Using Jakobson's formalist manifesto which examines systems in motion I examine simultaneous stasis and flow, thinking this through Henri Bergson's work on duration and simultaneity and Michel Serres's notion of homorrhesis. I analyse the fleshing-out of this theory through the work of Travis Alabanza and their show *Burgerz*. I discuss two examples of recent mobilisations of formalist frameworks in the work of James Williams and Armen Avenassian and Anke Hennig. I examine the ways in which the gender binary can be troubled through the splicing of words in the work of Quinn Eades's rewriting of Gertrude Stein's *Tender Buttons*.

In **Chapter 2**, 'Mythorefleshings' I trace a series of mythorefleshings, charting the ways that these feminist rewritings of mythological figures constitute what I have called a 'fictive public', taking up Michael Warner's work on publics and counterpublics. I discuss various versions of conceptual and narrative personae through the work of Maria Tamboukou's narrative persona and Gilles Deleuze and Félix Guattari's conceptual persona. Taking Adriana Cavarero's *In Spite of Plato* as an exemplary philosophical rewriting, I then discuss the figures of Penelope through Margaret Atwood; Arachne and Ariadne through Nancy K. Miller and Aritha Van Herk; Iphis through Ali Smith; Eurydice through H.D. and Kathy Acker; Lavinia through Ursula Le Guin; Medusa through Hélène Cixous; Circe through Madeleine Miller and Afrekete through Audre Lorde. Through more examples of synvariance I demonstrate that these figures can embody fictive publics of new alternative personae.

In **Chapter 3, 'A Field of Heteronyms and Homonyms: new materialism, speculative fabulation and wor(l)ding** I assess various theoretical areas drawing together fiction and philosophy: fictocriticism (Stephen Muecke), hyperstition (Simon O'Sullivan) and speculative fabulation (Donna Haraway) with a focus on utopia and uchronia in Afrofuturist writing and the agency of the heteronym and homonym (Kodwo Eshun) I discuss the use of science fiction or speculative fabulation as a type of 'worlding', taking the 'matter-realising' of both language and fiction as seen in theorists such as Haraway as well as afrofuturist writers absolutely literally. I consider the concepts of utopia, uchronia and personae together in order to think about the fabulation of reinvented futures and pasts. A worlding is a simultaneous materialisation of persona and topos, often rendered heteronymically. The numerous interstitial realms spawned from the splicing of science and/or philosophy and/or literature (CCRU's hyperstition, Donna Haraway's speculative fabulation, Stephen Muecke's fictocriticism, O'Sullivan's myth-science and fictioning) all explore different permutations of this, ultimately demonstrating that stories still matter, vitally.

In **Chapter 4, 'Sensorium',** building on comments from various scholars about the rich potential for new materialist scholarship within the realm of the sensory, I draw together topology (the mathematical study of spatial properties preserved under continuous deformation) with synaesthesia (the perceptual phenomenon in which stimulation of one cognitive pathway leads to automatic experiences in another). These phenomena are linked through a shared goal to displace Western Enlightenment ocularcentrism in favour of intra-sensory entanglements. This paper traces some of the onto-epistemological strands of topological embodiment, from Lacan's conception of the structure of human subjectivity as a topological space in the later *Seminars* to Serres's passionate 'topology of tailoring' to Grosz's feminist critique of the Möbius strip and several feminist developments and manifestations of the figure of the cortical homunculus. These various strands are explored speculatively in this chapter, via several sections pertaining to surfaces based on a series of alternative taxonomies segmenting our sensory existence: a hormone symphony, a new theorisation of the vowel space after Rimbaud, a speculative taxonomy of musical intervals in the diatonic scale, and a meditation on sirens and organs based in Blackpool.

The **Epilogue, A Hymn to Sol, or, She Rides the Tram in Different Voices, or, A Heliochronic Tram Journey on Blackpool at Sunset, or,**

Radio Blackpool (voices, multiple; deities, multiple), is an enactment of the queering of defamiliarisation through a gendered 'rewriting' of Joyce's chapter 'Oxen of the Sun' from *Ulysses*, which in its original version chronicles a stylistic journey of white male writers and thinkers in the English language from Anglo Saxon to Joyce's present day. This version echoes the chronological journey but replaces Joyce's stylistic chronology with a more diverse procession of voices.

CHAPTER 1

Synvariance

The history of a system is in turn a system.
                (Jakobson and Tynyanov 1928, in Matĕkja and Pomorska 1971: 79)

And ain't I a woman?
                (Sojourner Truth 1851, in hooks 2015: 160)

This chapter examines some of the implications of the first lines of the Introduction, which argue that language in its material strangeness has the power to advance feminist, queer, intersectional politics. In the Introduction I discussed the queer nature of the restless terminological propulsion: the proliferation of neologisms. Here I discuss the spatiotemporal movement and organisation of language when it is made strange; I present queer defamiliarisation as a reconfiguration of linguistic spatiotemporality. It is this reconfiguration that foregrounds language as matter, among other actions and gestures: stuttering, repetition, interruption, equivocation, neologism and diffracted or spliced morphemes. This chapter considers these linguistic operations in the light of categories of identity formation, with a particular focus on some of the ways that these operations can be defamiliarised or deformed.

The conventional axes underpinning structuralist linguistics are usually considered as that of the horizontal syntagmatic and vertical paradigmatic orders. The figures discussed in this chapter queer both the syntactic line and the paradigmatic order of their material-discursive frameworks. Synvariance is a queering (or a defamiliarising) of both syntax and invariance, which is to say a reorientation of both. *Syntax* generally constitutes the logical stringing-together of words in order to make sense. *Invariance* generally constitutes a principle of constancy or universality: that which does not vary. These two concepts are brought together here because they both constitute certain spatiotemporal presuppositions: syntax generally requires some kind of linearity, while invariance generally requires some kind of stasis. Some of the examples discussed in this chapter challenge the notion of temporal linearity or succession; others challenge the notion of invariance in language and in the world. Some do both at the same time.

What do structuralist lingustics and intersectional feminism have in common? In short: they both make use of axes, and the nature of these axes has been subject to critique. Does it make sense to perceive of language stretched across spatiotemporal axes? Does it make sense to perceive of categories of oppression organised along spatiotemporal axes? What does new materialism have in common with these questions? These questions form the basis of this chapter.

At their origin, both structural models of language and intersectional models for identity formation are, rightly or wrongly, read as requiring dual geometrical axes or categories: spatial and temporal axes for language, and race and gender for the intersectional model. Various dualisms spring to mind when thinking about these areas: the two main interlinking ones are *difference and sameness* and *movement and stasis*. Both dualisms are challenged when subjected to the type of critique that I will argue is common to both poststructuralism and new materialism. This critique, which aims to overcome both dualisms and rigidity of categorisation or separability in favour of dynamic systems, not only allows for movement within the system but requires a *constancy of movement* for the working of that system. In order to determine why this matters in our contemporary climate – theoretical, political, creative – it is necessary to analyse some of the ways that these frameworks have been subjected to critique and how these criticisms interrelate. The latter is perhaps the most pressing. How do abstract figurations of language borne out of early twentieth-century Russian formalism relate to intersecting categories of human disempowerment? Aside from the moments of defamiliarisation narrated in the Introductions, what more could these exceedingly different areas have in common before they are even subjected to critique? Let us look firstly at one figure from Russian formalist linguistics with more of a radical and playful perspective than he is generally credited with: Roman Jakobson.

Horizontal/Vertical

In her discussion of linguistic ontologies from Husserl to Derrida and beyond in *Quantum Anthropologies*, Vicki Kirby is aware of the contradictions and difficulties within even the originary Saussurean system of structuralism, pointing out that Saussure himself was troubled by the internal movements of his static system:

> Saussure's problem was that while he wanted to acknowledge a motivational coherence whose systemic implications conjured some working sense of a reference for a language community, he also wanted to concede that the identity of any datum was inherently plastic. However, if he understood that language involved a sort of living mutation *within* stability (indeed, this is what he meant by 'system'), he struggled to conceive how he might be investigating the workings of a general operation, a 'semiology' as he called it, rather than something peculiar to linguistics. (Kirby 2011: 45)

The problem of structuralism is one of how to account for plasticity *within* stasis, or mutation *within* stability as Kirby states here.

As the attempt to create a 'science' of language, structuralism may appear a predictably static system of binary oppositions, but Roman Jakobson's work from futurist to formalist to structuralist linguist is always concerned with the role of radical creativity powering these frameworks and in problematising the oppositions. According to François Dosse in his *History of Structuralism*, 'Jakobson hoped that linguistics would allow him to successfully bridge creation and science . . . Poetic language offered him a good starting point because, unlike daily language, which is shaped by elements external to its own logic and its heterotelic, poetic language is fundamentally autotelic' (Dosse 1997: 54). This opposition between heterotelic (having an extraneous telos) and autotelic (it is its own telos) summarises the general distinction between language as communication and what Jakobson calls the poetic function, which I will discuss below.

One reason why structuralism underpins contemporary disciplinary diffractions is its link between the humanities and the sciences, encapsulated in the originary aim to create a science of language through the identification of a synchronic system containing linguistic invariants. This link is not merely methodological, as Jakobson's work demonstrates. The linkages between poetics and both relativity theory *and* quantum mechanics are hinted at in Jakobson's works at numerous points. One such example can be found in his text *The Sound Shape of Language*, in which he writes about both invariance and relativity. Relativity theory, according to Jakobson here, is linked to Saussurian structuralism: in fact, Jakobson points out that Saussure's *Cours de linguistique générale* appeared in 1916, the same date as the first edition of Einstein's *General Theory of Relativity* (Jakobson 1979: 21). Jakobson's project is sharply different from Saussure's in terms of the roles of *stasis* and *succession* in the thinking of linguistic temporality: to put it simply, Jakobson aims for a critique of both. While Jakobson's quest is for linguistic universals in order to create a science of language, and he actually links this search to the transformation of classical mechanics into quantum mechanics, the link to quantum rather than relativity is important here because it demonstrates, amongs other things, the eternal impossibility of fixity or objectivity (both of which we see in Karen Barad's thought, discussed later in this chapter).

In much of his work Jakobson sets up a distinction between the vertical paradigmatic line of poetry and the horizontal syntagmatic line of prose. The poetry/prose distinction is famously discussed in Paul Valéry's 'Remarks on Poetry' in which prose is likened to walking and poetry is to jumping (Valéry; in West 1980: 50). The distinction between poetry and prose is important to consider in syntactical terms; however, there is also the very pragmatic aspect of the time, space and materials required to write prose compared with the comparative brevity of poetry. Lorde echoes and develops Virginia Woolf's infinitely-cited feminist classic text *A Room of One's Own*, in which Woolf states that 'a woman must have money and a room of her own if she is to write fiction' to incorporate her own experience as 'a forty-nine-year-old Black lesbian feminist socialist mother of two, including one boy, and a member of an interracial couple' to show that 'A room of one's own may be a necessity for writing prose, but so are reams of paper, a typewriter, and plenty of time' (Woolf 1929: 6; Lorde 1984: 114, 116).

Putting these concerns together complicates the picture of both Valéry's and Jakobson's formal or generic distinctions between poetry and prose. Lorde's are material, economic concerns, added to those of race, gender and others, which are not normally considered in considerations of the differences between poetry and prose. If we were to intuitively align poetry and prose with Lorde's *mythical norm* outlined in the Introductions or the imagined Other of this (much as Lorde outlines her own position, with the potential of further categories added), it would be easy to assign rational, horizontal, chronosensible Prose with the mythical norm whereas the *more* sensuous, *more* fleshly, *more* abstract, *less* rational Poetry with the other domain. Rather than reinforce this dualism, let us look more closely at the spatiotemporal complexities of the distinction by analysing ways in which it can be challenged. Gertrude Stein (discussed below) famously queers the syntactic line like no other, and yet Stein scholars would argue tirelessly that the spatiotemporal befuddlements in her writings are not meaningless: far from it. They create and perform their own meanings.

One of the ways that Jakobson describes his theory of the poetic function is to 'focus on the message for its own sake' (Jakobson 1981: 26). It is generally defined against another of Jakobson's functions, the referential function (heterotelic in Dosse's words above), which is language which refers to something external to itself.[1] This distinction makes sense to us: language that foregrounds itself above all else (autotelic in Dosse's words above) is generally understood as 'poetic' language. Rather than purely autotelic, however, I argue here that it is in fact the poetic function that allows us to go beyond language, precisely because through making language a strange thing of substance it conjures a beyond; it takes us somewhere new. It is language in its poetic function which allows it to advance what I outlined at the beginning of this chapter and in the Introductions: feminist, queer, intersectional politics. Rather than obfuscate, the poetic function connects reason with feeling to create new meanings. Kristeva underscores the significance of Jakobson's poetics in her essay 'Ethics and Language', in which she argues that it is his unique focus on poetic language alongside his other linguistic concerns that constitutes an ethical dimension of his linguistics. As Kristeva says, 'there is an *other* besides the irony of the learned man; there is the poem, in the sense that it is *rhythm, death,* and *future*' (Kristeva 1987: 26). On describing Jakobson's readings of Russian avant-garde poets Vladimir Mayakovsky and Velimir Khlebnikov in a Harvard lecture that he gave in 1967, Kristeva draws together the differing sounds, shapes and textures produced by these two poets and reproduced by Jakobson in his lecture with the stories of their aesthetic and political rebellion just before the Revolution. It is these material, personal, political concerns that create the 'science' of language in Jakobson's thought. The poetic function, which straddles and splices spatiotemporal axes, is the most rather than the least efficient function within the system to resist, rewrite and revolt. The historical, aesthetic and political context of the Russian avant-garde from which Jakobson emerged is one clear example of this at work but there are many other more recent examples, some of which I discuss below.

By Any Other Name a Rose Is a Rose by Any Other Name

Pareidolia: to see patterns where they, seemingly, are not.

It is impossible for me to read the word *pareidolia* without thinking of a proliferation of *doilies*. The most pointless of early twentieth-century

---

[1] NB: Laurent Binet's novel *The Seventh Function of Language* (2017) speculatively asks what it would have been like if a seventh function had been discovered by Roland Barthes before he died. Much hilarity ensues.

kitchen fripperies: decorative paper circles with intricate patterns of holes cut out of them; like obverse paper snowflakes, but actually the transfers for dustings of icing sugar snow to form further patterns on cakes. Patterns upon patterns. My grandma would place a doily over her Victoria sponges before shaking icing sugar over them, so there would be fractal dustings of sugar patterned across the top. My cognitive linking of the word *pareidolia* to the object *doily* is an example that appears to contradict Saussure's conception of the non-motivatedness of the signifier/signified relation (the relation between the word 'pareidolia' and the concept that it denotes is an arbitrary one), and rather affirms Jakobson's poetic function, which '*projects the principle of equivalence from the axis of selection into the axis of combination*' (Jakobson 1980: 27). The equivalence, or sameness, that is generally perceived on the vertical axis of *selection* (consisting of metaphorically and paradigmatically arranged lexical elements with common elements) is projected into the axis of *combination* (consisting of metaphorically and paradigmatically arranged lexical elements with differing elements) so that there are shared elements across the syntagm. The axes themselves are reconfigured. We generally create meaning through combinations of differential linguistic elements rather than shared metaphorical ones, but the poetic function reconfigures this. So when I link *pareidolia* with *doily* I create meaning through an alternative route. What this means is that within the poetic function, the relationship between language, space and time is fundamentally changed. The shared letters 'd-o-l-i' or 'd-o-i-l' in the respective words are in fact combined with my associations of their patternedness to produce a cognitive link: an analogy. Pareidolia for me *is* a doily, multifariously: the almost-fractal patterns cut into the circles of paper are replicated in the concept which happens to denote the perception of patterns which apparently are not there, even though the patterns of the letters 'd-o-l-i' and 'd-o-i-l' form the beginning of a sequence based on another logic – that of letter ordering.

What does this mean and why is it relevant? I have linked these words through their shared patterns of letters, sound and a common denotative feature of patterns. They are therefore linked semantically as well as sonically, though this is incidental. Are we able to make any sense of this? The shift here is once more to do with axes. Sonic linkages are due to resemblance (of sound) rather than difference, which is why they are paradigmatic and correspond to the vertical axis of combination. Our system of reason is forever linked to the other axis; the horizontal axis of differential selection. The differentiation between the syntagmatic and paradigmatic axes of language was developed considerably by Jakobson, and later set further in motion by others. Throughout his career Jakobson pointed out the need to consider *both* invariance *and* variation in *both* axes. As I have written about elsewhere, Jakobson refuses the Saussurian distinction of synchrony and diachrony and instead propounds both 'permanently dynamic synchrony' simultaneous with 'static invariants in the diachronic cut of language' (Jakobson 1985a: 374; see Palmer 2014). Before this refusal, the standard differentiation within linguistic study comes from Saussure's equation of synchrony with temporal stasis and diachrony with temporal movement: 'Everything that relates to the static side of our science is synchronic; everything that has to do with evolution is diachronic' (Saussure 2011: 81). Not only that, but for Saussure, the synchronic perspective is the *proper* linguistic perspective whereas everything else is exterior and contextual: '. . . the synchronic viewpoint predominates, for it is the true and only reality to the community of speakers. The same is true of the linguist: if he takes the diachronic perspective, he no longer observes language but a series of events that modify it' (Saussure 2011: 90). Everything outside of the synchronic snapshot or slice for Saussure is external to language, whereas for Jakobson, this exteriority is *within* the phenomenon that is language.

The concept of exteriority within phenomena is something that we see emerging in new materialist thought, as will be discussed later in this chapter in the work of Karen Barad. In between Jakobson and Barad, the question of exteriority *within* the phenomenon that is language occupies Derrida for much of the latter part of the twentieth-century: I am thinking here of the oft-quoted Derridean adage *il n'y a pas de horstexte* (there is no outside-text) from *Of Grammatology* (Derrida 1997: 158). If there is no outside-text, if we are thinking from a new materialist perspective, is the exteriority *within* the text? Where, then, does linguistic matter reside? It is worth pointing out here that Butler's *Bodies that Matter* (1993) is another source that highlights the importance of materiality within the signifier. If Derrida's provocative statement has previously appeared to gesture towards nothing but a proliferation of seemingly *immaterial* signifiers as opposed to a transcendental signified or referent, Butler shows us that in fact it is *not* that one cannot get outside of language in order to grasp materiality in and of itself; 'rather, every effort to refer to materiality takes place through a signifying process which, in its phenomenality, is always already material' (Butler 1993: 37). Butler demonstrates through this her keen awareness that language and materiality are not opposed, rather that materiality itself is part of the signifying process. As with Butler and Colebrook, Kirby similarly presents language as bursting the ideal/material opposition. Furthermore, Kirby points out the gendered nature of this 'outside' of signification, which is read as impenetrable 'matter' and therefore feminine. Kirby also reads Saussure's exclusion of all materiality from the signifier as phallocentric 'somatophobia', articulating instead a relation between ideality and materiality in the signifier as a 'productive entanglement' (Kirby 1997: 54–5).

In terms of syntax and rhythm, Stein's famous lecture 'Composition as Explanation' remains a wonderfully mind-befuddling, axis-stretching, language-spidering piece of prose. This text says more about linguistic spatiotemporalities through its execution or its articulation in time than any attempt to theorise, rationalise or explain it. 'The only thing that is different from one time to another is what is seen and what is seen depends on how everybody is doing everything' (Stein 2004: 21). Stein here achieves a prismatic effect through the repetition of function words and seemingly mundane phrases. The concept of 'everybody doing everything' is contingent rather than static; it differs each time and shifts our perception each time. The radically kaleidoscopic nature of Stein's work is due to the conceptual creation being done by the reader. What does this mean for my pareidolia-doily analogy? If we think about the effects of repetition written through and/or into the conventions of syntactical temporal unilinearity in the English language that we see in Stein's work, the element shared with the pareidolia-doily analogy is a moment of stuttering new or near-comprehension wherein something uncertain and new is produced. It is this stuttering moment of conceptual creation through the queering of the syntagmatic-paradigmatic axes where things dance with life, where things are defamiliarised and perceived anew.

My pareidolia doily is encircled all around with a patterned wreath of roses. We may take another brief example from Stein to follow the analogy further. 'Rose is a rose is a rose' (Stein 1922: 187). Trifold roses subsequently abound throughout Stein's *oeuvre*. Rose is a rose is a rose is a . . . if I repeat the phrase ad infinitum, does it mean something different to Stein's original line, pleasingly triangular in its structure? If it is quoted without being cited (see Ehrmann 1971) does it mean something different again? If we substitute 'rose' for another flower: 'sunflower', 'corpse flower', 'welwitschia miribalis', does it mean something different again? The trifold structure is open to infinite manipulation, sometimes literalising flowers' historic and euphemistic relation to female genitalia. Kathy Acker's Eurydice (who we will discuss further in Chapter 2) gives a nod to Stein: 'I can see them, roses, I once said

"A rose is my cunt"' (Acker 1997: 16). Jeanette Winterson tells us in *Written on the Body*: playfully, wryly, flatly: 'Sometimes a breast is a breast is a breast' (Winterson 1992: 24). Stein is certainly vastly quotable when it comes to syntactical play; her rose line crops up frequently in discussion of linguistic spatiotemporality due to its playful repetition but also perhaps due to its radical haecceity: its roseness. Indeed, Stein said that it was the first time that roses were red in the English language for a hundred years (Stein 1969 [1947]: vi). It happens that while reading for this book I encountered multiple occurrences of Stein's famous and beautiful line and further figurative deployments of flowers. As well as Acker's *Eurydice in the Underworld* and Winterson's *Written on the Body* they were also blooming in Hélène Cixous's 'Circe, or the Self's Opening', in Armen Avenassian and Anke Hennig's *Metanoia*; in Jacques Ehrmann's 'The Death of Literature'; in Stephen Muecke's 'The Fall'; in Stéphane Mallarmé's preface to René Ghil's *Treatise on the Word* and subsequently Maurice Blanchot's *The Work of Fire*; in Michel Serres's *Hermes*; in H.D.'s *Selected Poems*; and many more. Combined with a wild and overgrown garden full of sprawling roses screeching/scratching at the panes of my window, the repetition, no – let us call it what it is – the *patterning* of roses creeping, unfurling, *blooming* around the physical and psychical space forces me to perceive, create or employ (depending on where you, the reader, source the agency of the motif or even of the roses themselves) this pattern as instrumental to the overall thesis of the book. The logic of the doily would lead you to think that it is, in fact, a book about roses.

Going any further down this overgrown garden path is probably inadvisable; neural pathways strewn with roses are perhaps likely to distract more than they elucidate. And yet, what this example serves to demonstrate is the potential repercussions of applying paradigmatic logic to an argument, or Jakobson's poetic function, or my own logic of the doily, to an argument. Argumentation to us is so utterly and thoroughly powered by the syntagm, and yet it is through the reorientation of linguistic spatiotemporalities and the consequent imaginative labour that new neural pathways are forged and new concepts are created. I believe that the playfulness of Jakobson's thought is not given enough consideration, and it is his playfulness which allows us to see him testing the limits that he sets for himself. As a formalist and structuralist linguist with an early apprenticeship as futurist poet with pseudonym Aljagarov, with friends such as 'transrational' poets Velimir Khlebnikov and Alexei Kruchenykh, Jakobson's technical approach is consistently attentive to the possibilities of stretching, bending and testing the rigidity of the frameworks and axes he sets out before him. Put simply, Jakobson is concerned with *sameness* and *difference* in various manifestations, and how the opposition between sameness and difference can be challenged and complicated. This sameness and difference is written in different ways in different parts of his work, and pertains to the following oppositional pairs: *variance* and *invariance*, *syntagmatic* and *paradigmatic* orders of language, *synchronic* and *diachronic* perspectives on language and *stasis* and *movement*. I have written about these in more detail elsewhere (see Palmer 2014). Jakobson is consistently preoccupied with the conflation of two seemingly opposing temporal modes, or axes, in the thinking of language.

Stasis/Flow

As stated above, Jakobson's main critique of Saussure is to do with Saussure's treatment of linguistic temporality. Jakobson's development and complication of Saussure's thought is palpable as early as 1928 in his structural manifesto written with Yurij Tynyanov 'Problems in the Study of Literature and Language'. The line 'The history of a system is in turn a system' that opened this chapter alongside Sojourner Truth is from this text, and is perhaps the best way to grasp the argument put forward. Histories are systems themselves, and histories are dynamic therefore systems are dynamic. At every possible spatiotemporal juncture in the thinking of language there is the simultaneous possibility of a systemic dynamism and a dynamic system. The thought of Henri Bergson is relevant here, as Jakobson's thought on language and spatiotemporality is in line with Bergson's thinking of time as fundamentally indivisible and heterogeneous (see Bergson 2001). Bergson distinguishes in *Time and Free Will* between time as a homogenous medium reducible to space, and pure duration as a heterogeneous medium irreducible to space. Duration for Bergson is 'a mutual penetration, an interconnexion and organization of elements, each one of which represents the whole, and cannot be distinguished or isolated from it except by abstract thought' (Bergson 2001: 101). Without digressing too far into Bergson's theories here, there are two elements of Bergsonian duration relevant to Jakobsonian linguistics and Russian formalism more broadly: the revelation of the static 'present moment' to be a fiction, and the critique of a spatial perception of temporal succession. Bergson was important to a number of Russian formalists such as Viktor Shklovsky, Lev Yuakubinsky and Boris Eichenbaum: in fact, it has been claimed that much of the language of Shklovsky's 'Art as Device' in terms of 'automatization' and also distinguishing between ordinary and artistic perception is derived from Bergson. As James Curtis argues, the formalists associated the binary pairs of seeing and recognition, continuity and noncontinuity and deautomatisation and automatisation all with Bergson. Despite not always referring to him directly in their work, they implicitly demonstrate 'a Bergsonian paradigm' (Curtis 1976: 113). What these linkages show is that the Russian formalists were thinking about simultaneities and other spatiotemporal blind spots in language from the beginning; they were always already stretching and bending those axes.

Jakobson and Tynyanov's statement 'The history of a system is in turn a system' combines the two types of simultaneity that Bergson outlines in *Duration and Simultaneity*: the simultaneity of stases and the simultaneity of flows. Bergson distinguishes between the simultaneity of the instant and the simultaneity of the flow, wherein the former is required to chart simultaneous moments with clock moments, while the latter is required to chart two moments. Both of these are *relative* simultaneity for Bergson. The third type that Bergson discusses is what he calls *absolute* simultaneity, which is a simultaneity of two clocks. The opposition between movement and stasis is shown to be a reciprocity here, as synchronic (static) linguistics is inseparable from diachronic (dynamic) linguistics. This maps onto the concept of systems and evolution for Jakobson and Tynyanov.[2] As Krystyna Pomorska concludes in her 'Dialogue on Time in Language and Literature' with Jakobson in 1980, 'any verbal act, any phenomenon of language from phonemes to literary works, necessarily enters into a dual temporal frame: linear succession and strict simultaneity' (Pomorska, in Jakobson 1985a: 24). From his earliest to his last writings, Jakobson consistently attempts to make all simultaneities both stasis and flow, cementing his position as an early pioneer in the war on binary thinking from the very site where binary thinking began to infiltrate multiple scholarly fields: early structuralist linguistics. The imprint of pareidoliac logic in all its ludic glory consistently presents itself in Jakobson's work.

Repetition/Difference

HOT DOG OR BURGER?
Die quietly or die loudly? Splitting things up into two arbitrary categories has never worked ever since the beginning of time.
(Alabanza 2018: 13)

---

[2] For more discussion of this see Palmer (2014).

One of the linguistic phenomena I listed in the Introduction as illustrative of its materiality is repetition, and repetition is also a phenomenon that allows us to perceive difference within itself. Repetition itself produces difference precisely because language is material and contingent. Repetition is never, as poet-philosopher Denise Riley points out, an inert affair. Repetition is the simultaneity of different spatiotemporal modes: it is productive of both sameness and difference.

> Say it, read it, echo it often enough and at short enough intervals, and the word suffers a mutation, its thingness abruptly catapulted forward. It begins to look somewhat comical or grotesque in its isolation – and this folly soon seeps over the reader too, who may feel sheepish to be so greatly struck by the repeated thing-word. (Riley 2005: 122)

Here Riley narrates a moment which we could call queer defamiliarisation. Repetition brings the thingness of the word into sharp focus, while the sense of the word recedes. 'Whether by the enforced prominence of its sounds, or the odd look of the letters themselves, to see a word printed many times over on a page make it start out, and this exposed arbitrariness is indeed queer' (Riley 2005: 122). While it is more probable that Riley intends 'queer' to be understood in the broader sense of 'strange or unusual', that does not occlude its use for our more specified meaning here. What this passage from Riley shows us is that the queer operation of repetition is precisely what brings about the moment of defamiliarisation. Rather than diluted or divested of sense, the repeated item becomes supercharged.

Writer and performer Travis Alabanza's show *Burgerz* (Hackney Showroom, London, 2018) contains one such moment. The show itself is an iterative process of deconstruction and repetition, focusing on a moment of trauma experienced by Alabanza in which the performer had a burger thrown at them by a passer-by on Waterloo Bridge, while none of the many onlookers came to their defence or support. Near the beginning of the performance Alabanza repeats a two-word choice to the audience. Burgers or hotdogs? Burgers or hotdogs? Burgers. Hotdogs. Burgers. Hotdogs. In the context of binary gender presuppositions and the verbal and physical violence of discrimination, these food objects are placed in opposition to one another, hyper-saturated in anatomical symbolism which is not lost on the predominantly queer-presenting audience. Burgers. Hotdogs. Burgers. Hotdogs. Each night of this performance Alabanza re-enacts the incident with the burger through a staged deconstruction and reconstruction. The moment of burger-throwing is broken down and attended to prismatically: it is a freeze-frame moment subjected to Alabanza's passionate and vitriolic critique. Every element of the burger from container to condiment is examined, assembled, minced, sliced, pounded, fried, layered, boxed and eventually thrown – but not at Alabanza. Burgers. Hotdogs. This is a self-professed exercise in the reclamation of agency over a moment of abuse and suffering, and the fast-food items (which essentially involve variations of sized and shaped encasings of reshaped meat products sheathed in variations of sized and shaped bread product) are crude material signifiers demonstrating the utter arbitrariness of gender divisions. Burger. Hotdog. Are you a burger or a hotdog? Through the repetition the words are utterly defamiliarised; their automatised perceptions are lost and we are left with the sounds, the letters, the objects, the bread buns, the meat shapes. After this linguistic performance, all that is left is the dubious sense of a spectrum of bread-encased-meat-items, and the processes of categorisation and binary division rendered ridiculous.

A rose by any other name? This partial question, itself multiply chopped, sliced, mixed and minced from its Shakespearian roots, is perhaps particularly resonant for those outside of the dominant order of gender division. Would a queer/trans/non-binary/intersex human, by any other name, possess the same internal sense of themselves? Surely it is through sheer materiality of these moments that the divisions crumble and split. The next moment is creativity. 'Make me new': with masochistic fervour, Renaissance poet John Donne entreats the God he desires to break him down in order to remake him (Donne 1994: 252). Perhaps we can make this moment new. '. . . To dance again with life', Sara Ahmed says in her description of the reappropriation of old norms in queer family gatherings (Ahmed 2006: 164). To make anew: the moment by which sense is stripped of its habit and its material form is held, perceived and reshaped. This is queer defamiliarisation.

Every Term Must Be Supplanted by Another Term

The linguistic conflations of the distinctions discussed above – sameness and difference, stasis and movement, synchrony and diachrony – are hugely important when we think about a divisive category such as gender. When we create a new term we create a new category. We create a limit; we demarcate; we draw a dividing line between the thing and the not-thing. The living, breathing organism of language will forever be tied up with the equivocal and restless creation of identity categories, even in the same breath as the critique of the concept of identity itself. The categories and terms that have emerged within queer/trans* culture and are slowly making their way into the mainstream in some lucky places are steps on the way to what some would describe as the utopia of a post-gender world. They are both inclusive and exclusive. This leads us to the fundamental paradox linking up Jakobson's thought with the eternal movement of contemporary queer discourse: *it must create new terms*, if only to give the illusion of staticity, but with the full knowledge that those terms will soon be eclipsed for new terms, and a new system set up. The system can never be totalised, measured, finished or stopped; it is never complete. It never ends, yet every time a new term is created this creates the necessary illusion of an end. It is a dynamic, living, breathing, self-generating, self-thwarting system.

There is an image by the artist Tony Toggles that has been shared widely within queer, trans* and non-binary communities across social media platforms since 2014. A square image with a pink background, two speech bubbles and a human head. The question posed to the head: Are you a boy or a girl? The head's answer: No. This affirmative refusal of the conventional question demonstrates some of the ways in which poststructuralist understandings of language and gender literally beyond the binary can help those for whom the either/or option is utterly insufficient. We have come a long way in our thinking around bathrooms since Jacques Lacan's narration of the bar of urinary differentiation in 1957, though as I write these are increasingly worrying times for those existing outside gender norms.

I quoted Ezra Furman in the Introductions describing queer as 'continual transformation'. The proliferation of new terms for categories and typologies of orientation, gender presentation, sexual practice and style is another gesture which is both affirmative and negative. In practice, the proliferation itself betrays a gendered inequality that is a feminist issue. Isabel Waidner discusses gay taxa in the queer avant-garde novel *Gaudy Bauble* (2017), specifically that of certain notoriously (male) gay areas of London and the proliferation of animal types associated with particular styles and builds of gay human male. 'Is the derivative status of lesbians behind the unquestioned absence of the womanly Eagle on Kennington Lane? How many self-identified Ursulas per one-thousand Bears? Had there been a lesbian equivalent to the historical, hysterical, galvanising, generative, prolific, prohibitive, empowering, limiting, liberating, inclusive, exclusive, offensive Gay Zoo?' (Waidner 2017: 22). The continual transformation of queer taxa may be an affirmative gesture but the male categories of bear, otter, cub, pig and others have been accepted into at least some parts of mainstream culture while there is no established female equivalent to these animal categories. The problem with the ways that we go about refining the categories is analogous to the problematic and privileged position from which critiques of subjectivity in favour of difference emerges, which is analogous to the problematic and privileged position from which critiques of areas such as intersectionality emerge.

Variance/Invariance

The fluid is stable; the solid which wears away is unstable – Heraclitus and Parmenides were both right. Hence the notion of homeorrhesis.
(Serres 1982: 74)

Notwithstanding the somewhat different forms that the notion of 'fundamental affinities' takes in the arts and the sciences, the dominance of the search for the relationship over that for the related items themselves knits together the topological nucleus of this century's art and Einsteinian science.
(Jakobson 1985: 261)

Invariance: properties remain the same regardless of transformations in conditions of measurement. Invariance is a concept that filters through from mathematics and physics to linguistics and elsewhere, but its uses and understandings are entangled between these realms. The equation $E = mc^2$ was derived from the inconsistency between two principles: Newton's principle of the relativity of motion and Maxwell's principle of constancy of the speed of light. Whether geometrical in the first instance or topological in the second, both principles rely upon a notion of invariance. Jacques Monod describes the basic strategy of science as 'the ferreting out of invariants' (Monod 1972: 94). Linguistically we could say that formalism and structuralism are also constituted by the ferreting out of invariants, although the nature of this invariance differs according to which linguist we are consulting. Saussure's linguistic invariants would be more absolute than Jakobson's, for example. Both Jakobson's six functions of language (from which the poetic function discussed above is derived) and his general notion of invariance are relational; they exist in relation to their oppositional functions. In Jakobson's thought, as we have seen, invariance is more complex, as we have seen in his perception of system and evolution within language as co-constituted. As part of his ongoing critique of Saussurian linguistics, Jakobson consistently foregrounds the search for linguistic *invariants in the midst of variation*, as was discussed in the Introductions. Rather than a mere critique of the static side of the dualism (invariance) in favour of the dynamic (variance), Jakobson prefers to see these oppositions as reciprocally determined.

Both the ambiguous nature of invariance and its creative potential can be further perceived if we look at some of the ways that the term figures in both linguistic and non-linguistic terms. In an essay discussing various types of creative translation and transposition, Jakobson calls equivalence in difference 'the cardinal problems of language and the pivotal concern of linugistics' (Jakobson 1971: 233). What Jakobson describes as 'equivalence in difference' is the reciprocity of variance and invariance. The specific type of linguistic invariance that Jakobson proposes is described by his collaborator Linda Waugh as relational invariance, meaning that '. . . there is associated with any item in any language certain defining characteristics which remain no matter what alterations of or influences on that item there may be as it is used in various contexts or situations' (Waugh 1976: 68). As Waugh outlines, the focus on relationships between elements in a system rather than the elements themselves filtered through in the early twentieth century from relativity theory. Relational invariance is therefore the invariance associated with each sound in the linguistic system of which it is a part. This relational invariance is what links language with science and mathematics, and as Waugh points out, the science of invariance is topology. Jakobson's invariance is equivalence under isomorphic transformations: its form is topological. Interestingly, Jakobson conducted a seminar on physics and linguistics with Niels Bohr in the 1950s at MIT, in which concepts such as invariance would no doubt have been discussed in detail. Jakobson cites Bohr in his paper on Einstein, drawing attention to what Bohr describes as 'the exigencies of relativistic invariance' (Bohr 1958: 72). Through Bohr and Jakobson, physics and linguistics were united in what Jakobson describes as 'the search for and structure of the ultimate constituents of both the physical and the linguistic universe, the 'elementary quanta' (Jakobson 1985a: 263). It is interesting that both Bohr and quanta have taken centre stage again in recent years due to the work of physicist Karen Barad, who reads Bohr in order to think about quantum physics and the entanglement of matter and meaning (Barad 2007). Barad is discussed later in this chapter.

In her entry on invariance in the *Posthuman Glossary*, Vera Bühlmann asks how we can think of invariance while remaining faithful to 'a derivative, differential and functional view on sexuation (ontologies: genderedness, queerness, nomadicity, "bodies-that-matter") rather than a structural or homeostatic, symmetry-based and equational view rooted in identity (metaphysics: principles, laws, axioms, elements, atoms' (Bühlmann, in Braidotti and Hlavajova 2018: 213). We might also ask: how can we advance any argument about a particular understanding of invariance while remaining with the poetic function, pareidoliac logic, or the logic of the doily discussed earlier? Instead of or alongside patterns of roses we search for conceptual patterns. The relation of variance with invariance in Jakobson's thought could be perceived as similar to other thinkers' articulations of the relation between difference and sameness and/or movement and stasis, whether in language, outside language or both. After all, if patterns are nothing but the repetitions of shapes, then conceptual patterns are nothing but the repetitions of conceptual shapes. Another thinker we could turn to who traces the lines between linguistic and non-linguistic understandings of concepts such as invariance is Michel Serres. In *Hermes: Literature, Science, Philosophy* (1982) Serres discusses the concept of the living organism as a dynamic system demonstrating both sameness and difference, stasis and flow, variance and invariance.

> The living organism, ontogenesis and phylogenesis combined, is all of times . . . Homeorrhetic means at least that: the rhesis flows, but similarity pushes upstream and resists. All the temporal vectors possessing a directional arrow are here, in this place, arranged in the shape of a star. What is an organism? A sheaf of times. What is a living system? A bouquet of times. (Serres 1982: 75)

In order to talk about the dynamism of a system Serres coins the term *homeorrhesis*. This term is a variant on the more conventional homeostasis (steady internal conditions maintained by living things), but instead of stasis we have rhesis – movement. Serres draws on the figure of the eternally flowing river and draws Parmenides (the world as an invariant) together with Heraclitus (the world as flux), as we see in the quotation at the beginning of the chapter. Serres uses the concept of the living organism (which we can read as both linguistic and non-linguistic) as being of multiple temporalities. This constitutes a critique of temporal unilinearity of a kind different to the syntactical play of Stein discussed above. The figures that Serres employs to illustrate the complex temporal interweavings of living organisms are themselves organic, and funnily enough, the flower motif is also repeated here, among stellar organisms too. All arrangements are non-linear but are complexly spatialised. The organism, the bouquet, the doily, the spatialised Steinian sentence: living arrangements requiring the interdependence of variance and invariance.

Zombie Signs/Metanoia

Is it wise to follow the pattern further, deform the shape further, discover more roses? An invariance of variance *in language* is another articulation of the continual transformation described in the Introductions and narrated above. It is a language that constantly shifts, wherein the constant *is* the shift. Repeated variances of invariances. If form is deforming itself then the conceptual (topological) shape (the co-constituence of variance and invariance) retains its properties under deformation. Onwards we go. Jakobson and Serres are by no means the only thinkers to have challenged synchrony, succession or stasis in the sign. Here I will briefly discuss James Williams's process philosophy of the sign, and Armen Avenassian and Anke Hennig's 'retroformalist'-inspired concept of metanoia. Both of these examples inject their own dynamic versions of the sameness/difference and movement/stasis relations into formalist and structuralist figurations, permitting a more mobile and politically valent framework of language and world.

James Williams achieves this through the creation of a speculative process philosophy of the sign. Echoing Braidotti's words, Williams's Deleuzian reading of the sign is 'a critical and creative approach designed to allow for shifts between established pictures' (Williams 2015: 8). A shift in Williams's thought here is a change of intensity, and in the sign, meaning is created precisely by a change in intensity. It is the shift that creates meaning. For Williams the sign is a process; it is a matter of intensities and relations. Meaning is therefore a change of intensity between signs. This is another sharp distinction from conventional synchronic structuralism comparable to that of Jakobson discussed above; the focus is on the shift rather than on fixity. Williams sums up the dialectical progression of conventional synchronic structuralism thus:

> In order to function reliably language must tame the process of signification by fixing it. Signs become settled in a closed language which is only set in motion through the intervention of speech in a discontinuous movement between closed states of language and intervening stages of openness in speech. (Williams 2015: 113)

The process sign, for Williams, is very different and turns away from structuralist aspects of the sign such as the signifier/signified distinction and its arbitrariness. Williams's process sign is a multiplicity. Instead of the classic synchronic cut we see in Saussure, Williams's process sign is continuous and intensive, with no aspects of duality and all structures mobile. It is therefore thoroughly Deleuzian in its articulation.

> A sign might appear dead, but it is just running at low intensity for selected relations or even running at high intensity but in a way we are not conscious of. Continuous processes cannot be disentangled and reassigned into clear categories of inert form and living use according to dualist distinctions. (Williams 2015: 17)

Rather than create another dualism (alive/dead), Williams suggests that signs are *the living dead*; they are 'self-generating and self-dividing zombies'. He then suggests a game wherein a shape is cut out of a postcard, and then the postcard with its cut-out hole is placed against a background or substratum so that two worlds are juxtaposed. 'There is no world that is not a zombie world for any other, ready to rise from the tomb and become a matter of urgent critical demands and creative openings through the medium of signs' (Williams 2015: 32). The result of the zombie postcard game is to create new shifts in perception and new lines of connectivity.

I take a postcard with an appealing image of thick entangled colourful material tubes, worms or wires bursting out from a surface – Anna Ray's *Margate Knot* (2016) – fold it in half, cut out a rough trapezoid shape, and hold it up to the window pane in front of me. Moving it to fit each pane of the window creates a new sign. Nodding outside towards the bottom of the window are the dark, wrinkled buds of rose hips, thorned stems and bright green leaves, enshrined or enshrouded by the postcard frame: a mass of intestines, elongated maggots, bendy multicoloured cotton buds, electrical cords or alien eels. Incongruity! The garden outside is in Tooting, South London, a safe Labour seat and a wild rectangle of garden where squawking wild parakeets (imported during a moment of hyper-imperialism over a century ago) alongside native birds almost drown out the constant hum of the A214. At the time of writing – twelve days before the UK may clatter out of Europe – there is a sense of a collective throwing-up of hands in the air in despair at the futility of each political non-manoeuvre, at least in cosmopolitan London. The postcard hails from the district of Thanet in Kent, the district which houses Margate and the Turner Contemporary gallery where this artwork was exhibited in 2017 and where there was a 63.8 per cent Leave vote in the 2016 referendum. The postcard image takes me momentarily to Margate or Hackney-on-Sea as it is cynically called due to an influx of artists fleeing from gentrified East London; colourful streaks of patterned Technicolour clothing against the grey of sea and sky on the otherwise quaint and quiet Kent coast; flashes of paint on a natural landscape like the parakeets which flash green against the dark boughs of trees. Moving the postcard up towards the sky the frame captures the silhouette of the tall hanging silver birch, empty of leaves (it is March) and the sign is crying; the world is dying. Each time the postcard is placed somewhere else against the garden scene the splicing of the organic with the inorganic sprouts new melancholy, so much so that each single wire in Ray's image appears to resonate with a slightly different tone of sadness. With each movement and clash of systems, a tangled cacophony.

The perception of interdependence or perhaps interpenetration between the sign and its substratum is a Deleuzian manoeuvre which removes the hard boundaries between things and their environment. Williams criticises the separation of the sign from its signifying process: '. . . we cannot distinguish the sign from the process of signification' (Williams 2015: 112). Later on in the book Williams suggests another physical rendering of his process philosophy, this time deliberately *not* making any cuts so as to remain within a topological figuration. Rather than the Saussurian example of the cutting out of a two-sided piece of paper, the sign according to Williams's process philosophy would employ the topological properties of a thin rubber sheet stretched out in the wind, not cut, but with lines drawn on it according to an initial selection. 'Directions and singular point shift and move according to the stretching of the sheet. This is the sign: not the stasis of a two-sided cut but rather the dynamism of lines in motion determined by an initial selection and diagram of movements' (Williams 2015: 119). Williams's topological presentation is useful because it points to the need for more dimensions in the thinking of language. This in itself is not new, but is important, and we will see more on this in Chapter 4.

Are there any more roses to be found? Williams argues that 'to speculate is to create new signs' (Williams 2015: 27). This process of speculative sign-making also underpins Armen Avenassian and Anke Hennig's book *Metanoia: A Speculative Ontology of Language, Thinking and the Brain* (2018). In *Metanoia* roses still abound. Avenassian and Hennig take Stein's famous line discussed above and consider the material qualities – the redness – of the roses in the line. In their account the particular aspects of the rose are opened up, attended to and examined prismatically: the rose's rosiness, its flowerness, its redness – all are scrutinised with a scientific precision that is simultaneously both synchronic and diachronic. Through a discussion of rose and colour taxonomies and focusing on the metaphoric development of the red rose since the Middle Ages and finding its apex in Romantic literature, they trace the recursive movement of 'rose' between word and world. For them, as Stein herself stated, the formula for *a rose is a rose is a rose*, which they write as 1 > 2 > 3, permits the Romantic metaphor to actualise itself.

> The *poietic* circle does not trace a movement from a concrete expression and back again. In the circle, all three dimensions of the sign combine: redness does not become manifest at any point along the length of the sentence. Rather, redness grows out of language, into whose paradigm the metaphor has entered . . . (Avenassian and Hennig 2018: 67)

The process that they are detailing here is an aesthetic experience, but it is not just that: it is a shift, analogous to the shifts outlined in the Introductions: 'It is about encountering a changing object, an encounter in which we suddenly cross the line into the future' (Avenassian and Hennig 2018: 164). What they describe in this account of metanoia is a movement of defamiliarisation itself. Recursion here is designated as the type of movement they advocate between language and the brain: it is circular and refers to itself. As with many of the mobile structures described in this chapter, metanoia too is a constancy of movement. For Avenassian and Hennig, recursion is a linguistic invariant but it is mobile: it is a movement. As with Deleuze and Guattari's continuous variation (discussed below) and other, recursion is the only way that an invariant can be thought: through a constancy of movement. They describe this movement in three parts:

> First, the reader's thought is not just addressed by the language of a certain thought. In metanoia, you go beyond what you thought up to this point. Second, you seek a new language for this and find it where you change your own world, where you take the place of its referent. Third, you determine yourself anew and become an other. (Avenassian and Hennig 2018: 45)

In this schema, formalist and structuralist conceptions of language morph into something more mobile, contemporary, radical and unfixed. This is done through innovative readings of Jakobson among others. They too read Jakobson and Tynyanov's 'Problems in the Study of Literature and Language' in terms of the interweaving of diachrony and synchrony, and find that even as far back as this, not only are system and evolution reciprocally dependent but this is a methodological perspective. The stone is stony; the tree greens; the rose is red: recursively, each and every time as if for the first time: such it is to defamiliarise and perceive anew.

Axis/Assemblage

One important aspect of the various mobilisations of invariance in linguistics discussed so far is the assertion that language does not happen in a vacuum: language is social and therefore contingent. As well as being simultaneously syntagmatic and paradigmatic, the dynamic line of language that Jakobson traces is simultaneously both creatively autonomous and context-bound. As Jakobson's collaborator linguist Linda Waugh states, 'One could say that the poem provides its own "universe of discourse"', but she also warns against perceptions of complete autonomy or self-referentiality: 'a poem does not exist in a vacuum: it is part of a general historico-cultural context and indeed depends on that context for its interpretation' (Waugh 1980: 72). This argument is developed in the 'Postulates of Linguistics' plateau in Deleuze and Guattari's *A Thousand Plateaus*. Context changes, and meaning is dependent upon context, which means that variation itself is constant: it is the constant. This is the concept of continuous variation that they outline. Deleuzian feminist Tamsin Lorraine gives a good example of this when she suggests the hypothetical situation of a feminist philosopher delivering a paper at a conference. The hypothetical paper strays into the realm of performance art. Depending on the audience, the paper will be accepted as 'philosophy'. The tension created from this situation either increases or decreases as the speaker either tones down the performative element to placate the audience or is asked to stop speaking by a moderator. The point is that the possible variations on this line of continuous variation are not actualised but are nevertheless real. 'The lines of continuous variation that insist in the speech acts and actions that actually manifest are specific to particular social fields at given times' (Lorraine 2011: 14). Having given a few performative conference presentations myself in the past few years I can relate to this, particularly as part of Le Tomatique alongside Vikki Chalklin when handstands, flumping, falling, plastic lobsters, bread batons, marshmallows, clown braces and stick-on false-eyelash goatees have been our aids. At feminist and new materialist events the reception has been generous: people want to be woken up and jerked out of their postprandial conference snooze, which is precisely what the movement of defamiliarisation seeks to enact.

Deleuze and Guattari's linguistics orbit around the concept of the *order-word*, which takes J. L. Austin's work on performative utterances – specifically illocutionary speech acts – and extends this to all language.[3] The order-word, for Deleuze and Guattari, is a figure that

---

[3] Austin makes a temporal distinction between perlocutionary and illocutionary speech acts: while illocutionary acts do what they say in the moment of saying, perlocutionary acts produce certain consequences which follow on. See Palmer (2014) for a discussion of this related to the temporality of the manifesto; see Austin (1962) for the original elucidation.

operates for all of language in that *all* language performs and enacts itself, which makes *all* language, to echo Rosi Braidotti's words on the 'double-edged vision' of feminist theory, an act both creative and critical (Braidotti 2006: 273). This could lead us to state that all propaganda can be read as poetry, and all poetry can be read as propaganda. The order-word itself is a constant variable, and language itself is continuous variation. Language is not a homogenous but a heterogeneous system, meaning that it is composed of variables throughout. 'We cannot content ourselves with a duality between constants as linguistic factors that are explicit or potentially explicit, and variables as extrinsic, non-linguistic factors. For the pragmatic variables of usage are internal to enunciation and constitute the implicit presuppositions of language' (Deleuze and Guattari 2004: 94). Variables are inherent to enunciations; enunciations form assemblages; assemblages relate to the incorporeal transformations of the function: this is Deleuze and Guattari's pragmatics. Deleuze and Guattari return to the Stoics in their critique of language, and pick up some of Deleuze's formulations around bodies, causes and incorporeal transformations. Rather than form and content, Deleuze and Guattari look to the work of Louis Hjelmslev and distinguish content and expression, which are woven into one another continually.

> The independence of the form of expression and the form of content is not the basis for a parallelism between them or a representation of one by the other, but on the contrary a parceling of the two . . . forms of expression and forms of content communicate through a conjunction of their quanta of relative deterritorialization, each intervening, operating through the other. (Deleuze and Guattari 2004: 96–7)

How might we mobilise continuous variation, or the Deleuzo-Guattarian perception of language as assemblage, in order to think about the aim stated at the beginning of this book: to advance feminist, queer, intersectional politics? Jasbir Puar's call to read the framework of intersectionality in terms of assemblage in *Terrorist Assemblages* (2007) is one exemplary articulation of this. Following both Jakobson and Deleuze and Guattari as discussed above, her work also relies on the perception of dynamic systems. Puar mobilises the intersectional model so that it is able to account for more variation, providing a critique of the intersectional model on a number of counts. Firstly, the presumed separability of its components, to which an assemblage possesses the advantage of understanding forces as interwoven. Secondly, intersectionality presupposes stable categories of identity over space and time, whereas assemblages would perceive these as mutable. Thirdly, she argues that intersectionality is compliant with state-enforced segregation through positionality. Rather than perceiving assemblage as entirely supplanting intersectionality, however, Puar points out in 'I would rather be a cyborg than a goddess: Becoming-Intersectional in Assemblage Theory' that rather than oppositional we should perceive them as 'frictional' (Puar 2012: 50). Puar demonstrates that in Crenshaw's original formulation (after the Combahee River Collective) the figure is always a dynamic one: the traffic intersection is always already an event. Rather than decry intersecionality for its shortcomings it is possible to mobilise it. Puar's Deleuzo-Guattarian angle is useful for doing so. A politics that recognises the dynamic processes occurring within and between bodies is required.

Intra-Acting/Intra-Secting

In the work of Karen Barad, the relationship between the linguistic and the material is reconfigured into

> a causal relationship between specific exclusionary practices embodied as specific material configurations of the world (i.e., discursive/(con)figurations rather than 'words') and specific material phenomena (i.e., relations rather than 'things'). (Barad 2003: 814)

Barad's materialist and posthumanist performativity places phenomena (which she defines as ontologically primitive relations utterly distinct from both Kant's phenomena and the phenomenologist's phenomena) before any pre-existing relata: the relations come first. Meaning is produced through 'specific agential intra-actions' which enable phenomena to become determinate. An intra-action enacts what Barad calls an *agential cut*, which does separate subject and object, but only at a local level rather than pre-existing the phenomenon entirely. In contrast to the Cartesian inherence of a subject-object distinction Barad proposes the concept of *exteriority within phenomena*. In contrast to the status of apparatuses as neutral, stable and static, Barad posits apparatuses as implicated, dynamic and inseparable from their outside. It is intra-activity which constitutes the world's ontological 'differential mattering' for Barad. Words and things are utterly entangled in Barad's thinking of intra-activity. Discursive practices are, for Barad, causal intra-actions which are both cause and effect in their articulation. They are 'not speech acts, linguistic representations, or even linguistic performances', which perhaps separates Barad's thought from that of Deleuze and Guattari.

What Barad is pointing to here is that discursive practices are material and materiality is discursive; the two are 'mutually implicated in the dynamics of intra-activity' (Barad 2003: 22). The reciprocal determination of the material and the discursive here is very clear, which is why it is surprising that new materialism has somehow gained a reputation for privileging the material over the discursive – owing much, perhaps, to decontextualised interpretations of Barad's opening line to her article 'Posthumanist Performativity' (2003): 'Language has been granted too much power' (Barad 2003: 801). Prior to Barad's arguments here and in *Meeting the Universe Halfway* (2007), in *The Promises of Monsters* Donna Haraway discusses the concept of the material-semiotic derived from actor-network theory in order to discuss the 'material-semiotic "actor"' in order to highlight the object of knowledge as an active part of the apparatus of bodily production (Haraway 2004: 68).

Is it possible to mobilise this for the thinking of the axes of difference as outlined above? Does it make sense to think of *intra*-sectionality? For feminist scholars and theorists of gender, Barad develops Butler's notion of performativity thus: 'performativity is not understood as iterative citationality (Butler) but rather iterative intra-activity' (Barad 2003: 828). Performativity extends beyond the merely human and discursive into the posthuman and material-discursive. It is not only us that enact and/or are enacted through language; we are the same as the matter around us, and *everything* is constituted through the process of ongoing intra-activity. There is no separation between subject and environment, and consequently no separation between epistemology and ontology, which is why onto-epistemology is Barad's term of choice for the practices of knowing and being.

In order to tackle the question of whether Barad's work is useful to think through a dynamic reconfiguring of the problems faced around frameworks of intersectionality, it is perhaps helpful to look at some of her sources. Barad uses the operation of reading and writing diffractively to challenge the ways that difference is thought. As a practice, diffractive reading has developed within new materialist thought primarily by Iris van der Tuin (see van der Tuin 2011, 2014a, 2014b; Dolphijn and van der Tuin 2013). In 'Diffracting Diffraction' (2014) Barad presents and diffracts the work of multiple thinkers in such a way that their thought is demonstrated to be productively entangled rather than opposed. Barad reads Trinh Minh-ha and Gloria Anzaldúa diffractively alongside quotations from others including Derrida, Haraway and her own work, in order to present ways in which difference might be thought to figure differently (Barad 2014). The writing itself enacts a diffraction pattern, forming oscillations and waves which diffract further and further, creating more and more new oscillations and waves as it goes. There is still very much a sense of deconstructionist postmodern textuality here: quotations upon quotations show very clearly that this work still operates within the domain of the intertextual even in its material-discursive presentations.

> To survive in the Borderlands
> you must live *sin fronteras*
> be a crossroads.
> Mestiza consciousness. Marrano consciousness. Trans/queer/intersex consciousness. Transmaterialities (Anzaldúa 1987: 195 and Barad 2014: quoting Barad 2015 (then forthcoming))

In this fragment we see Barad setting Anzaldúa to work with Barad herself, and in this concluding part to the article the text is a patterning of quotations and fragments, an eddying or perhaps an intra-action itself. Both Anzaldúa and Minh-ha are vital to Barad's diffractive writing practice here: they are the backbone to Baradian diffraction's socio-political engagement. The Mestiza and Marrano figurings and the intra-lingual poetry from Anzaldúa's *Borderlands* as well as the transmaterialities from Barad's 2015 work are the material-discursive phenomena which are intra-acting. These behave, as Barad points out, with Bohrian complementarity: atoms behave like waves, whereas elsewhere atoms know themselves as particles. They perform themselves differentially; they intra-act. As well as Anzaldúa's Mestiza and Marrano consciousness, Minh-ha's work in encapsulating the refiguring of difference in the thinking of otherness is fundamental to Barad's thought. Rather than the 'apartheid type of difference' which views difference 'not as a tool of creativity to question multiple forms of repression and dominance, but as a tool of segregation, to exert power on the basis of racial and sexual essences', Minh-ha advocates 'difference as understood in many feminist and non-Western contexts ... is not opposed to sameness, nor synonymous with separateness' (Minh-ha 1988). This filters very directly into Barad's notion of exteriority within phenomena. It is important to point out that Anzaldúa's and Minh-ha's texts are Barad's tools; they are her apparatus. Just as much as Niels Bohr's physics, these writings, which come from places of multiple disenfranchisement and experiment in differential intra-textuality, are the entangled roots of Barad's work and should be acknowledged as such.

Barad has suggested ways of avoiding what she perceives as the Euclideanisation of intersectionality, described as such because the figure that it uses – the common notion of the intersection – is one drawn from recognisable Euclidean geometry. Barad writes in 2001: 'Identities are not separable, they do not intersect. Rather, identity formation must be understood in terms of the topological dynamics of intra-activity' (Barad 2001: 99). Elizabeth Grosz later similarly criticises the classificatory framework of intersectionality because it still has recourse to sameness. As she states, intersectionality

> actually attempts to generate forms of sameness, similar modes of access to social resources, through the compensation for socially specific modes of marginalization (for migrants, access to translation services; for battered wives, access to shelters, and so on) . . . No voice ever represents a group, category, or people without dissent; and no categories are so clear-cut and unambiguous that they can be applied willy-nilly, without respect for the specific objects of their investigation. (Grosz 2011: 94)

Not only is intersectionality too static in Grosz's summation, but it also forbids both fuzziness and movement within and between intersections.

More recently, 'superdiversity' has been introduced as a potential improvement on intersectionality for thinking political differences. A Special Issue of the *Dutch Journal for Gender Studies* (Geerts et al. 2018) discusses this in detail. Faten Khazaei cites the work of Candace West and Sarah Fenstermaker in their critique of intersectionality due to its perception of power relations as static and ahistorical, and that it 'does not consider the continuous reformulation and situatedness of gender, class, and race' (Khazaei 2018: 10). Khazaei discusses superdiversity (a term introduced by Steven Vertovec in 2007) as accommodating of variations in aspects such as migration patterns, education, work skills and experiences. As Khazaei states, 'the potential of superdiversity to name the heterogeneity within the multiple axes of differentiation is the key to establishing a dialogue with intersectionality' (Khazaei 2018: 13). Khazaei concludes by suggesting that the two frameworks can inform one another. This suggests that the concept of one framework's struggle for dominance over another is redundant, and the diffraction of them together will not only bear more fruit but is necessary to accommodate for the complexities of difference in the world.

In *Meeting the Universe Halfway* (2007) Barad gives an example of a thinker whose work presents identity formation in precisely this topological fashion: Leela Fernandes, in her book *Producing Workers* (1997) which discusses the ways that gender, class and culture intra-act in the context of the Calcutta Jute Mills. As Fernandes argues, 'we cannot simply acknowledge that social categories such as class, gender and community occasionally "intersect" with each other. When we choose to analyse particular phenomena through the lens of one or the other category, we may ourselves inadvertently be producing political boundaries that simultaneously rest on and circumscribe other categories' (Fernandes 1997: 161). What is required, then, as Barad states, is an understanding of structures as material-discursive phenomena and of identity formation as 'a dynamics of changing topologies of space, time and matter' (Barad 2007: 240). It is topology that is required, according to Barad, to allow us to think these things fully. It is not enough, she argues, to think about the social 'constructedness' of certain geometrical figures. 'Questions of size and shape (geometrical concerns) must be supplemented by, and reevaluated in terms of, questions of boundary, connectivity, interiority, and exteriority (topological concerns)' (Barad 2007: 244). Topological concerns will be further discussed in Chapter 4, but for now it is important to note that Barad makes a political case for their relevance in the modelling and thinking of identity formation.

Boycunt/Logic of the 'As'

'Like and like likely and likely likely and likely like and like' (Stein 2004: 221). Gertrude Stein's trick of creating sense where it appears not to be is often down to sentences consisting almost entirely of polysemic function words. These words sometimes give the impression of doubly articulating themselves, though it is often the ambiguity, the hovering between different uses, that creates the movement of sense. 'It is very likely that nearly everyone has been very nearly certain that something that is interesting is interesting them' (Stein 2004: 21). Here we see the repetition of 'interesting' operate with a different sense each time: repetition as difference. 'Interesting' as adjective shifts to 'interesting' as present continuous; 'interesting' as intransitive becomes 'interesting' transitive. This shift, which takes place somewhere outside this cluster of letters i-n-t-e-r-e-s-t-i-n-g, changes the meaning entirely. Similarly, the repetition of 'nearly' produces different effects each time: while both are suggestive of approaching a limit or telos, the first 'nearly' is approaching a numerical limit whereas the second is approaching a feeling (of certainty). Homonymy, which I will discuss further in Chapter 3, is not only important but is generative of meaning. It worlds as it words.

Stein's placing of these words close to one another highlights their equivocal nature, but in fact we do not need repetition to highlight equivocation. The shift can be expressed within one lexical item. The phrase in this subtitle, 'logic of the "as"', is my gesture towards what Deleuze describes as a logic of the AND, in which the conjunction ('and') operates as a copula ('to be'), a manoeuvre I have discussed elsewhere (Palmer 2014). I am suggesting something different but related here: a logic of the 'AS'. As well as operating as a comparative adverb, a conjunction, a pronoun, a preposition, the word 'as' often demonstrates analogical movement. Along with 'like', these words signify the movement of a simile. In Stein's 'Composition As Explanation', for example, we take this title to mean that there is an analogy being drawn between composition and explanation. The word 'as' is the linking word that heralds the simile, or comparison, or substitution: it is composition = explanation but somewhere in between. This in turn heralds the shift itself – from *explanation*, which would generally be understood as syntagmatic, to *composition*, which is not strictly paradigmatic but suggests a more spatialised type of arrangement.

> Books contained tenses like closets full of clothes, but the present was the only place we were alive, and the present was like a painting, without before or after, spread to be sure, but not in time; and although ... the present was not absolutely flat, it was nevertheless not much thicker than pigment. (Gass 1979: 69)

As William H. Gass points out, in Stein's *Tender Buttons* the crucial word is *change*, and with every material shift that takes place in the text, from restorative processes such as cleaning and mending to quantitative changes in sewing, decorating, cooking, and these processes are constantly compared structurally to writing.

> Words can be moved about like furniture in their sentences; they can be diced like carrots (Stein cuts up a good number); they can be used in several different ways simultaneously, like wine; they can be brushed off, cleaned and polished; they can be ingeniously joined, like groom and bed, anxiety and bride. Every sentence is a syntactical space (a room) in which words (things, people) act (cook, clean, eat or excrete) in order to produce quite special and very valuable qualities of feeling. (Gass 1979: 79)

I am suggesting, then, that Stein's entire argument is encapsulated in this title: it is not quite 'Composition IS Explanation', but the logic of the 'as' presents this as a possibility, hovering within the word. The best way to express this analogical movement or shift between 'as' and 'is' might be through a speculative attempt at a Steinian sentence.

As as is, and as is is, and as is as is are all the same, because an as can be as an is can do, which is to say as can do.

All this sentence is doing is placing the movements of 'as' and 'is' side by side to demonstrate that they might be similar, and in doing so, there is a suggestion that 'as' may acquire the status of a verb ('as can do'). 'As' is more onto-epistemologically fluid than 'is'; it permits an understanding of categories as mobile and shifting, resists finality, and ultimately constitutes an opening rather than a closing of terminological boundaries.

I want to conclude this chapter by suggesting that a logic of the 'as', the shift within the 'as', demonstrates the affirmation of queer language, shift language, language in transition. It is precisely the equivocation of 'as', drawn from a critique of linguistic linearity in favour of more complex assemblages, that allows for one lexical object to operate as shift and differ within itself. We know from word blends and neologisms that this is possible, and the significance and proliferation of these will be discussed later in the book. For now, let's take one example. In the conclusion to his poetry collection *Rallying* (2017) Quinn Eades draws inspiration from the text from Stein's *Tender Buttons* (1914) to write his own version *Tender Bodies*, which includes the subtitle 'Boycunt'. 'Boycunt' operates according to 'as' rather than 'is'; it is a deliberate (yet uneven, almost synecdochic, part-for-whole, wholeboy for cuntpart) splicing of conventionally oppositional anatomical terms. 'Boycunt' expresses and affirms equivocation from within; it does not seek a teleological end but rather is shift, as shift: it shifts. The text includes some of Stein's original lines in italics interspersed with Eades' own visceral and heartwrenching prose. Stein's line 'The difference is spreading' takes on a different meaning in the context of a transitioning body. The inventorial household nature of Stein's text becomes an emotional inventory; an inventory of love. 'My boycunt is a red leaf and we fuck it together' (Eades 2017: 148) writes Eades, and from the flipping of geometrical and corporeal externalities and internalities bursts forth new angles, new axes, new assemblages. Composition as kaleidoscope: queer defamiliarisation as the splicing of language.

CHAPTER 2

Mythorefleshings

> ... the mythic figure has the power to express in a concentrated way the symbolic order that shapes it. Indeed it is within the symbolic order that the figure takes on a signifying name (a proper name). It does this with a kind of immediate, story-like allusiveness, coming to life in a vital, paradigmatic way.
>
> (Cavarero 1995: 1)

> Raped, appraised, marked down, Bloom takes her place among Bella-Bello's equally bastard boarders: Zoe (life), Kitty (kitten), Flora (vegetable). Brothel blossom, she uncovers a pistil.
>
> (Cixous 1975: 394)

> before I am lost,
> hell must open like a red rose
> for the dead to pass.
>
> (H.D. 1983 [1925]: 55)

> Beneath my feet were the bones of a thousand years. I thought: I cannot bear this world a moment longer.
> *Then, child, make another.*
>
> (Miller 2018: 247)

Mythological figures are presented as archetypes, but to consider these archetypes as originary or universal means accepting that the female figures that we encounter in translations of Ovid or Homer or even those mentioned by philosophers such as Plato are silent and/or only exist in relation to their masculine counterparts. They are either raped and then often punished for being raped, or they are mothers or wives belonging in the home, or they are enchantresses who lure heroes to their deaths. In her work *In Spite of Plato: A Feminist Rewriting of Ancient Philosophy* (1995), Adriana Cavarero gives voice to four female mythological figures who are mentioned in passing in the works of Plato, often as metaphorical conduits for the denouement to a metaphysical argument. For example, in her account of the character of Penelope (who we know from Homer's *Odyssey* and subsequent rewritings, as I will discuss below), Cavarero begins with an excerpt from Plato's *Phaedo* wherein Penelope's role as weaver (and unweaver) operates as a fleshly metaphor for the task of philosophy itself. Penelope's task of weaving and unweaving is rendered a pointless exercise in Plato's analogy, because the *unweaving* symbolises precisely what the soul should not do; it should not return to the body but rather strive to contemplate truth and the divine by following discourse, until death finally frees it. Of course, Penelope's unweaving is all but pointless: it saves her from the suitors and carves out a space for her that is free from wifely duties yet remains in the domestic space expected of a woman of her time. In unweaving, Penelope rebels: she challenges the space and the time meted out to her. As long as she is unweaving she is, in Cavarero's words, 'anomalous' (Cavarero 1995: 12): as long as she continues to weave and unweave, she is no one's wife.

Cavarero's project in *In Spite of Plato* is a rewriting: she begins each chapter with a fragment from Plato which mentions a female mythological character, and then refleshes the character from a new angle, with a new lens. You might say she defamiliarises these characters in order that they are perceived anew. You might also say that she frees them from the yoke of the patriarchal logos from which they emerge. In this chapter I chart several other comparable mythological rewritings, refoldings and refleshings. These three 're-' prefixes suggest that the processes of writing, folding and fleshing have already been done and are now being *re*done. These processes are presented here as feminist writing strategies that are simultaneously rewritten, refolded and refleshed within and between themselves. Here I discuss various literary writings and their reimaginings in order to demonstrate that (and I will use that threefold grammatical structure again): *rewriting can be refolding can be refleshing*. I posit rewriting as an embodied affirmation of a chorus of feminist voices, examining a number of strategic reworkings of mythological texts that result in a multiplication of personae and also a reworking of the constantly deforming conceptual shapes that emerged in Chapter 1: acts of defamiliarisation that are also deformation. While the Introduction focused more on the 'de-' prefix, the affirmative gesture of the negative prefix, I am now examining the affordances of the 're-' prefix. I listed the operations of (de)construction, (de)familiarisation, (dis)identification, (dis)orientatation and (de)formalism. I argued that these movements of abstraction or moving away are in fact affirmations which allow things to be perceived anew. The 're-' process focuses more on the thing being perceived anew: the process of its revisioning in an act of rewriting which I argue is simultaneously a refolding and refleshing. The folding is derived from the defamiliarised dimensions that I have already discussed, what we could call a queer topology of proximities and distances which operate according to dimensions which are defamiliarised beyond conventional Euclidean geometries.

In theorising the paradoxical relations between the private sphere, the public sphere and the notion of counterpublics, Michael Warner echoes the notions I discussed in the Introduction and in Chapter 1 relating to *constancy of movement* and *eternal transformation*, both of which, as we have already seen, relate to the deformation processes to which topological shapes are subjected. Warner talks about 'the unending process of redefinition' (Warner 2002: 14), another variant of this constant variation. To belong to a public, one speaks in a certain way, shares certain beliefs or is constrained by certain ideologies. A counterpublic emerges in opposition to a hegemonic or normative public. The imagining of a public, Warner states, is what allows us to conceive of collective acts or decisions or social groupings. And yet, 'publics exist only by virtue of their imagining. *They are a kind of fiction that has taken on life*, and very potent life at that' (Warner 2002: 8; my italicisation). This description, amongs many descriptions, is what has allowed me to conceive of this theory existing within the fictive frame or perhaps on the mobile edge of the fictional world, or the lip of the world, as Stephen Muecke describes it and which I return to in Chapter 3. To conceive of publics *as a fiction* is what leads me to think the possibility of a *fictive public*. This would be a group of personae: we could perhaps call them ontologically translucent in the sense that they are versions of myths. They are deformed, destabilised, defamiliarised, rewritten, refolded and refleshed. I sketch these duplicitous characters below. These fictive publics share qualities of other configurations of publics and counterpublics in that they are it is both familiar and estranged, close and distant, a multiplicity and a unity. To conflate these oppositional tendencies I develop and affirm a paradoxical relationality inspired by the assertion that publics presuppose a proximity of strangers (Warner 2002).

Laurent Berlant and Michael Warner's article 'Sex in Public' takes up Warner's work on publics and counterpublics and thinks this through a specifically queer lens. For them writing in the late 1990s, queer was newly utopian, a 'world-making project' in which new coded forms of intimacy were necessary because all the existing forms were heteronormative. 'Making a queer world has required the development of kinds of intimacy that bear no necessary relation to domestic space, to kinship, to the couple form, or to the nation' (Berlant and Warner 1998: 558). As I have already stated, the concept of 'queer' is constituted by a paradox: the simultaneous desire for and resistance to terminological separation and division. A similar constitutive paradox inheres within some literary publics in the sense that a common or collective radical praxis risks losing its radical nature through its ascendance. 'Dissolution of genres and transgression of borders has become the rule, rather than the exception' (Forslid and Ohlsson 2010: 431). With these paradoxes in mind, the figures I draw together here are collectively different in the sense that they share their 'countered' nature. Importantly, the nature of this counteredness is in a reversal of agency or the removal of a symbolic gag. The countering is therefore a feminist strategy. The lacunae of audible femaleness as in ancient patriarchal discourses such a myths are obvious to us now as feminist researchers, and naturally we want to make those silent female voices speak. We make them speak through the creation of another fictional being or version of the original, and together these unsilenced personae constitute a new type of counterpublic: a fictive one.

Mythological figures are endless sources of fascination for artists and writers, which results in a deformation and multiplication of mythological personae. What makes the figures under discussion here a *public* are the unifying and yet estranging notions of gender and sexuality. Through the interlinked processes of rewriting, refolding and refleshing, gender imbalances are redressed, silenced female voices are unsilenced and the result is a fictive public consisting of a plurality of rewritten female figures who may go by the same name but matter differently. These personae are both the same and different as the prototypes from which they spring. A public is *'poetic world making'* (Warner 2002: 422). In this chapter I literalise that concept, drawing together a host of fictive personae who collectively make up an enfleshed, emancipatory subjectivity. The concept of 'enfleshed' materialism is something that Braidotti develops in *Metamorphoses: Towards a Materialist Theory of Becoming* which thinks through the body to provide an alternative perception of the subject giving priority to 'issues of desire and the erotic imaginary' (Braidotti 2002: 5). Here I continue and extend this project to think about *re*fleshing – what happens when the enfleshed subjects of mythological narratives are reimagined and rematerialised through gestures of queer defamiliarisation.

Feminist rewriting or revisionism is not a new strategy or discourse, particularly in terms of the rewriting of canonical 'greats'. The figures I discuss here are Afrekete, Arachne, Ariadne, Callisto, Circe, Eurydice, Iphis, Lavinia, Medusa and Penelope, but there are many other names who could have equally been the focus. They are mythological staples;

they are typologies themselves. Their stories are comfortable in the sense that we know the perspective from which we are generally meant to perceive them, and the gesture of revisionism involves making them uncomfortable. The making-strange required here is an act of rewriting, refolding and refleshing, which is at the same time an act of defamiliarisation. Here I focus on mythological figures but this is also inextricably tied to the form of the language in which these characters' stories are articulated. Synvariance, or the deliberate variation or defamiliarisation of the syntactic line as discussed in the previous chapter, is relevant here too, as we will see by the end of the chapter.

Personae: Conceptual, Narrative, Collective?

A 'persona' is a useful term for encapsulating multiple narrative concepts of 'role' or 'character' outside of conventional narrative spaces. This has been explored by philosophers such as Deleuze and Guattari, who believe that philosophy relies on conceptual 'personae' to enact the concepts it creates. As they state in *What Is Philosophy?*, 'Even Bergsonian duration is in need of a runner' (Deleuze and Guattari 1994: 64). As I have written elsewhere (Palmer 2014: 129), the conceptual persona in Deleuze and Guattari's terminology lifts an utterance or a being out of its particular enactment and makes it universal; it changes *parole* to *langue*. These concepts are just as ripe for the revisionist strategy. Maria Tamboukou develops the concept of the conceptual persona drawn from Deleuze and Guattari into the *narrative persona* when writing about the women artists in her study. The narrative personae 'become mediators through whom narrative as philosophy mobilizes thinking and narrative as art produces affects' (Tamboukou 2010: 181). The narrative persona demonstrates how we might use a person's story in order to demonstrate the movement of a concept. Simon O'Sullivan similarly develops the concept of *fictioning* in art practice in which art 'speaks back' to its progenitor through becoming something entirely other and untimely. 'For the I is indeed a stranger, but it is only through a specific practice that this stranger can foreground itself from the habitual and familiar' (O'Sullivan 2014: 5). This will be returned to in some detail in Chapter 3.

Braidotti also develops Deleuze and Guattari's concept of conceptual personae when she outlines the need for what she calls 'figurations', which are critical, creative and alternative dramatisations of the subject. It is here that we see critique and creation as explicitly entangled: 'Critique and creation strike a new deal in actualizing the practice of *conceptual personae* or figuration as the active pursuit of affirmative alternatives to the dominant vision of the subject' (Braidotti 2013a: 164). Before examining some examples of these personae, however, we can take a brief look at Deleuze and Guattari's own list of conceptual personae and determine how these might be queered or gendered. Deleuze and Guattari's list leaves no room for the female:

> The destiny of the philosopher is to become his conceptual persona or personae, at the same time that these personae themselves become something other than what they are historically, mythologically, or commonly (the Socrates of Plato, the Dionysus of Nietzsche, the Idiot of Nicholas of Cusa). (Deleuze and Guattari 1994: 64)

A useful literary addition to the list here might be Virginia Woolf's Orlando. Orlando both is and is not Vita Sackville-West; Orlando is both a conceptual and a narrative persona embodying the materiality and fluidity of gender. Rosi Braidotti and Derek Ryan both read Orlando as personifying a queer new materialist vitalism. The following excerpt from Braidotti regarding the Virginia-Vita-Orlando relationship is worth quoting in its entirety:

> In other words, one's affirmation of the life that one is shot through with is materially embodied and embedded in the singularity that is one's enfleshed self. But this singular entity is collectively defined, interrelational and external: it is impersonal but highly singular because it is crossed over with all sorts of 'encounters' with others and with multiple cultural codes, bits and pieces of the sticky social imaginary which constitutes the subject by literally gluing it together, for a while at least. (Braidotti 2006: 198)

The type of embodied relationality outlined here is precisely the rewriting/refolding/refleshing to which the title of this chapter refers. What I would like to suggest here is a different kind of collective persona: a *fictive public*. A fictive public could be described as a collective of personae engendered by myth and reimagined as a multiplicity. Both conceptual *and* narrative, the fictive public is constituted by versions of mythological figures who have been rewritten in order to enable the silenced females of the original narratives to speak.

Arachne

Spiders scuttle their way across most of the chapters of this book; from Bataille's 'spider or spit' comment in the Introduction to Eva Hayward's topological arachnoid sensoria in Chapter 4. Deft and swift personae themselves, they have somehow woven their way in. In mythological terms, spinning and weaving are feminine activities associated with both materiality and artifice and are personified by a number of female figures. The *Odyssey*'s Penelope, discussed further below, weaves and unweaves a shroud for her elderly father-in-law in order to escape the unwanted attentions of the suitors clustering around her while Odysseus is away. Comparably, Ariadne possesses the spun thread that leads Theseus in and out of the labyrinth, while Arachne's hubris in the weaving stakes results in her being transformed into a spider. Nancy K. Miller's concept of 'arachnology' is defined as

> a critical positioning which reads *against* the weave of indifferentiation to discover the embodiment in writing of a gendered subjectivity; to recover within representation the emblems of its construction ... more broadly the interpretation and reappropriation of a story, like many in the history of Western literature that deploys the interwoven structures of power, gender, and identity inherent in the production of mimetic art. (Miller 1986a: 272)

Miller reminds us of the literature-as-web analogy with which Woolf presents us in *A Room of One's Own* and suggests that within the web of women's texts we may find 'marks of the grossly material, the sometimes brutal traces of the culture of gender, the inscriptions of its political structures' (Miller 1986a: 275).

What is interesting is that traditionally Arachne and Ariadne are both silenced and punished for overreaching their positions. The conflation of Arachne and Ariadne to 'Ariachne' in Shakespeare's *Troilus and Cressida* has been debated by many literary critics in the last century (see, for example, Bate et al. 1996: 292 n. 39). Whether a deliberate or mistaken blend of these almost-homonymic names, the result is rather ambiguous. J. Hillis Miller applauds the coinage as a 'splendid portmanteau' and an excellent vehicle for a deconstructive reading:

> She is both and neither at once. To the similarity and dissimilarity of stories in the same mythical or narrative line must be added the lateral repetition with a difference of distinct myths, here called attention to by the accidental similarity of the names. This clashing partial homonymy perfectly mimes the relation between the two stories. (Miller 1992: 14)

While the laterality of the repetition is a useful aspect to be foregrounded here, Miller does not lament the fact that a conflation of two distinct figures here amounts to the elimination of both. Prohibited from their own individual subjectivity, Arachne and Ariadne fade. To this equation, then, we might rather add the possibility of rewriting Ariachne as an entirely new persona with her own voice; rather than eliminating the possibility of the other two she adds another persona to the public. Homonymy and its sibling heteronymy are further discussed in Chapter 3.

More recently, Arachne has been recast as restless Canadian travelling sales rep Arachne in Aritha Van Herk's novel *No Fixed Address* (1986). Rather than spinning or weaving, Van Herk's Arachne peddles women's underwear and drives along the roads on a voyage of self-discovery. 'From Calgary roads spider over the prairie. Arachne pores over Thomas' maps, the lines enticing her to quest beyond the city's radius' (Van Herk 1986: 163–4). The verb 'spider' appears a number of times in the novel, standing for a type of nomadic wandering which transforms the act into something else entirely. While spinning and weaving are a means to an end, the 'spidering' encountered here is an autonomous movement that is an end unto itself. Furthermore, Arachne's desire to move beyond the lines meted out for her on maps is palpable throughout the novel. Van Herk's Arachne therefore continues and develops the project of Arachne the spinner, but instead of being transformed into a spider as punishment for overreaching she rather has the agency of her own transformation, which, like Braidotti's becoming-nomadic, does not have an end point.

Penelope

As I mentioned at the beginning of the chapter, Adriana Cavarero's *In Spite of Plato* (1995) 'steals' four female figures from classical myth – Demeter, Penelope, Diotima and a Thracian maidservant – and reappropriates them elsewhere so that they are able to speak for themselves. Once decontextualised, these figures 'literally stand before us, surrounded by the male code of ancient cast that has imprisoned them in its tenacious metaphysical web' (Cavarero 1995: 9). The symbolic problem of female 'voicelessness' within the patriarchal Logos of classical mythology so eloquently articulated in Cavarero's text is forgrounded and literalised in Margaret Atwood's retelling of the story of Homer's Penelope, *The Penelopiad* (2005). As Atwood's Penelope says:

> The difficulty is that I have no mouth through which I can speak. I can't make myself understood, not in your world, the world of bodies, or tongues and fingers; and most of the time I have no listeners, not on your side of the river. Those of you who may catch the odd whisper, the odd squeak, so easily mistake my words for breezes rustling the dry reeds, for bats at twilight, for bad dreams. (Atwood 2005: 4)

Atwood's Penelope is very much aware of her status within her society as fleshly currency, and the way that she articulates this again literalises and foregrounds her own corporeality: 'And so I was handed over to Odysseus, like a package of meat. A package of meat in a wrapping of gold, mind you. A sort of gilded blood pudding' (Atwood 2005: 39). Rather than affirming her corporeality, however, this description renders her as passive flesh: she objectifies herself as she demonstrates her awareness of her role in the exchange that takes place. Atwood's female voices throughout *The Penelopiad* are all too aware of their limitations; their comments betray a weary cynicism that does not seek to rail or rebel but merely acknowledges the injustice of the system of which they must play their part.

In her reading of Penelope, who sits and waits unendingly for her husband Oysseus' return in Homer's *Odyssey*, Cavarero suggests that perhaps Penelope does not *want* him to return; perhaps in her endless weaving and unweaving she is defining a space for herself that will be usurped as soon as Odysseus returns. It is through the unweaving of what she has already woven that Penelope disrupts both patriarchal symbolic and spatiotemporal orders meted out to her. As Cavarero puts it, she 'contradicts and renders vain the work of the loom, tailoring for herself an unpredictable and impenetrable time and space' (Cavarero 1995: 16).

Perhaps the most significant rewriting, refolding and refleshing that takes place in Atwood's *Penelopiad* is not that of Penelope but that of the role of the 'chorus', which Atwood chooses to give to the twelve maids who were hanged after being raped by the suitors who had been trying to gain Penelope's hand in marriage. This double injustice is remythologised in bold colours by Atwood. There is the added factor of class in the namelessness of these maids; they are not named even in Atwood's text, but rather continue to operate as symbols, despite the fact that they are given the chorus role (traditionally an omniscient narrative position which arguably holds more power than any single character). Atwood deforms the form of her own narrative throughout this text; she moves through Penelope's retroactive first-person narrative to skipping-rope chants to an anthropology lecture and a courtroom videotape transcript. All of the formal experiments come in the sections narrated by the chorus, none of whom are named. Atwood's most speculative section is perhaps the anthropology lecture, wherein the maids consider, then reject, alternative narratives for themselves. They consider the world as if they, along with Penelope (the thirteenth, making one for each lunar month), had been a matrilineal moon-cult which had been overthrown by a group of 'usurping patriarchal father-god-worshipping-barbarians', after which its leader Odysseus would then marry the moon-cult's High Priestess, Penelope. An imagined member of the audience's accusation of 'unfounded feminist claptrap' is denied and the narrative is continued for a few more pages before it is then finally rejected:

> ... you don't have to get too worked up about us, dear educated minds. You don't have to think of us as real girls, real flesh and blood, real pain, real injustice. That might be too upsetting. Just discard the sordid part. Consider us pure symbol. We're no more real than money. (Atwood 2005: 168)

There is a bite of sarcasm in these words from the maids which is absolutely justified and in fact operates as a challenge. *Don't worry your heads about us, O academics.* The fact is that Atwood's *Penelopiad* is more about the hanged maids (homonymous with handmaids) than anyone else. These silenced and wrongfully punished women are, as chorus, almost centre-stage – not quite, but their unconventional position as chorus, plus the multiple modes through which their stories are articulated, renders them even more in need of rewriting than Penelope and means that their collective voice is the one that we must listen to most urgently.

In her account of Penelope, Cavarero also draws attention to the maids, and also within her own writing Cavarero herself acts as weaver, drawing together the disciplines of Platonic philosophy with the feminine craft of weaving itself. While philosophy separates body and mind, weaving draws them together. I mentioned in the Introductions the knitting-together of reason and feeling, or sapience and sentience, through George Eliot and other thinkers. Cavarero here attributes this also to Penelope's actions as a weaver: 'The interweaving of intelligence and the senses is where all humans exist as part of their gender ... A woman like her handmaids, Penelope holds their intertwined thoughts and bodies in a home of their own, leaving elsewhere the masculine exercise of death' (Cavarero 1995: 30).

Iphis

> ... the imagination doesn't have a gender.
>
> (Smith 2007: 97)

Ali Smith's *Girl Meets Boy* transplants the Iphis/Ianthe myth to Inverness in the year 2007. In Ovid's *Metamorphoses* Iphis is disguised as a boy and falls in love with Ianthe. Part of the Canongate *Myths* series which also contains Atwood's famous *Penelopiad* (2005), this novella queers its very own narrative line through syntactical playfulness. Iphis is reconstituted as Robin, a gender-fluid political activist with whom Anthea, reluctant employee of evil bottled water company Pure, falls in love. As Kaye Mitchell points out in her queer reading of Smith's text, the central motif of *Girl Meets Boy* is a material element: water. Rather than the predictable association of water with the feminine, Mitchell reads it as dismantling the gender binary and standing for a type of sexual desire that is quite literally fluid. Water and watery language 'eschews the logic of penetrating/penetrated (and thus, by extension, of masculine/feminine), so that erotic experience renders the body liquid, malleable but forceful: finally, watery motifs here express the saltiness of bodily fluids, a body dissolved in desire, the boundaries between bodies likewise dissolving' (Mitchell 2013: 70). If we recall the removal of boundaries between subject and environment discussed in the previous chapter, water as an element exists within, without, between and through bodily boundaries. Stacy Alaimo discusses an example of this phenomenon, which she calls 'transcorporeality', in *Bodily Natures* (2010), citing Sandra Steingraber's narrative of the material ecologies of motherhood in *Having Faith* (2001). Alaimo focuses on a moment in which Steingraber drinks water which then becomes blood plasma and suffuses through the amniotic sac, in order to demonstrate that in her theory of transcorporeality 'her body, the habitat for her developing child, is inextricably linked to the wider world . . . Steingraber imaginatively transforms a medical test for genetic 'abnormalities' into a poetic exploration of how the substances of the vast world flow through her body as well as her daughter's body' (Alaimo 2010: 103–4).

Smith's use of water's universal pervasiveness in *Girl Meets Boy* is much more sexualised, culminating in a series of syntactically parallel questions while narrating the lovers enthralled in their first night together:

> Was that what they meant when they said flames had tongues? Was I melting? Would I melt? Was I gold? Was I magnesium? Was I briny? Were my whole insides a piece of sea, was I nothing but salty water with a mind of its own, was I some kind of fountain, was I the force of water through stone? (Smith 2007: 102)

Requiring no answer, these questions encapsulate Alaimo's theory, which sees the body as co-extensive with its material environment. Not only this, but the *transitional* nature of the language, the bodies and the elements invoked are both vital aspects here. Already a queer narrative, Ovid's *Metamorphoses* is queered further in Smith's linguistic virtuosity.

The process of metamorphosis itself is rendered real and physical, again through the language describing the sexual act: 'I was hard alright, and then I was sinew, I was a snake, I changed stone to snake in three simple moves, stoke stake snake, then I was a tree . . .' (Smith 2007: 102). The list 'stoke stake snake', another example of synvariance, literalises the material process of metamorphosis lexically. The words are pre-existing, but the syntax eschews the syntagmatic line and becomes serial. Another example of synvariance Smith employs to literalise language's transformative power is the 103 word sentence consisting of the repeated phrase 'I was . . .' or 'we were . . .' with a different noun or descriptive noun phrase.

> I was a she was a he was a we were a girl and a girl and a boy and a boy, we were blades, were a knife that could cut through myth [. . .] were the tail of a fish were the reek of a cat [. . .] can we really keep this up? (Smith 2007: 103)

The elimination of any conjunctive word between the phrases in favour of *another* phrase very much conjures up the sense of eternal becoming, queering not only the metamorphoses of Ovid's text but also queering *becoming* in the Deleuzian sense, becoming as developed by Nietzsche (Deleuze 2010. This is another example of the synvariance discussed in Chapter 1, and also the *continual transformation* already discussed, celebrated in the exuberance of the syntactical proliferation. The stretching and bending of the spatiotemporal linguistic axes is mirrored in the stretching and bending of the categories of identity formation, from gender spectra to time travel to olfactory dimensions to infinite edges and cuts and non-human animals. This is desire in all its exhilarated and multifarious openings, beginning, eddies and tributaries, an infinite precipitation of possibilities.

Eurydice

Understandably, the form of the question is a common feature in modern retellings of myth as humans retroactively apply reason to the seemingly arbitrary actions of the gods. W. B. Yeats concludes his famous poem by asking the enigmatic question of Leda after Zeus rapes her in the form of a swan: 'Did she put on his knowledge with his power / Before the indifferent beak could let her drop?' (Yeats 1963: 127). The Leda who exists in this poem, however, is still silenced. Yeats's Leda only exists through an inventory of body parts: thighs, nape, breast and fingers. Comparatively, the form of the question also inhabits the almost-contemporaneous 'Eurydice' in H.D.'s poetic reimagining of the story of Orpheus and Eurydice, but this time Eurydice does have a voice. H.D.'s Eurydice is rightly enraged and bombards the silent Orpheus with questions:

> why did you turn?
> why did you glance back?
> why did you hesitate for that moment?
> why did you bend your face
> caught with the flame of the upper earth,
> above my face?
>
> what was it that crossed my face
> with the light from yours
> and your glance?
> what was it you saw in my face?
> the light of your own face,
> the fire of your own presence?
> (H.D. 1988 [1925]: 52)

It has been argued that while H.D.'s Eurydice refuses to accept her own death and is able to express her rage in her own language, she also 'obeys the imperative of a gaze that cannot be escaped' (Bruzelius 1998: 458). While H.D.'s Eurydice acknowledges that the contingency of her own existence rests solely upon the gaze of Orpheus, she does not seize the opportunity to reverse her position and become the subject rather than the object of the gaze.

Turning to another rewriting, Kathy Acker's Eurydice in *Eurydice in the Underworld* (1997) demonstrates a good deal more agency than H.D.'s, and takes control of her own environment. She refuses to play the role Orpheus lays out for her (he describes her as 'the sexiest, the hottest piece of flesh I had ever encountered' (Acker 1997: 26(); instead she is a subject in control of her own sexuality with a voice and a sharp, precise understanding of the material agency of language and desire. Written at the end of her life after a double mastectomy, Acker casts her Eurydice as also dealing with the aftermath of surgery, while her useless partner Orpheus is unable to care for her and is only interested in when they can start having sex again. The sense of feeling like passive matter, operated on and then fucked, is brutally clear in Eurydice's character. She gains agency through her perception, defamiliarisation and re-articulation of the world.

There is something of the world-making in Acker's Eurydice: when we perceive the world through her, it is refleshed at every moment. Acker's Orpheus cites Maurice Blanchot and his essay on Orpheus, and together with Blanchot reduces Eurydice to the role of the that-which-cannot-and-simultaneously-must-be-seen. For Blanchot's Orpheus, and also for Blanchot himself, Eurydice is 'the profoundly dark point towards which art, desire, death, and the night all seem to lead' (Blanchot 1981: 99). She is the centre of the night; the point to which he cannot or must not look. It is as though Orpheus does not really want her, except in the guise of the dark impossible point of art: the infinite. While Blanchot focuses on this point of impossibility in Orpheus as artist, Acker's Eurydice here articulates her own unique vision of a defamiliarised environment:

> The countryside: Silver here is everywhere an object, and swamps. Pale greens and browns mix with branches; in this place objects and colors have the same status. Sky can be seen either through, or falling through, wood: inside the colors is a house. (Acker 1997: 15)

This beautiful passage demonstrates precisely the *matter* of which Blanchot speaks or pronounces the impossibility of speaking. Eurydice's artistic perception here flattens the ontological hierarchy of colours and objects. While Blanchot's Eurydice is the muse who calls forth a creative flow of inspiration: 'To look at Eurydice without concern for the song, in the impatience and imprudence of a desire which forgets the law – this is *inspiration*' (Blanchot 1981: 101), Acker's Eurydice is her own inspiration. Her agency is precisely sourced in her defamiliarising gaze, which encompasses all. 'She lives in her own world because she makes the whole world hers' (Acker 1997: 1). Through this and throughout her wild, sensuous, sexual, learned, battered, capricious/serious, lofty/guttural, gritty, granular and stunning prose, Acker creates anew. Every sentence makes a world.

One more recent visitation to the Eurydice myth queers not Eurydice but Orpheus, whose trans*chronic persona we will mention briefly here by way of a contrast:

> *The figure, now transforming through a seemingly indiscriminate series of sex and silhouette, first male then female then both then neither, and so on, then raised a finger to hrs blackened lips. Paused again. Lights flickered again against the roiling sky and the now retracting angelic-demonic-cybernetic-chthonic-xenosonic form.* (Blake 2018: 180)

Charlie Blake's Orpheus is deformed, destabilised, defamiliarised, and rewritten, refolded and refleshed into an 'Orpheus machine' which again demonstrates the movement of *eternal transformation* that is queerly topological.

Lavinia

Ursula Le Guin's *Lavinia* is the deliberate fleshing out of a fairly marginal character, whose role is to wait and see. This rewriting is interesting because of the placement of Vergil, the poet, within the fictive frame. This enables Lavinia to talk about her own story with its creator and hers. Lavinia talks to the poet in the sacred space about her fate; he foretells some details about her forthcoming marriage to Aeneas which ultimately prevents her from agreeing to marry Turnus, the suitor favoured by her mother. Lavinia is well aware of the disservice done to her in terms of an insubstantial narrative portrait and voice: 'If you'd met me when I was a girl at home you might well have thought that my poet's faint portrait of me, sketched as if with a brass pin on a wax tablet, was quite sufficient' (Le Guin 2008: 5).

The poet wonders aloud why he has revisited the world of the living in order to communicate with Lavinia rather than any of his other characters, for example Aeneas. His conclusion is telling: 'Because I did see him. And not you. You're almost nothing in my poem, almost nobody. An unkept promise' (Le Guin 2008: 63). The lack of depth in the poet's portrayal of Lavinia compared to that of Aeneus suggests a different kind of 'seeing' altogether – a seeing that is a not-seeing, or the seeing without seeing which recognises (in Shklovsky's terms). As the poet realises the gendered nature of his creations, so too does Lavinia realise the difference between her reaction and her husband's if he had been presented with the fact of his own fictionality. 'It has not been difficult for me to believe in my fictionality, because it is, after all, so slight' (Le Guin 2008: 119). The question of narrative agency – as opposed to narrative predestination – is left deliberately ambiguous. Lavinia has some knowledge of the textual nature of her existence, and yet is simultaneously unable to alter her own fate. She is given a voice and is yet still denied agency, but only in the same way that all of the characters are simultaneously denied it. She appears to be the only character in the unique predicament of knowing both her fate and her fictive status. The relationship between literature and mythology, however, is necessarily constituted by an ambivalence in terms of the reciprocal levels of fiction, metaphor and literality. Consequently, it matters less that Lavinia knows she is not 'real', and that her fate is predetermined by a poet-author, than it would in contemporary times. It is Lavinia's centrality in this narrative, as well as her relative freedom of movement for a girl of ancient Roman times, which is striking here in its revolutionary nature. Lavinia and her friend run for miles through the countryside. 'I was all dirt and dried sweat' (Le Guin 2008: 116). Not only is she rewritten as an entire character with agency, she is also permitted a messy corporeality that directly challenges the ideal embodiment of femininity of the time. Here we can feel the *refleshing* of Lavinia take place as she is rewritten in the narrative.

Medusa

Long perceived by the male gaze as an aesthetic horror, the figure of Medusa is particularly applicable for feminist rewriting. Susan Bowers proposes that we perceive Medusa and other figures with the *female* gaze in order for women to reclaim their own sexuality. Here women would learn 'to see clearly for themselves' (Bowers 1990: 218). Looking further back into now canonical feminist mythological revitalisations, Hélène Cixous infamously invokes the figure of Medusa in her exultant manifesto for a corporeal, relational, feminine writing.

> Write! and your self-seeking text will know itself better than flesh and blood, rising, insurrectionary dough kneading itself, with sonorous, perfumed ingredients, a lively combination of flying colors, leaves, and rivers plunging into the sea we feed. (Cixous 1976: 889)

The problems we can now see with this influential text have been pointed out by many, including a rising star of trans* literature, Juliet Jacques, who rightly points out that the alignment of women's writing with a 'dark Africa' feels 'Orientalist and appropriative', and 'differences of race, nation, class, ability, sexual orientation or gender identity' are only mentioned in passing or not at all (Jacques 2014). With an awareness of this, however, Cixous's Medusa remains a useful historical example of a feminist philosopher's appropriation of a maligned female figure in order to foreground the vital materiality of women's writing. It is possible to perceive not one but several laughing Medusas, affirmed in all their snake-haired glory.

Circe

'What a long slog through centuries of misogyny', comments Judith Yarnall in the conclusion to her documentation of the literary transformations of the enchantress Circe (Yarnall 1994: 194). Yarnall points out that Circe has remained for the most part voiceless, apart from some twentieth-century incarnations such as in Margaret Atwood's 'Circe/Mud Poems' in *You Are Happy* (1974). As Yarnall points out, 'In most of her literary incarnations, Circe has been as mute as the virgin Mary, that other magical shaper of flesh and blood whose ponderings of heart remain unworded' (Yarnall 1994: 182). This was indeed the case when Yarnall wrote this book in 1994. However, the very presence of Circe's voice – its material texture and quality – is one of the most foregrounded aspects of Madeleine Miller's 2018 rewriting of Circe. As a baby, Miller's Circe is noticed for her voice: 'the strange, thin sound of my crying'; as a child her cousins mock her: '*Her voice is as screechy as an owl*'; when talking to her captive uncle Prometheus: 'My voice was thin in the echoing room'; later when talking to Hermes: 'My voice is not pleasing to others. I am told it sounds like a gull crying' (Miller 2018: 4, 6, 16, 81). While her voice does not sound quite as it should, its very presence is hugely noteworthy in its very sounding. Miller's *Circe* retells her story from her own unique and unforgettable voice which resonates and reverberates throughout the novel.

In most accounts since Homer, Circe is famous for transforming Odysseus' crew of sailors into pigs. In Miller's account the act is done in self-defence: she is alone on the island, and once the sailors realise this, their intent changes to one of rape. One of them rapes her before she manages to transform them all. The nature of this transformation and a polyphonic, perhaps *caca*phonic proliferation of symbolic notes is resonant throughout James Joyce's 'Circe' episode in *Ulysses*, which sees Leopold Bloom visiting a brothel and undergoing several transformations himself. Bloom is suddenly both female and swine, utterly dominated by brothel madame Bella, who has also changed gender and become Bello. Scholars have noted that the word χοίρος in Greek means both young pig and female genitalia, and that Joyce would have been aware of this (see Vanderbeke 1998: 63).

Joyce uses the word 'sowcunt' in his Circe episode, an approximation at a translation of the double meaning of the Greek word which resonates interestingly with the word 'boycunt' that we encountered at the end of the previous chapter. '*Her sowcunt barks*', he writes of Bella the whore, who transforms into the male Bello as Bloom is transformed into both female and pig (Joyce 1998: 517). The sadomasochistic and gendered nature of this episode is striking: it is as woman and as animal that Joyce's Bloom is humiliated by the whore Bello who has been rendered male. It is interesting that the term 'pig' now carries different homosexual meanings in male gay culture. A pig is 'defined by raunchiness, hedonism, and insatiability, a guy who will dive into a stinky armpit and lick it out because the taste and smell drive him nuts on the deepest primal level. That's a pig', says a sex worker interviewed for an article in *The Voice* about the so-called 'ass menagerie' of gay male terminology (Theory 2016). In some ways Joyce's transformed Bloom prefigures aspects of this terminology.

Hélène Cixous writes about Joyce's Circe episode and plays upon the idea of continual transformation that it evokes. At the brothel, as Cixous says, 'everything is endlessly transformed', including, in particular, Leopold Bloom himself, who 'passes from one state to another through repeated falls, collisions and fascinations, projected everywhere, then withdrawing, and reprojecting himself, backward-buggering, de-figuring metaphorical productions by sudden actualizations . . . Bloom collects, real piggy bank for the forbidden; all imaginable follies and filth fall into his body through the slot' (Cixous 1975: 393). Part becomes hole and flower becomes genitalia; Bloom-as-cunt becomes synecdochically an everywhere. As female, Bloom's nature as blooming flower is magnified: 'In so far as Flower Bloom has more than one calyx, the feminization is exuberant, the phantasmic body fecunt on all sides' (Cixous 1975: 396).

Circe lurks behind all these transformations. As enchantress she has agency over them, and she orchestrates metamorphoses according to her will. Miller's Circe is aware from birth of how little she matters in the world of the gods that she is born into. She knows that she is different from others in her family. There is not even a name for what she is. She does not look or sound the way she should: her status as outcast is evident from infancy. 'I was nothing, a stone', Circe says of herself (Miller 2018: 18). However, a stone in this world may be otherwise. When her captive uncle Prometheus says of the Harpy who has been torturing him 'Her cruelty springs fast as weeds and must any moment be cut again', Circe notes the reversal of agency in his expression. Another kind of transformation. Prometheus is the one who is being cut but his words make the opposite appear to be the case. Circe appreciates the incantatory power of words perhaps from this moment: 'as if his words were a secret. A thing that looked like a stone, but inside was a seed' (Miller 2018: 18). It is she, Circe, who is the seed: she observes herself as a being encased in a world of murk and depths but not a part of it. 'I was not a part of that dark water. I was a creature within it' (Miller 2018: 19).

Callisto

Hal Coase's play *Callisto: A Queer Epic* (2017) attends to the myth of Callisto, the Greek nymph from Ovid's *Metamorphoses* who is raped by Zeus disguised as Artemis and is then turned by Zeus' wife Hera into a bear (and subsequently a stellar constellation) as punishment. Coase splices four storylines across four spatiotemporal dimensions: London 1680, Worcester 1936, Los Angeles 1979 and the Moon 2223. Drawing on some historical figures (Restoration opera singer Arabella Hunt and her 'husband' Amy who is disguised as a man and then discovered and imprisoned, and mathematician codebreaker Alan Turing who was prosecuted for homosexual acts and eventually committed suicide), as well as fictional ones (Tammy who wants to be a porn star in 1970s LA, and beings of the future Lorn and Cal, human and AI, residing on the Moon and creating a new virtual world), the rapid shifting of the dialogue and the way that the language itself shifts creates new multidimensional shapes of transformation. What comes through in these rapidly shifting times, locations, dimensions and interrelations is transformation and perception itself, couched in and constituted by the language of each dimension. In 1930s Midlands England, Alan Turing spars awkwardly, painfully and philosophically with Isobel, the mother of his recently deceased lover Christopher. In 1970s Los Angeles, porn stars Lola and Tammy fall in love and run away from Callisto Studios after killing Lola's abusive husband Harold. In seventeenth-century London, singer Arabella and her partner Amy discuss passing as a man: '. . . the manliness is all in the motion', Amy jokes (Coase 2017: 12), provoking a laugh from the queer audience. Later a nurse subjects the imprisoned Amy to a forceful search, taking the speaking casually/profoundly of gendered linguistic variance and invariance:

> See – an apple is a pomme is a mela – I learnt that on the wharf. All's one. And if my dear apple could speak, what says it then? 'I am an orange!' Matters not. 'Tis an orange, then. It tastes like an apple. It looks like an apple. It smells like an apple. It calls himself an orange – God bless it. (Coase 2017: 42)

The use of the objectifying and dehumanising 'it' alongside the male pronoun – 'It calls himself an orange' – is particularly resonant for those existing outside the gender binary, for whom 'it' is not an absurdity but an unwanted and malignant assignation.

In the future, Lorn and his AI companion Cal appear to be the only beings left in the world in 2223. Their shorthand, staccato dialogue communicates wide-eyed love and hope in an utter void. Figurative world-making is literalised here: Lorn is supposedly building a new world in his mind, called the Bliss, as he sleeps and Cal watches over him. Lorn is also teaching Cal about human life and emotions, though Cal knows, understands and feels more than he appears to. Their discussion often revolves around colours, emotions and their manifestations in language:

> CAL: So plus-plus colourful.
> LORN: Yeh.
> Is colourfulmost.
> CAL: Colourfulmost!
> Yeh.
> Colourfulmostest?
>
> (Coase 2017: 48)

While the Orwellian Newspeak-style language is clipped and short, Lorn and Cal's navigation of it is nuanced and delicate. The fact that these two beings appear to be the only beings left in the world doesn't seem to matter to them; they are happy in their playful discourse which includes games of assigning colours to abstract emotions, some of which Cal has not yet experienced, such as hope.

> LORN: K. Like . . . Yellow is . . . Surprise an joy an closeness – true closeness – an exciting an kindness an beeches an hope an laughter –
> CAL: Hope?
> LORN: O. Um . . . Like . . . Is-like figuring something thas not cert but if things were best – if you could – you'd make sure cert. Is-like being excited for laughter.
> CAL: Aha. I figure it.
> LORN: Yeh?
> CAL: Got it. Cept laughter's blue so . . .
> LORN: Laughter is like the least blue mote there be.
> CAL: No bickery!
>
> (Coase 2017: 76)

Nowhere more in the play than in this conversation do we see the very act of making and remaking the world *laid bare* – in the Russian formalist sense – through the almost-lovers of the future, human and posthuman, painting the abyss they see before them through the assignation of colours to emotions they have not even yet felt, such as hope in a hopeless universe. The inclusion of 'mote' as utter grammatical archaism expressing a vehement modality yet also denoting the smallest particle, atom or grain of sand, works multifariously here. As with the other examples, it is through language *made strange* that new worlds are not just reimagined but made entirely anew.

Afrekete

Afrekete Afrekete ride me to the crossroads where we shall sleep, coated in the women's power.
(Lorde 1982: 252)

In Chapter 31 of Audre Lorde's *Zami* (1982), Audre meets a woman called Afrekete. Lorde describes *Zami* as a 'biomythography': as a text, its functions are multiple in that it charts both her own life story and creates a new mythology sourced in Yoruba mythology. It is here that our rewritings, refoldings and refleshings must conclude their journey.

As scholars have noted, *Zami* rewrites both Eurocentric and African archetypes. One of the most eloquent articulations of an intersectional feminist response to second-wave white feminist mythological revisionism within second-wave feminism can be found in Lorde's 1979 open letter to Mary Daly. Her questions regarding the lacunae that she found in Daly's *Gyn/Ecology* are resonant not just with Daly's text but speak for European mythological writings in general.

> Why doesn't Mary deal with Afrekete as an example? Why are her goddess images only white, western European, judeo-christian? Where was Afrekete, Yemanje, Oyo, and Mawulisa? Where were the warrior goddeses of the Vodun, the Dahomeian Amazons and the warrior-women of Dan? (Lorde 1984: 67)

The non-inclusion of these figures in Daly's text, writes Lorde, is a deliberate choice of Daly's and is all the more damaging coming from a thinker with supposedly shared feminist ideals. Countering Daly's exclusionary radical feminism, the figure of Afrekete reverberates through Lorde's mythobiography *Zami*. Lorde's Afrekete, possibly derived from the Dahomean names *Aflakete* and *Aflekete*, also sounds like the Greek goddess Aphrodite but goes beyond her. Lorde invokes the name Aphrodite in *Zami* only to note her inadequacy. Afrekete also sounds like Hecate or Hekate, goddess of witchcraft, liminality, trivia and triple crossroads. Afrekete is both Lorde herself and Kitty, the lover she encounters at the end of the book. Lorde describes Kitty/Afrekete with the Yoruban goddess Oya as well as the West African trickster god Esu/Elegbara. In writing Afrekete into her narrative Lorde revisions both West African and European mythology, but it is important to note that her invocation is not merely symbolic or metaphorical; for Lorde, 'these deities' names serve not only as poetic metaphors, but are at once metaphors and vessels of powerful, archetypal energies . . . They are meant to function not only aesthetically but also magically' (Connor et al. 1997: 218).

A number of scholars have presented Afrekete simultaneously as a trickster figure and as Lorde herself (see Provost 1995; Ball 2001; Rawlings 2007). Afrektete is both mythic and real, self and other, female and male. Afrekete's invocations throughout *Zami* are italicised which lends a dreamlike, incantatory yet tangible and textured quality to her voicings: '*And I remember Afrekete, who came out of a dream to me always being hard and real as the fire hairs along the under-edge of my navel*' (Lorde 1982: 249). It is precisely through the breaking down of dualistic conceptions that Lorde presents and personifies the figure of the trickster in Afrekete, as Kara Provost has noted: 'With their verbal dexterity, indeterminacy, gender ambiguity, and ability to mediate seeming contradictions, I believe Afro-Caribbean trickster figures – particularly in the incarnation of Afrekete – offer Lorde both a model survivor/fighter and particular linguistic strategies which aid her struggle against oppressive beliefs and behaviours' (Provost 1995: 47).

MawuLisa, thunder, sky, sun, the great mother of us all; and Afrekete, her youngest daughter, the mischievous linguist, trickster, best-beloved, whom we must all become. (Lorde 1993: 225)

MawuLisa, celestial *lwa* (deity or spirit) of the Vodou pantheon, is alternately depicted as linked to female (Mawu) and male (Lisa) twins and as a single gynandrous or transgendered divinity (see Conner et al. 1997: 228). MawuLisa is important to Lorde, particularly as she is the mother of the trickster Afrekete. Trickster figures historically embody the breaking of taboo and interstitial inherence: they are 'paradox personified' (Babcock-Abrahams 1975: 148). In her folklorist's study of the trickster figure, 'he' (and the trickster is referred to as male within Babcock-Abrahams's account) is aligned with the marginal and the deviant. She uses Victor Turner's work on the concept of liminality to align the trickster with three principles which are then ripe for Lorde to take up herself and rewrite, refold and reflesh: (1) they fall in the interstices of social structure; (2) they are on its margins; or (3) they occupy its lowest rungs. Of course, some members of society may identify with all three of these, and later theories of intersectionality which hit the mainstream mindset by the end of the 1980s with Kimberlé Crenshaw's article on the topic (Crenshaw 1989) would allow for multiple aspects such as these to be thought together. While the trickster figure may have remained primarily male in European and Anglo-American literature, this is not the case with African-American literature. Lorde's trickster is both divine and human and operates to give voice to Black female experience while avoiding the pitfalls of Western imperialism, and as

L. H. Rawlings has shown in her extensive study of the trickster trope within Black feminist writing (Rawlings 2007).

> *To the journeywoman pieces of myself.*
> *Becoming.*
> *Afrekete.*
>
> (Lorde 1982: 5)

Lorde's statement above, which ends *Zami*, suggests that Afrekete is a being-to-come who is part of all of us. M. Charlene Ball draws a comparison between Afrekete and Virginia Woolf's Judith Shakesepare from *A Room of One's Own*: 'a figure not yet present but looked for in the future' (Ball 2001: 77). These figures are not only futural and speculative but also embody hope for change: through their articulation they affirm the possibility of someone like them existing, outside of the patriarchal and Eurocentric confines of their time. The hypothetical yet affirmative nature of these becoming-beings relate to the discussion of uchronia in Chapter 3.

Paradoxical Relationalities: Intimacy and Estrangement

In order for rewritings such as those detailed above to happen, a particular kind of relationship to the 'original' version must be affirmed. I argue here that what is required is a paradoxical relationality requiring simultaneous proximity and distance. Following Nancy Fraser's famous conception of subaltern counterpublics (Fraser 1990), Michael Warner's conception of publics as presupposing a 'relation among strangers' is a key beginning point (Warner 2002: 217). The very concept of a proximity of strangers is paradoxical in itself, but is nevertheless vital in the thinking of gender, race and other issues, as Sara Ahmed has shown. Ahmed reimagines the relation between proximity and estrangement in *Strange Encounters* so that 'the definition of the nation as a space, body or house *requires the proximity of "strangers" within that space*, whether or not that proximity is deemed threatening (monoculturalism) or is welcomed (multiculturalism)' (Ahmed 2000: 100).

Both Hélène Cixous and Adrienne Rich pre-empt more recent theories of relationality in the thinking of feminist rewritings. 'There must be ways, and we will be finding out more and more about them, in which the energy of creation and the energy of relation can be united' (Rich 1972: 23). The so-called 'relational turn' of the past couple of decades has been documented and explored in feminism and literary theory (Schapiro 1994), psychoanalysis (Mitchell 2000), new materialism (Barad 2003), affect theory (Venn 2010) and continental philosophy (Benjamin 2016). Prior to these explicit documentations, however, Cixous is already advocating a feminist materialist relationality in 'The Laugh of the Medusa' when she asserts that writing is

> precisely working (in) the in-between, inspecting the process of the same and of the other without which nothing can live, undoing the work of death – to admit this is first to want the two, as well as both, the ensemble of the one and the other, not fixed in sequences of struggle and expulsion or some other form of death but infinitely dynamized by an incessant process of exchange from one subject to another. (Cixous 1976: 883)

A *paradoxical* relationality, then, is thus due to a conflation of the opposing vectors of proximity and distance. This is particularly relevant when considering new materialist thought in relation to the feminist project of radical rewriting I outlined at the beginning. We want to be proximal; we want to be close to, preferably to touch the thing we are apprehending in order to perceive it anew. And yet at the same this strategy for perception requires a critical distance. So we are pulling in opposite directions at the same time. The concept of the fold (Deleuze 1988) has been useful for two analogical figurations relevant to this discussion: for dissolving the internal/external dualism in the thinking of subjectivity, and for figuring relationality. Elspeth Probyn (1993) acknowledges the importance of pleating or folding when both constituting and dismantling internality and externality in terms of the self. The figure of the fold demonstrates the reciprocity of the processes of subjectification and objectification. Through Deleuze (1988) and Foucault (1988), Probyn demonstrates that folding is always refolding: 'The act of "pleating" or "folding" ("la pliure") is thus the doubling-up, the refolding, the bending-onto-itself of the line of the outside in order to constitute the inside/outside – the modes of the self' (Probyn 1993: 129).

Gendered Perception: Queer Defamiliarisation

In the introduction to their volume on feminism and classical myth *Laughing With Medusa: Classical Myth and Feminist Thought* (2006), Vanda Zajko and Miriam Leonard cite Monique Wittig's *Les Guérillères* (1969) and Elizabeth Cook's *Achilles* (2001) as two exemplary modes of feminist rewritings. It is noteworthy that the section they highlight from Cook's novel involves the following line (about Helen): 'Not one of them has ever seen her' (Zajko and Leonard 2006: 2). As they rightly point out, Helen is a figure infamously constructed by the male gaze. Helen operates as the catalyst for an entire war through the mere image of her face, and yet no one has 'seen' her. This suggests to us that the nature of the 'seeing' proposed by Cook is more nuanced. According to Shklovsky, not a figure known for progressive proclamations about gender but hugely important for theories of modernist artistic perception, *seeing* is a truly creative act as we discussed in the Introductions. *Seeing* is opposed to *recognition*, which is a mode of perception that requires no autonomous thought. In the process of recognition, outlines and symbols are predicted, rehearsed and recognised; no creative labour is required.

Let us turn back now to Helen. Cook's line suggests that one has 'seen' Helen in the Shklovskian sense. Helen is traditionally recognised without being seen; she is perceived automatically, synecdochically, as the face that launched a thousand ships. The task, then, is to build another Helen: a Helen made strange. The way to do this is through giving her a voice. This is precisely the process we witness with Lavinia as outlined above: the poet's admission that he did not 'see' Lavinia.

It is my ongoing project to queer the concept of defamiliarisation and present it in terms of material enactments. The creation of a fictive public is one such gendered enactment: the telling of new stories, and in doing so, the creation of new voices. As we have already seen, Braidotti writes about defamiliarisation as a political strategy in her book on the posthuman (Braidotti 2013a). According to Braidotti, we *must* defamiliarise: she imbues this term with contemporary political potency. Braidotti's description of the defamiliarisation process is precisely what is involved in the creation of the fictive public I have outlined: with each persona, '. . . the subject becomes relational in a complex manner that connects it to multiple others' (Braidotti 2013a: 167). What I am calling a queer defamiliarisation, then, can go beyond the linguistic and the aesthetic to critique the dominant mode of perception of the human subject. As feminists we can understand that a queering of defamiliarisation itself, considering its now canonised and institutionalised position within modern aesthetic theory, constitutes quite a radical rewriting, refolding and refleshing.

Conclusion: Syntaxa/Parataxa

Increasingly, I find myself drawn to poetics as a mode of expression, not in order to move away from thinking rigorously but, on the contrary, to lure 'us' toward the possibilities of engaging the force of imagination in its materiality. (Barad 2012: 14 n. 24)

The role of the imagination in the thinking of a fictive public is clearly of vital importance, from conception to expression. The very matter of Barad's own materialist writings shows us, in fact, that conception and execution are inseparable in their mutual entanglement. As Warner states in the quotation at the beginning of this article, what is required for the thinking of what he calls 'strangerhood' is *constant imagining*. The conception of a fictive public requires just this: a constant imagining and a creative execution. The cementation of this concept and the conclusion to this chapter is therefore unashamedly creative in its execution: it consists of a list. The listing of names as a feminist intervention is not new; in fact, it is interwoven through the text of Monique Wittig's *Les Guérillères* (1985). The word LACUNAE punctures the narrative throughout, and what fills these lacunae are a fictive public of female names, throbbing through the pages.

AIMEE POMA BARBA
BENEDICTA SUSANNA
CASSANDRA OSMONDA
GENE HERMINIA KIKA
AURELIA EVANGELINE
SIMONA MAXIMILIANA
(Wittig 1985: 21)

The systematicity of the list is a device Wittig uses throughout her narrative. The subversion of syntax, or 'synvariance', is one type of defamiliarisation, as was discussed in the previous chapter. The defying of syntactical convention within the framework of a narrative packs a symbolic punch as a feminist intervention. One concluding list is therefore required, consisting of the rewritings, the refoldings and the refleshings discussed in this chapter. The multiplicity of rewritings, refoldings and refleshings that constitute the fictive public, united by name yet defamiliarised, are listed below. Our task going forward is therefore to affirm and to create.

AFREKETE AFREKETE MOTHER TO ALL ARACHNE THE WEAVER SPINS ARACHNE THE DRIVER ARIACHNE QUEER CHILD OF ARACHNE AND ARIADNE CALLISTO FUTUREPAST CALLISTO EVERYPLACETIME CIRCE SPEAKS CIRCE TRANSFORMS CIRCE CUTS EURYDICE THE SEEN BECOMES EURYDICE THE SEER EURYDICE DESIRES REMAKES THE WORLD HELEN UNSEEN HELEN BEYOND CATALYST IPHIS ACTIVIST BEYOND DISGUISED BOY IPHIS AS BOY AND GIRL AND GIRL AND BOY AS GIRL AS IPHIS LAVINIA MERE BLUSH LAVINIA FLAME-HAIRED OMEN LAVINIA SPEAKS RUNS SWEATS MEDUSA NO LONGER SNAKE-CHAINED MEDUSA GUFFAWS

CHAPTER 3

A Field of Heteronyms and Homonyms: New Materialism, Speculative Fabulation and Wor(l)ding

But what about making the world, this world, the old one?
(Le Guin 1981: 46)

The imagination is a tool of resistance . . . Welcome to the future.
(Womack 2013: 24)

. . . Black existence and science fiction are one and the same.
(*Mothership Connection*, dir. Akomfrah, 1995)

We wield 'science fiction' voice and word to manifest world-paradigms necessary for our survival. Empire does not welcome this. *Ride with us against empire.*
(Metropolarity Collective)

Prologue: THE FIELD

In a Taiwanese restaurant in downtown Sydney, a group of IT managers were quizzing her about the field she worked in. Haltingly, she surmised that the field was probably several interconnecting fields, and that her own background was both literary and philosophical, and that words mattered, and that language in its material strangeness had the power to advance feminist, queer and intersectional politics. She said that new materialism was a field concerned with the matter that made up the world.

One of the IT managers had a glint in his eye. He wanted, he said, to know a bit more about this field. Where was the field? How big was the field? Who created the field? Who else was in the field? Was camping allowed in the field?

In a similarly ludic vein she addressed his queries earnestly, seriously, one by one, and between them sprouted a Field of unknowable dimensions. The meandering directions of the furrows ploughed in The Field were expressed via the medium of rapid-flowing arm movements;

the colour of her interlocuter's tent in his agreed patch of The Field was agreed upon; they discussed the implications of holding raves in The Field; the merits of camouflage versus fluorescent clothing in The Field; the presence of cows in The Field; what the cow ate in The Field. He began to ask her whether he would actually be permitted in The Field, but then stopped himself. If The Field operated according to a flat ontology, owned by both everyone and no one, he reasoned, then why would he need to ask her permission?

> She said: all are welcome in The Field.
> She did not say: Fredric Jameson might call The Field a formalist's prison-house.
> She did not say: Lewis Carroll's generic 'it' usually described as 'a frog or a worm', might well be found in The Field.
> She did not say: Noam Chomsky might call The Field a furiously sleeping colourless green idea.[4]

Fields, then, she thought later on as she switched off the light, are clearly unstable concepts with differing material realities. All well and good, but beyond a quasi-Wittgensteinian highlighting of the limits of our articulation of the boundaries of abstraction and concretion, what was it about this reduction of the concept of the academic field that might be useful? Maybe it could be useful because it demonstrated the unique position of new materialism and speculative fabulation to enact worlds; to verb nouns; to story stories; to make matters matter; or to world wor(l)ds . . .

Fictocriticism; or, Flowers at the Lip of the World

We shape something when we utter it. Symbolism posits this shaping as a deferral, but it does not need be seen this way. Flowers have abounded in the previous two chapters: roses have bloomed. 'I say: a flower! and, outside of the oblivion where my voice relegates no outline, as something other than known calyxes, musically rises the idea itself, suave, the absent one of all the flowers' (Mallarmé 1886, in Blanchot 1995: 30). The step beyond this is the materialist disavowal of symbolist substitution in favour of realisation: the actual presence of the absent flower. We utter it into being; we breathe redness into the rose. Pioneer of Australian fictocriticism Stephen Muecke refers to Mallarmé's flower in his essay 'The Fall':

---

[4] Jameson (1972), Carroll (2001), Chomsky (1957: 15).

> We fall for the one who resembles a flower; this is the operation of a romantic percept as old and as complicated as the bouquet. But to know the structure of the plant (or the text) as a concept, is to be able, incredibly, to climb out again, wet, dripping, exhausted, on the lip of the world again. (Muecke 2002: 112)

This chapter examines the 'lip of the world', as Muecke puts it, as the moveable boundary between fiction and reality, and the concept of wor(l)ding as the problematisation of the distinction between 'lip' and 'world'. The absent/real flower is the like the field that emerged from the conversations outlined above. It could be posited in terms of a projected ideality: a utopia, uchronia or perhaps a combination of the two. As both *ou-* and (incorrectly) *eu-topos*, utopia is both not-place and good-place. Similarly uchronia operates as the temporal version of this. One of the meanings of to *speculate* (etymologically, to observe; later, to pursue truth through thinking; later still, to pursue profit through market value buying/selling), therefore, may be to operate as though the posited *ou* of utopia/uchronia has been granted ontological stability beyond its original projection.

Where are we? We're in London and it's May 2017. We're standing outside Birkbeck University. The title of the conference being held today is Dystopia Now. The conference asks some general questions. In an era of global turbulence, what pertinence do fictional dystopias have? Is dystopia a key genre for our time?
 I don't attend the conference but I have seen it advertised in various places. I think about dystopian objects. I imagine an exhibition called Dystopia Now accompanying the conference and displaying relevant objects emblematic of the dystopian now. Signatures of our combined ruin. What would be included. An orange blonde hamster hairpiece, perhaps. A bleeping smartphone. A bus saying LEAVE. A Big Red Button. A shredded declaration. A detention centre. A deportation vehicle. A burnt-out building. We could go on.
 The material realisation of a linguistically or symbolically deferred object inhabits the transversal, interpenetrating world of speculative fiction, speculative fabulation, science fiction and a number of other related areas. The blending of these worlds is an ongoing process. There is now nothing unusual about a text that blends elements of fiction, poetry, scientific discourse and philosophical reasoning. Muecke summarises the state of things with respect to the interpenetration of these worlds: 'The whole artifice of literary criticism was built up in order to do one thing really; to unmask the secrets of art. And the fiction was always there re-enchanting the world by putting on the beautiful masks again and again' (Muecke 2002: 108). This chapter positions diverse expressions of speculative writing as wor(l)ding; it considers these processes and their

contemporary political valency. And for this endeavour we begin predictably, alebit briefly, with Heidegger, whose grammatical iterations and idiosyncracies form an important part of his ontology, if only to depart from him.

Worlding from Heidegger to Haraway

Heidegger's work sometimes includes sentences comprising a noun which is then refracted into multiple grammatical forms. *'Das Ding dingt'* [The thing things] he states in What Is a Thing?' (Heidegger 1967), drawing our attention to the link between the noun *Das Ding* [the Thing] and the word *bedingen,* to cause or condition. He then performs a similar etymological linkage with 'worlding' and 'world' in 'The Origin of the Work of Art' (Heidegger 1971):

> The world is not the mere collection of the countable or uncountable, familiar and unfamiliar things that are just there. But neither is it a merely imagined framework added by our representation to the sum of such given things. The *world worlds*, and is more fully in being than the tangible and perceptible realm in which we believe ourselves to be at home. (Heidegger 1971: 44–5)

The work of art, for Heidegger, sets up a world. The performativity of the noun that repeats itself as a verb or gerund; the world's worlding is the setting up of the world. What, then, is the relationship between wording and worlding? In what ways could we say that the linguistic signifier 'worlds'?

Zoom backwards. Where are we? We're in Paris and the year is 1971. Every utterance makes a world. Jean-François Lyotard takes the aesthetic modernist critique of transparent and realistic representation and shows us that there is indeed a world in a word. The sign is thick, he says. Words are not just signs. This makes me think. The fictionalisation of reality and the realisation of fiction are precisely what the spatio-temporal zoomings-around of science fiction and now the dystopian present are showing us.

Lyotard argues for the 'thickness' of the signifier in *Discourse, Figure* which lends a certain sense of materiality to the signifier relevant to the present discussion. For Lyotard, language possesses a 'world-function' which worlds as it words:

> ... out of what it designates, every utterance makes a world, a thick object waiting to be synthesized, a symbol to be deciphered, but these objects and symbols offer themselves in an expanse where showing is possible. This expanse bordering

discourse is not itself the linguistic space where the work of signification is carried out, but a worldly type of space, plastic and atmospheric, in which one has to move, circle around things, make their silhouette vary, in order to utter such and such signification heretofore concealed. (Lyotard 1971: 83)

Hang on a minute. You're telling me fiction is real and reality is fiction? That's right. That's what I'm telling you. Dystopia Now. Signatures of our combined ruin. Let's collect some more.

It is clear that what Lyotard is gesturing towards is a materiality of language. This is the worlding which occurs in all wording: we could write wor(l)ding. The materiality of language is consistently interrogated throughout this book, and it is far from a simple concept. As Butler points out in *Bodies That Matter*, it is important to distinguish between the materiality of the signifier and the materiality of the signified, and then between the materiality of the signified and the materiality of the referent. 'Apart from and yet related to the materiality of the signifier is the materiality of the signified as well as the referent approached through the signified, but which remains irreducible to the signified' (Butler 1993: 38). What is important here, however, is that for Butler the signifier does not signify without a set of larger linguistic relations that deploy it. This is elucidated in Butler's conception of the lesbian phallus, in which many body parts or 'body-like things' can metonymically comes to symbolise the phallus (Butler 1983: 56). Butler's lesbian phallus finds a more concrete or material realisation in Kathryn Bond Stockton's word-dildo (Stockton 2015, 2019). Stockton renders Butler's lesbian phallus *more* material: in a brief autobiographical anecdote in her 2015 article the word 'lesbian' *itself* is figured a dildo inside both her and her partner. 'We have been dildoed by the sign "lesbian" . . . the word like a dildo' (Stockton 2015).

As Stockton writes later, provocatively, deliberately, in her book *Avidly Reads Making Out* (2019), some words are weightier, heavier or more impactful than others. Historically perceived as a literary device dating from Renaissance metaphysical powerhouses such as John Donne, the conceit is an elaborate, extreme or even surreal extended metaphor used for hyperbolic effect. 'Perhaps the word "dildo" has arrested you. Perhaps it hits you differently than my other words. Maybe you like it. Maybe it repels you. Or just jolts you. It is now in you' (Stockton 2019). This utterance is strikingly – yes, arrestingly – resonant with Austin's descriptions of performative language in the sense that something is done through its enunciation, though the relationship is somewhat different in that the words perform something different – there is a gap, perhaps – between the words and the thing that is heralded or being done. Stockton's reading-as-barebacking, word-as-dildo analogies operate as vivid conceits for our present arguments concerning the materiality of the signifier. As Stockton writes earlier:

> Gay male barebacking is like dildoing is like kissing is like reading: it's a fetishizing of sign and surface that must get inside us . . . the word births in us, with us, and through us, as we take it in: courtesy of us, it's allowed to breed an intimate estrangement of itself. (Stockton 2015)

Estrangement, both is and as queer defamiliarisation: it is these words we must focus on here, in the moment of arresting luminosity when the word-thing arrives within our perceptual field. If we think of the process of barebacking narrated multifariously in Stockton's texts – deliberate thrillseeking unprotected sex – it sets off a chain of reactions which will differ in each reader, but the very process of perception without the contra-ceptive sheath of linguistic prescriptivism. Put simply, meaning is untethered; the seeds, semina, are without their protective husk. Or, more crudely, amorphous sausagelike stuff of meaning is squeezed out of its sack. Whichever conceit-strewn pathway is chosen, it is precisely queer defamiliarisation that Stockton elucidates here; precisely through a conception of the materiality of words. What Stockton describes as tumescence of words – their getting fat inside us – is the process of shifting our perception of those words as they are perceived anew. It is through writing, mattering and making strange that this striking image – the word inside us: wor(l)d.

In order to determine what constitutes a process of wor(l)ding, the environment from which it emerges in its contemporary guises, and most importantly its political valency in terms of reimagined futures and pasts, I will now look at a number of manifestations of wor(l)ding, all related to science fiction in different ways: from Haraway's material-semiotic and later the heteronym Terrapolis; to ontologically unstable signs on the street; to Afrofuturism's alternative realities, futures and pasts.

'We are not immediately present to ourselves. Self-knowledge requires a semiotic-material technology to link meanings and bodies' (Haraway 1988: 585). We know from Haraway's earlier work that the conjoining of the material and the semiotic is important in understanding her work. In 'The Promises of Monsters' (1992) Haraway uses the term 'material-semiotic actor' to highlight the object of knowledge as an active part of the apparatus of bodily production (Haraway 2004: 67) Pointing towards the poem as an object with language as an actor, Haraway describes bodies as objects of knowledge and 'material-semiotic generative nodes' (Haraway 2004: 68). This move is about the insertion of the discursive and the artificial into nature and biology. In this context, it should not be forgotten that it is literature to which Haraway turns as her model for what she calls the apparatus of bodily production, using specifically Katie King's description of the 'apparatus of bodily production' (Haraway 2004: 68). This model is extended out to encompass the production and reproduction of bodies and other objects of value in scientific knowledge projects. This is the inspiration for Haraway's concept of the material-semiotic actor. In 'The Promises of Monsters' Haraway charts the relationship between science fiction and a series of concepts that we could now claim are distinctly new materialist. 'Science fiction is generically concerned with the interpenetration of boundaries between problematic selves and unexpected others and with the exploration of possible worlds in a context structured by transnational technoscience' (Haraway 2004: 70). Science fiction also informs Haraway's reading of Trinh T. Minh-ha's concept 'inappropriate/d others' (1986/7): 'If Western patriarchal narratives have told that the physical body issues from first birth, while man was the product of the second birth, perhaps a differential, diffracted feminist allegory might have "inapprioriate/d others" emerge from a third birth into an SF world called elsewhere – a place composed from interference patterns' (Haraway 2004: 70).

Zoom forwards. Where are we now? We are outside Archway underground station, London, December 2015. Another signature. A noticeboard outside the tube entrance which declares. 'When something goes wrong in your life just yell "PLOT TWIST!" and move on'. Another signature.

So we yell 'PLOT TWIST!' and move on. Where do we move onto? We move onto New York. It's December 2016. We're standing outside a bookstore. Another signature. A sign outside the bookstore declares. Post Apolcalyptic Fiction has been moved to our Current Affairs Section'. A joke, a signature, fictioning reality. So. Fiction is real and reality is fiction. And we're at the bad end of the bookshelf.

And yet.

It is clear that when Haraway is sketching out her version of worlding that she is keen to separate her term from that of Heidegger: 'Finished once and for all with Kantian globalizing cosmopolitics and grumpy human-exceptionalist Heideggerian worlding, *Terrapolis* is a mongrel word composted with a mycorrhiza of Greek and Latin rootlets and their symbionts' (Haraway 2016: 11). Wor(l)ding for Haraway manifests itself in the SF sense: 'a risky game of worlding and storying; it is staying with the trouble' (Haraway 2016: 13). Some of her earlier thinking around the conception of worlding can be seen in her *Companion Species Manifesto* (2003) as in her subsequent reference to Whitehead's process philosophy, specifically concerning his theory of prehensions. 'Reality is an active verb, and the nouns all seem to be gerunds with more appendages than an octopus' (Haraway 2003: 6), and of course tentacularity rears its tendrils later for Haraway not merely as a figure but as an active mode of thought. Here we are explicitly made aware of the noun-as-gerund, active world*ing*, which in Haraway's *Staying with the Trouble* is put into effect in the creation of Terrapolis: 'a story, a speculative fabulation, and a strong figure for multi-species worlding (Haraway 2016: 10). As speculative fabulation and as heteronym (both terms discussed below), Terrapolis is Haraway's own particular 'matter-realising', to use Braidotti's words, (Braidotti 2013a: 95) of The Field.

And yet.

The bad end of the bookshelf presupposes the existence of the good end. Signatures of our collective hope. We have to look for it in the same place. From dystopia to utopia. The spatiotemporal zoomings-around of science fiction and fiction science. Projected spatiotemporal coordinates will save us. Utopia Now. Who creates Utopia Now? The dreamer projected as realist. A world reworlded.

Zoom backwards. Where are we? We're back in London but it's the year 1516. We're reading Latin. We're reading Thomas More explaining a fictional island society. The dreamer projected as realist. Thomas More did science fiction early. We don't agree with everything this dreamer projected but we love the enthusiasm and the sheer audacity to dream. We all want to leap naked into fountains. Don't we? Science fiction now. Utopia as the not-place that we dare to think. But we said spatio-temporal. What about the not-time. Extend utopia to uchronia. Uchronia now! Speculate. To speculate requires hope. Hoping as worlding and reworlding. Fictioning as mythopoesis.

Agential Realism and the Material-Discursive

The shifting of noun to infinitive to gerund in the various theorisations of worlding (world – to world – worlding) is also an important constituent part of Karen Barad's agential realism. Akin to Haraway's use of the gerund in the term world*ing*, Barad speaks of matter*ing*.

> In an agential realist account, matter does not refer to a fixed substance; rather, *matter is substance in its intra-active becoming – not a thing but a doing, a congealing of agency.* (Barad 2007: 151)

Barad's account of agential realism works by means of entangling the material with the discursive. For Barad, matter 'is not a linguistic construction but a discursive production in the posthumanist sense' (Barad 2007: 151). Matter itself for Barad is always simultaneously a noun and a verb, because matter means mattering – or as she writes, matter(ing). The wor(l)dings discussed here are matter(ings). The shift from materiality understood as thing to materiality understood as a doing is most clearly outlined in Barad's agential realism, which emerges from her unique reading of Niels Bohr's work. Bohr's development and critique of classical physics culminates, in Barad's words, in the following result: '*the nature of the observed phenomenon changes with corresponding changes in the apparatus*' (Barad 2007: 106). For Barad, Bohr thus demonstrates the inseparability, or entanglement, of the phenomenon and the apparatus, of matter and meaning. Epistemologically: '*No inherent/Cartesian subject-object distinction exists*' (Barad 2007: 114). Barad's reading of Bohr's epistemological framework results in the following statement: 'Referentiality must be reconceptualised. The referent is not an observation-independent object but a phenomenon' (Barad 2007: 120). Bohr, according to Barad, situates practice within theory, and as a result, the processes of 'method, measurement, description, interpretation, epistemology, and ontology are not separable considerations' (Barad 2007: 120–1). Barad's reading of Bohr demonstrates that instead of taking words and things as separate and even opposing kinds of existents, we can take hold of both these existents simultaneously. Agential realism for Barad is a posthumanist theory of performativity that understands the primary ontological unit as phenomenon. Phenomena for Barad are 'dynamic topological reconfigurings/entanglements/relationalities/(re)articulations of the world' (Barad 2007: 141). It is precisely this inseparability of matter and discourse that can allow wor(l)ding to take place.

Zoom forwards. Where are we now? We're in Santa Cruz, California, and the year is 2016. SF – science fiction, speculative fabulation. Topos and chronos fabulated speculatively. Notice the word play. SF, science fiction, speculative fabulation, will save us. Donna Haraway remakes the Earth as Terrapolis populated by vermin, critters and string figures. Multispecies alliance. Haraway says: 'Recuperation is still possible, but only in multispecies alliance, across the killing divisions of nature, culture, and technology and of organism, language and machine. The feminist cyborg taught me that; the humanimal worlds of dogs, chickens, turtles and wolves taught me that; and in fugal, fungal, microbial, symbiogenetic counterpoint, the acacia trees of Africa, the Americas, Australia, taxa, teach me that' (Haraway 2016: 117)

Uchronia and Utopia. The dreamer as realist.

Speculative Topoi: Afrofuturism as Uchronia

> Ustopia is a word I made up by combining utopia and dystopia – the imagined perfect society and its opposite – because, in my view, each contains a latent version of the other. (Atwood 2011: 66)

We could say that the 'fields' referred to so far are speculative topoi, of which a speculative spectrum already exists: from utopia to dystopia. As Margaret Atwood states above, it is possible for these to be conflated. The concept of dystopia is just as prevalent in discussions of contemporary world politics as it is in literary academia. In May 2017, for example, a conference called Dystopia Now was held at Birkbeck University in London. It is no longer surprising nor is it an exaggeration to say that dystopia *is* now. We see signatures of dystopia now everywhere. The Dystopia Now conference was held by the Centre for Contemporary Literature, but the topic bleeds outwards into all aspects of life. Dystopia really is now. The blurring of fiction and 'real life' is hardly a new phenomenon, but there are signs of a more intense perception of dystopia, heretofore understood exclusively in terms of a future-looking literary genre, as already happening in our reality, right now. Consider the statement below, which we may have encountered already in another spacetimemattering . . .

Post Apocalyptic Fiction has been moved to our Current Affairs Section

This statement was written on a blackboard outside a New York bookstore in 2016 and was shared widely on social media. The literalisation of the radical genre-shift from fiction to 'real-life' demonstrates the incredulity with which humans are currently facing the world, and the increasing applicability of categories of fiction to lived experience. One effect of this phenomenon is the potential for categories of fiction to have material effects on lived experience. As a genre, science fiction has the potential to foretell scientific developments in the 'real' world, and the nature of speculation makes it harder to see where the fiction ends and the real begins. What is interesting about this kind of writing is that it relates real life to fiction in a very direct way. It demonstrates that the blurring of these realms is no longer confined to academic spheres. Perhaps dystopia is no longer a speculative topos; perhaps it has already been taken up in processes of wor(l)ding.

Wor(l)ding is, then, a particular blending of the material and the semiotic that can be perceived in what we call science fiction, speculative fiction, SF. Among other things, this transdisciplinary blend is apt to blur the boundaries between subject and environment, just as in Barad's agential realist account discussed above. Science fiction is particularly useful in demonstrating the multifarious inseparability of subject and object. As Margaret Atwood outlines in the introduction to her book on the topic, SF in its multiple contested forms and subgenres deals with 'those imagined other worlds located somewhere apart from our everyday one: in another time, in another dimension, through a doorway into the spirit world, or on the other side of the threshold that divides the known from the unknown' (Atwood 2011: 8). Science fiction is constituted by the wor(l)ding of an alternative topos; the 'SF world called "elsewhere"' mentioned by Haraway and quoted above. It comes as no surprise to those for whom 'other' has been an identifiable political category that the reimagining of these 'elsewheres' carries particular political-subjective applicability. This is why Afrofuturism is so important to this discussion; the wor(l)dings discussed below afford and create alternative spaces for those denied their place in the spaces already existing.

Zoom back one year. Where are we now? We're in Bamako, Mali. It's June 2015. A collaborative project of sound and image. An exhibition called Uchronia: The Unequivocal Interpretation of Reality. To hope is to speculate. A question both speculative and political: What would have happened if it had been a Malian emperor rather than Christopher Columbus who had discovered America? Even asking this question dislodges the signatures of our combined ruin. To hope is to make and remake the world. Afrofuturism makes utopia and uchronia now. To hope is to reimagine futures past.

The alternative reimagining of pasts is sometimes called uchronia, although spatial or geographical descriptors are still widely used.[5] In June 2015, photographer Maciek Pozoga and musicologist Christopher Kirkley collaborated on an exploration of sound and image called *Uchronia: The Unequivocal Interpretation of Reality*. Exhibited in Bamako, Mali, the premise of the exhibition was speculative and political: what would have happened if a Malian emperor rather than Christopher Columbus had discovered America? This story was a development or continuation of a story that Pozoga had read about online, namely that in 1311 the Malian emperor Abubakari II left West Africa to explore the Atlantic Ocean. Pozoga's aim with this project is described by Helen Jennings wanting 'to capture a sense of surface disorientation through the lens of folklore and science fiction thereby creating a space where it's the Azawad rebels and imperialist hangover that are unreal' (Pogoza and Jennings 2016). While the *Uchronia* exhibition speculates on historical narratives in order to produce a uchronia, other examples of Afrofuturist art and literature speak of a more mythological temporality.

The cycle of birth, death and renewal is given an Afrofuturist treatment in Tonya Liburd's poem 'Contemplation' (2016) by means of a mythic intertwining of trees, earth and ancestral spirituality. The speaker of the poem digs herself an early grave, fatigued with the feeling that the entire earth amounts to an 'elsewhere' for her. In a few lines the entirety of human civilisation's trajectory of racial injustice is charted: '. . . as human civilization went on and on . . . black-skinned men / pounded spikes, hammered tracks . . . everything controlled by pale-skinned men, who miser'd / knowledge / and had guns.' The poem's speaker becomes entwined with the roots of trees and the earth itself; 'rich loam attached to my eyelashes'. At the end of the poem the speaker rises newly empowered, 'a creature of the Earth like any other', and is deferred to by the men she comes across, 'elder to eldest' (Liburd 2016). The poem draws to a close as the speaker is bestowed with a 'new purpose'. This is Afrofuturist writing as wor(l)ding; the creation of an alternative poetic world which has implications beyond the text.

Let's go back to another future past. Another audacious individual who hoped to remake the world. Where are we now? We're in Oakland, the east side of San Francisco Bay, and the year is 1974.

---

[5] Coined by Charles Renouvier in *Uchronie (l'Utopie dans l'histoire): Esquisse historique apocryphe du développement de la civilisation européene tel qu'il n'a pas été tel qu'il aurait pu être* (2018 [1876]).

The satellites are spinning
A new day is dawning
The galaxies are waiting
For planet Earth's awakening
            (Ra 2005: 331)

Whose are these words? They're the words of Sun Ra, jazz genius space traveller Afrofuturist and world creator. The dreamer projected as realist.

Afrofuturism is a highly pertinent example of wor(l)ding because the world as it stands is already experienced as an elsewhere by people of colour. 'I'm black. I'm solitary. I've always been an outsider', states Octavia Butler in the *LA Times* in 1998. This spawns the need for new alternative topoi. This is the argument of Sun Ra, Afrofuturist pioneer, in the classic film *Space Is the Place* (1974):

> I'm not real. I'm just like you. You don't exist in this society. If you did, your people wouldn't be seeking equal rights. You're not real. If you were, you'd have some status among the nations of the world. So we're both myths. I do not come to you as a reality; I come to you as the myth, because that's what black people are. Myths.

Ra is persuading the black youths of Oakland to join him, arguing that they may as well create their own reality because they do not currently have the status of 'reality':

> since this planet for thousands of years has been up under that law of death and destruction, it's moving into something else which I choose to call MYTH, a MYTH-SCIENCE, because it's something that people don't know anything about. That's why I'm using the name MYTH-SCIENCE ARKESTRA, because I'm interested in happiness for people, which is just a myth, because they're not happy. I would say that the synonym for myth is happiness. Because that's why they go to the show, to the movies, they be sitting up there under these myths trying to get themselves some happiness. (Sun Ra, in Sinclair 2010: 28)

It is important to point out that the multidirectional temporal aspect of Ra's Afrofuturism is evident in his constant use of ancient Egyptian mythology as already on display in his name, which is taken from the Egyptian sun god Ra. For Ra the Afrofuturist, while ancient Egypt remained 'his single lodestar where African mythology was concerned' (Lock 1999: 74), this turn to ancient Egypt was in essence future-oriented.

Sofia Samatar's epic piece 'Notes Toward a Theory of Quantum Blackness' contains statements such as 'All models of quantum blackness attempt to develop a new geometry' (Samatar 2016). As the author states in a brief prefatory comment, the poem is about 'blackness as gravity'. The scientific hypotheses are used speculatively, as pointers towards alternative types of thinking, but the message is clear: the existing structural systems are racially unequal and therefore new systems must be invented. 'Blackness cannot be integrated with quantum mechanics at very high energies. At lower energies, it is ignored; to address energies at or higher than the Planck scale, a new theory of quantum blackness is required.' The language of scientific observsation and measurement is woven among the objects and signs of racial injustice and slavery, rendered in phrases such as 'the curvature of space-time is caused by the unequal distribution of mass/energy, and 'Plot the distance between bullet and flesh . . . Between throat and hair. Between hunger and time of day.' These interweavings both critique and affirm scientific methodologies.

Samatar's poem is acknowledged as part of a larger conversation involving the Black Quantum Futurism Collective. An artistic and literary collaboration between Camae Dennis and Rasheedah Phillips, the Collective outlines Black Quantum Futurism (BQF) as a practice in three modes: Future Visioning, Future Altering and Future Manifestation. According to Phillips, a BQF creative (she uses the noun to describe someone operating from a BQF perspective) 'exploits the fact that the future can alter the present and the present can alter the past' (Phillips 2015: 19). The use of 'quantum' here is careful; in *Black Quantum Futurism Theory and Practice Vol. I*, Phillips produces a 'BQF Correspondence Chart' in which various quantum phenomena are presented alongside African spiritual and religious phenomena, as well as physical descriptions and real-world correspondences. For example, wave-particle dualism described in physical terms is mapped onto the Ancient Egyptian concept of the Tuat, Ka and Qeb (Ankh Amen) and then described in certain 'real-world' manifestations (Phillips 2015: 76–7). These impressive trans-historical wor(l)dings are uchronic in the sense that the unit of quanta is speculatively sourced in ancient times, thereby achieving precisely the 'elsewhere' of a future-present-past 'retrocausality' that Phillips outlines.

Steampunk is another uchronic subgenre of science fiction that has been given an Afrofuturist makeover in recent times. Nisi Shawl's *Everfair* (2016) rewrites parts of history in order to create alternative futures. The novel explores the horrific Belgian colonisation of the Congo through imagining how things could have been if the native populations had learned about steam technology earlier. The utopian/uchronic Everfair is a haven for not only the native populations of the Congo, but also for slaves escaping from other colonised places. As Shawl notes at the beginning:

> The steampunk genre often works as a form of alternative history . . . I like to think that with a nudge or two events might have played out *much* more happily for the inhabitants of Equatorial Africa . . . Of course steampunk is a form of fiction, a fantasy, and the events within these pages never happened. But they *could* have. (Shawl 2016: 7)

The modality of the '*could* have' in Shawl's excerpt above is important; it speaks of a vital contingency which is discussed further below. To what degree, then, are Afrofuturist steampunk fiction and quantum blackness material-semiotic actors or causes? We need only to look as far as the proliferation of Afrofuturism itself to discern material effects: films, comics, poetry, fiction, theory, visual art and music to name just some examples of this flourishing. If we take 'material' in its financial understanding, the commercial success of the film *Black Panther* (2018) and the artist Janelle Monáe demonstrate this very clearly. *Black Panther* contains another uchronic wor(l)ding wherein the fictional nation Wakanda, in possession of the invaluable element of vibranium (somewhat resonant with Flann O'Brien's omnium, discussed below), flourishes and yet masequerades as a third-world country to the outside world. Janelle Monáe's vast inventiveness in terms of her own personae includes a heteronym itself, in messianic ArchAndroid Cindi Mayweather (*The ArchAndroid*, 2010). As Monáe states in an interview:

> . . . to me the android will represent a new Other – just like any of us who've ever been considered 'the minority' at some time can feel like 'The Other!' And so I'm basically asking people to think about whether we'd DISCRIMINATE against this new 'Other' . . . And what makes the ArchAndroid herself very special is that she represents the MEDIATOR between the have's and the have not's, the minority and the majority. (Monáe 2015)

The alignment of the android with Other is precisely why the function of the heteronym is of particular use within Afrofuturism: it allows the 'have nots' to reimagine and reinvent. In Harawayesque, material-semiotic terms, articulations such as these are themselves signifiers with material effects in the world.

So. We must try to render it here. How? Speculate, shore up knowledge, look forwards back. Back to what. To the what we know. Hope was a goddess called Elpis. Pandora's jar. The one left inside. The good one left inside lid shut. What else. The steadfast anchor. Tied to what. Tied to rock in shifting sea bed monster. Try again. Sedimented between Faith and Desire. Sludgy bedfellows slippery rope. A wet knot is stronger. A wet dust is sludge. A sand is sharp. Clutch and clench. Clench is down and screw is up. Keen is forward. Keen is lean. Are we converging or diverging. Can we hope back or is that nostalgia. Do both. Hope forward back.

Wor(l)dings: Speculative Fabulation, Hyperstition, Fictioning, Myth-Science

Where else can we find comparable processes of wor(l)ding, and what are the factors that differentiate them? In the 1990s, Warwick's CCRU (Cybernetic Culture Research Unit) defined what they called hyperstition as the process in which 'fiction is not opposed to the real. Rather, reality is understood to be composed of fictions – consistent semiotic terrains that condition perceptual, affective and behavioural responses . . . Rather than acting as transcendental screens, blocking out contact between itself and the world, the fiction acts as a Chinese box – a container for sorcerous interventions in the world' (CCRU 2001: 278). Hyperstition has been discussed and perceived at various significant points wherein a fictophilosophical concept is created: for example, Luciana Parisi describes both Laboria Cuboniks' Xenofeminist Manifesto as 'an exercise in hyperstition: a thought experiment or an enabler of the future' and Haraway's cyborg figuration as 'a radical hyperstitional attempt at exposing the alien or denaturalised fabrication of gender' (Parisi 2017: 215, 217). Citing Haraway, Simon O'Sullivan draws our particular attention to the transition from 'world' to 'worlding' that we see in her work and compares this with his own examination of the transition from 'fiction' to 'fictioning' (Gunkel, Hameed and O'Sullivan 2017: 13). The temporal paradox of science-fictioning, according to O'Sullivan, is 'how to be in the world but not wholly of that world; the important part being that there is no attempt to solve this paradox, rather it is made manifest. This is fictioning as mythopoiesis: the imaginative transformation of the world through fiction' (O'Sullivan 2016: 6). As O'Sullivan and others are aware, we can trace this fictioning-as-mythopoiesis back to Bergson and *fabulation*, sometimes translated as myth-making, such as in *Two Sources of Morality and Religion* (1932). This myth-making faculty for Bergson is not merely the imagination; it is 'a very clearly defined faculty of the mind, that of creating personalities whose stories we relate to ourselves.' *Fabulation*, or its English translation myth-making, for Bergson is no less than a 'fundamental demand of life' and 'to be deduced from the conditions of existence of the human species' (Bergson 1974: 184). Myth-making links up ancient tales with contemporary novels and, according to Bergson, the entire development of the human race. 'If the human species does exist, it is because the very act which posited man with his tool-contriving intelligence, with the necessary continuation of his intellectual effort, and the danger arising from such a continuation, begot the myth-making function' (Bergson 1974: 186). While Bergson's function here has a religious purpose, Ridvan Askin analyses the Bergsonian concept of fabulation as taken up by Deleuze and Guattari in his theory of differential narratology and demonstrates that in Deleuze and Guattari the concept is secularised. Askin goes further than Deleuze and Guattari in his presentation and use of the 'fabulation function', widening its scope from merely fabulation as fiction to a more general Deleuzian speculative narratology in which fabulation's true function is 'the production of stories in the general sense of narrative rather than in the restricted sense of fiction' (Askin 2016: 69). For Askin, narration is by definition creative and speculative. 'It all boils down to this: in order to narrate, one has to make use of fabulation. In order to speculate, one has to tell a story' (Askin 2016: 70).

For a literary example of such imaginative transformation let me briefly turn to a work which we might call speculative in the above sense and which definitely aggravates the boundaries of the absurd, with the full knowledge of definitions being a slippery illusion of solidity in a watery landscape *and* with the knowledge that it wouldn't have been called that at the time of publication: Flann O'Brien's *The Third Policeman* (1967). The fictional and almost-but-not-quite-nonsensical philosopher de Selby's identification of a speculative element is relevant to this discussion and deserves a place in the speculative Field: omnium.

> 'You are omnium and I am omnium and so is the mangle and my boots here and so is the wind in the chimney.'
> 'That is enlightening,' I said.
> 'It comes in waves,' he explained . . .
> 'Some people,' he said, 'call it energy but the right name is omnium because there is far more than energy in the inside of it, whatever it is. Omnium is the essential inherent interior essence which is hidden inside the root of the kernel of everything and it is always the same . . .
> Some people call it God.' (O'Brien 1967: 109–11)

What we have here is a playful speculative typological conceptual persona for the driving force that illuminates, energises and infuses everything. Omnium: one name for all. While the book was not published before the 1960s, it was written in the 1940s. De Selby almost proposes a kind of speculative vitalism which makes very direct reference to Bergson's philosophy in terms of his notion of the *durée* in order to reanimate a tantalisingly partial Bergsonian world: human existence *is* a succession of infinitely brief static experiences, and therefore a journey *is* a series of infinitesimal pauses. As well as its pleasing neological inventiveness, the engagement with (then) contemporary philosophical theories and the knowing use of a fabulation function is interesting.

More recently, these earlier examples of wor(l)ding have been refigured, refabulated and reformed. In Elizabeth de Freitas's piece in the 2017 special issue on new materialism of the *Minnesota Review*, her Laboratory of Speculative Sociology is to be understood in a number of different ways simultaneously. It is 'not only or essentially a thermodynamic system but also a quantum event, by which all individuation of object or person is the effect of wave diffraction and temporal permutations', she maintains (de Freitas 2017: 117). When de Freitas writes, in the past tense, that 'Gradually, researchers turned to a more haptic conception of diffraction, one more truly based in the feeling of intensity when two waves meet' (de Freitas 2017: 117), there is a sense that this knowingly fictional fragment might actually foretell the future trajectory of new materialist research into diffraction. This would then be the very action of speculative fabulation: the fiction materialises the real. To elucidate further how speculative fabulation engenders its own materiality, which can then have real spatiotemporal consequences, I will now turn to the use of heteronyms and homonyms.

Off we go. Where are we now? New Cross, South East London, 1998. More Brilliant Than The Sun. Kodwo Eshun and heteronymic soundplay. Eshun welcomes us to the reworded reworlded Futurrhythmachinic Discontinuum. Acid house, Phuture with a Ph. Sound and shape effects worlding through a synthesis of elements. The signature of the name splinters into its material fragments. Eshun says: 'Ph is to sound as silver is to vision. Ph is the silver prefix, the word concentrate' (Eshun 1998: 94)

Wor(l)dings: Heteronymy, Homonymy, Contingency

What place might '-nym' word-creatures occupy in the Field? Surely this suffix (meaning name, from the Greek *onoma*) leads to a relatively limited nomenclature-type of thinking. Homonyms – words which have the same pronunciation and spelling but are different in meaning – and heteronyms – words which have the same spelling but different pronunciation and meanings – both have potential to create a speculative proliferation of material-semiotic realities, as the examples below demonstrate. Both homonymy and heteronymy reduplicate worlds through words.

> *Don Quixote* is is an accidental book, *Don Quixote* is unnecessary. I can premeditate writing, I can write it, without incurring a tautology. (Borges 1962: 50)

J. L. Borges's short story 'Pierre Menard, Author of the *Quixote*' (1939) makes use of a homonym-like process in which identical articulatory marks or sounds made by the character Pierre Menard produce a replica of Cervantes's *Don Quixote* which is *somehow different* from the original. It is not a tautology. The difference between the identically written texts, according to the fictional reviewer, is their temporal position. The events taking place since the original publication of Cervantes's work contribute palimpsestically to the richness of the allusions to be found in the rewrite, and the result is an argument for the significance of context. Things matter differently according to their position, which is why the relation between the *Quixote* of 1605 and the *Quixote* of 1939 is that of heteronyms. A rewriting, identical, but not a copy. Like Foucault's heterotopias, heteronyms demonstrate a spatiotemporal, material-semiotic heterogeneity.

The Borgesian process of productive repetition with difference has provoked further twenty-first-century iterations. In 2016 artist Ami Clarke replicated a chapter of former options trader Elie Ayache's book *Blank Swan: The End of Probability* (which is itself inspired by the Borges story), and argued that this did not constitute a copy. Economic speculation requires the prediction of future events, which is yet another type of wor(l)ding, another type of field. Ayache's *The Blank Swan: The End of Probability* (2010) is a critical response to Nassim Nicholas Taleb's *The Black Swan: The Impact of the Highly Improbable* (2007). Taleb's imagined polar worlds of Extremistan and Mediocristan are speculative topoi; they are toponyms. Perhaps they are heterotopias. The supreme law of Mediocristan is as follows: '*When your sample is large, no single instance will significantly change the aggregate or the total.*' Called a 'utopian' province by Taleb (with speculative tongue firmly in speculative cheek), single events do not really affect the scale of the topos as a whole. The supreme law of Extremistan, by contrast, is as follows: '*In Extremistan, inequalities are such that one single observation can disproportionately impact the aggregate, or the total.*' Variation within distributions is far less constrained, making it harder to make reliable predictions from data. According to Taleb, wealth and almost all social matters are from Extremistan (Taleb 2007: 32–3). The title of Taleb's work, *The Black Swan*, pertains to an unpredictable improbable event which is then explained and made to seem less random. Taleb suggests both Google and 9/11 as examples of black swans.

Elie Ayache's response book *The Blank Swan* counters these ideas very directly; rather than discussing probability, Ayache discusses contingency. Quantum mechanics, for Ayache, is the 'Black Swan of all Black Swans' (Ayache 2010: 15). The following description he provides echoes Barad in its foregrounding of the inseparability of phenomena and context.

> The quantum phenomenon has the peculiarity of not being separable from its context of manifestation. Depending on the experimental set-up (or context of experiment) the quantum object may disclose itself either as a particle or as a wave, and there is no way we could counterfactually argue, in one context, what the object may have been in the other. (Ayache 2010: 15)

For Ayache, it is contingency which must be compared with writing: for him 'the writing process and the pricing process are two special kinds of processes that do not take place in possibility or in probability, like the traditional stochastic processes' (Ayache 2010: xv). Ayache argues that neither possibility nor probability are sufficient strategies for the paradoxical dimension wherein one can do something different than predicting history, which is impossible, or replicating it, which is empty. It is contingency, as advocated in Meillassoux's *After Finitude* (2006), which Ayache believes is the necessary mode of thinking. Meillassoux points out that contingency means that anything may happen, even that the invariants of the world remain invariants: 'Contingency is such that anything might happen, even nothing at all, so that what is, remains as it is' (Meillassoux 2006: 63). Contingency is similarly defined by Robin Mackay as 'the attempt to think events that take place but *need not take place*: events that could be, or could have been, otherwise' (Mackay 2011: 1). It is clear that contingency and narrative are vitally linked, but how might this be useful for the thinking of material-semiotic realities? In terms of contingency and narrative, it is interesting that Michael Jay Lewis defines contingency in this context as either 'accident' or 'apposition', both of which are significant for the wor(l)ding function. Whether one or both of these understandings of contingency are employed, its role in narrative as creation of concepts is clear and expressed by Lewis in terms of schemas: 'The translatability of the significance of one schema (a fictional one) into the logic of the next (a non-fictional one) is indicated, in part, by the ability of factors such as contingency' (Lewis 2012: 101).

The dreamers projected as realists. What do they all say. They say you can. Something. From nothing. Something from nothing. Worlding is hoping and every utterance makes a world. If post apocalyptic fiction has been moved to the current affairs section then we must inject the bookshelves with reworked definitions. Spawn new subgenres. Fiction as worlding. Politically valent reimagined futures and pasts. Alternative spaces for those denied their place in the places that already exist.

Contingency is also an important factor when thinking through the literary function of the heteronym, as we see in Alain Badiou's reading of Fernando Pessoa. The literary heteronym is a concrete but fictional alter-ego, in contrast to a pseudonym, which is but a 'false name' that is, a different name for one and the same person. 'And so I created a non-existent coterie, placing it all in a framework of reality', writes Fernando Pessoa in his letter of 1935 to Adolfo Casais Monteiro (Pessoa 2001: 257). Pessoa's use differs significantly from the linguistic understanding of the heteronym, in which words have the same spelling but different pronunciations and different meanings. Famously, Pessoa developed scores of alternative personae who were cast as distinct characters and authors with their own distinct biographies, works, styles and theories. Some were poets; some were critics. Ricardo Reis, Alberto Caeiro and Álvaro de Campos all are and are not Fernando Pessoa. Pessoa's heteronyms, for Badiou, are 'opposed to the anonymous inasmuch as they do not stake a claim upon the One or the All, but instead originarily establish the contingency of the multiple . . . For the real universe is at once multiple, contingent, and untotalizable' (Badiou 2005: 44). It is interesting in Badiou's description that 'contingency' is highlighted here too. Again, it is literary writing that is presented as the medium of contingency. Badiou describes Pessoa's works as 'thought-poems' and reserves the highest praise for his *oeuvre*, placing Pessoa before any philosopher of modernity, attributing to him simultaneously Platonic and anti-Platonic trajectories and describing his poems in philosophical terms: 'a veritable philosophy of the multiple, of the void, of the infinite. A philosophy that will affirmatively do justice to this world that the gods have forever abandoned' (Badiou 2005 [1998]: 45). Every heteronym is therefore a wor(l)ding, and this is where a creative and generative philosophy can begin to be thought.

Fragments shored? T. S. Eliot I will raise you your fear in a handful of dust and give you Ursula Le Guin.

Where are we? Portland, Oregon, 1989. Le Guin tells us something. She says: 'To make a world you start with an old one, certainly, to find a world, maybe you have to have lost one. Maybe you have to be lost. The dance of renewal, the dance that made the world, was always danced here at the edge of things, on the brink, on the foggy coast' (Le Guin 1989: 48).

So. For what may I hope?
At best still hope for not.
At best hope to stand against the tide.

Another example of a discussion of the function of the heteronym can be found in Kodwo Eshun's *More Brilliant than the Sun: Adventures in Sonic Fiction* (1998). This text is full of rhetorical flourishes similar to those we see in Haraway, including a literary heteronym for the world. Haraway's heteronym for the world in *Staying with the Trouble* is Terrapolis (2016), whereas Eshun's in *More Brilliant than the Sun* is the Futurhythmachinic Discontinuum (Eshun 1998: 10). A wor(l)ding; a peopled world; both homonym and heteronym functioning synecdochally not just as signature but as what we might call entireosphere. Eshun takes his inspiration from Sun Ra's myth-science in populating a future-past of the world of electronic music that both is and is not our recognisable world.

What are we doing on the foggy coast as we stand against the tide?

We are building a sandcastle. Sandcastles are irrational. We build them anyway.

Eshun builds on the avant-garde and jazz foundations laid down by Ra in the 1970s, moving the musical genres forward into the realms of disco, breakbeat, house and techno. It is on the subject of early acid house music where Eshun's language really shifts into a gear of phonetic matter*ing* (to use Barad's term) that demonstrates the power of wor(l)ding. He calls upon the strategies of both homonym and heteronym while enacting their powers of wor(l)ding in the creation of his replica world of the Futurythmachinic Discontinuum (Eshun 1998: 10). In this context, he writes about the pioneering acid house DJ Phuture:

> OJ Pierre's heteronym Phuture substitutes the 'f' in future for the 'pH' of the chemical formula and the ph of phono. Ph makes the phuture sound synthetic and phono-chemical. Ph is to sound as silver is to vision. Ph is the silver prefix, the

word concentrate. The future becomes a phuturistic Pharmatopia. With Phuture, the sound of the future separates from the look of the phuture. Vision and sound, heteronym and homonym, split off, run away from each other. (Eshun 1998: 94)

Zoom forwards. Where are we now? Senate House Library, London, November 2017. Ali Smith is giving the annual Liberty lecture. A tumbling wonderland of words and worlds. A sandcastle. She feeds us fragments to shore us against the ruins some of the many divisive recent words of Theresa May who told us during this year that if we believe we're a citizen of the world then we're a citizen of nowhere. If ever there were words to stamp on the sandcastle of someone's hope those are they. However. Smith tells us all: If you're a citizen of the imagination you're a citizen of everywhere.

Eshun's language does not just evoke; it renders material. Sound and shape effects wor(l)ding through a synthesis of elements: the polysemous, polysensory Ph mentioned above is a prime example. The signature of the name splinters into its material fragments. Not only is the sign thick; the sign is also sharp. Fragments shored against our ruins, or perhaps, fragments assembled to make and remake the world. As Ursula Le Guin so beautifully states:

To make a new world you start with an old one, certainly. To find a world, maybe you have to have lost one. Maybe you have to be lost. The dance of renewal, the dance that made the world, was always danced here at the edge of things, on the brink, on the foggy coast. (Le Guin 1989: 48)

Screw it up further. Make a path with shells. These fragments you have shored. Count stones. When you write that something can come from nothing but you don't know what the something actually is. When you look at a piece of Abstract Art (Capital A Capital A) and you know that you Feel Something (Capital F Capital S). When you bend towards tend towards. Something. When you utter something purely to fill the. Nothing.

Hope sandwiched between Faith and Desire? They are all a kind of breathing-in. The prickling on the back of the neck when the breathing in is accompanied by a thought of something that moves you and keeps you going. Pneuma. Inspiration. Not just for lofty white men in ivory towers consumed by the thought of divine or unreachable Muses. Inspiration keeps us alive. To inspire, to be inspired, we have to breathe in – we have to keep going, so that's what we are all doing, we're all breathing in, because it's the only thing left to do.

Epilogue: THE FIELD

The sultry February night was thick with shimmering halfsmearings, halfsmatterings, as she surfed between sleep and waking at the lip of the world. Propped up on the nightstand was a postcard emblazoned with the words WORD THE WORLD BETTER (Foley 2017).

It struck her that personae and topoi . . . or, in the neologononsensical night, persoi and toponae . . . of Haraway and Eshun were not so different. To wor(l)d was to populate the Field with heteronyms and homonyms. Haraway's strings and critters crawled, knotted, entwined themselves around The Field of Terrapolis, as did Eshun's silver prefixes, punctuating, perforating, aerating The Field of the Futurrhythmachinic Discontinuum. To wor(l)d was to fabricate and fabulate, without knowing the outcome, because it was the only thing left to do.

CHAPTER 4

Sensorium

I who outside the musical scale
(*moi qui hors de gamme*)
(Césaire 1986: 55)

... we describe the anatomy and histology of a previously unrecognized, though widespread, macroscopic, fluid-filled space within and between tissues, a novel expansion and specification of the concept of the human interstitium.
(Benias et al. 2018)

Histology, from *histos:* the web of the loom.

In March 2018 scores of articles in science magazines announced the discovery, published in *Scientific Reports* by a team of pathologists at NYU School of Medicine, of (almost) a new organ within the human body. Behold the interstitium. Lurking under the skin, just below the surface, are a series of interconnected fluid-filled compartments supported by a meshwork of strong and flexible connective tissue proteins: strong, flexible shock absorbers. What was previously thought to be merely dense tissue now appeared to be a new subcutaneous dimension of interconnected spaces: new worlds. The spaces are full of fluid to protect what lies underneath them. Without the fluid the compartments collapse, 'like a building with the floors suddenly knocked out, leaving the whole structure to flatten like a pancake' (Gibbens 2018).

There are several things we can take from this announcement. Both the concept of newly discovered secret compartments netted together under the skin and the imagined perception of these compartments flattened like a building are imaginative manoeuvres requiring spatial deformations. Imagining this new 'organ' requires a kind of imaginative proprioception beyond our conventional sensory systems; the systems themselves would require deformation. The interstitium is an in-between world of new complexity; it is the addition of a dimension.

Interstitia then – two, in fact – line and bolster this chapter, which draws together topology (the mathematical study of spatial properties preserved under continuous deformation) with synaesthesia (the perceptual phenomenon in which stimulation of one cognitive pathway leads to automatic experiences in another). The consideration of a topology of the senses is derived from an apprehension of the limitations of geometric systems, segmentations and scales: particularly for those existing at the margins, interstices or outside these systems altogether. Just as Aime Césaire writes in 1949 that he exists 'outside the musical scale', so too writes Hortense Spillers of the 'great black hole of meaning', the 'cul-de-sac' of unarticulated of black female sexual experience: 'unvoiced, misseen, not doing, awaiting *their* verb' (Spillers 1985: 74; 77). As with the creation of new voices and new worlds, so too must we perceive of new categories of spatiotemporal, corporal and sensory distribution.

Deforming the Senses

Why and how could sensory organisation be conceived of topologically? Here I present synaesthetic entanglements as a stretching and bending of the systems of Western ocularcentric sensory segmentation: a queer defamiliarisation of the senses. I trace some of the onto-epistemological strands of topological embodiment, from Lacan's conception of the structure of human subjectivity as a topological space in the later *Seminars* to Serres's passionate 'topology of tailoring' (Serres 2016: 228) through Susan Stryker's topological poiesis of the trans body and Eva Hayward's arachnid and coralline sensoria through marine tentacularity and haptic perception. I discuss the ways that haptics and optics might be thought together, and the operation of touching corporeal surfaces and the complexity of this operation in some non-human animals such as the spider and the octopus. The chapter ends by thinking acoustics and optics together with a speculative navigation of sirens and organs as instruments, agents or interfaces of variegated sensory stimulus. The first Interstitium opens up the concept of the human corporeal surface, making the surface of the body of Lewis Carroll's Alice operate as conceptual persona. The second Interstitium considers a series of attempts at taxonomical defamiliarisation or speculative taxonomies as examples of ways that we could rethink the ways that we categorise our existence.

Synaesthesia is the condition wherein the senses are experienced as other senses. The *dérèglement de tous les sens* or derangement of the senses prescribed by Rimbaud and constitutive of much of twentieth-century artistic experimentation is of course a speculative attempt at the synthesis of a condition experienced involuntarily by some people (Rimbaud 1966: 306). As an eternally nonsynaesethetic synaesthetophile, my own vain attempts to approximate this condition are documented at the end of this chapter.

Among other famous artistic figures, Russian abstract painter Wassily Kandinsky appears to have experienced this. In his 1911 text *Concerning the Spiritual in Art* Kandinsky discusses the psychic effects of colour beyond that of association. He saw in the attempt to use one sensation to describe another nothing less than the abstract dawn of the future of art. We can understand intuitively that colour can awaken a physical sensation due to semantic links, but Kandinsky points out that this is not a universal thing, and further that there are examples which refuse to be semantically or logically classified.

> Many colours have been described as rough or sticky, others as smooth and uniform, so that one feels inclined to stroke them (e.g., dark ultramarine, chromic oxide green, and rose madder). Equally the distinction between warm and cold colours belongs to this connection. Some colours appear soft (rose madder), others hard (cobalt green, blue-green oxide), so that even fresh from the tube they seem to be dry. (Kandinsky 2008: 60)

Kandinsky sketches out his own speculative taxonomies for colour tones, assigning certain colours to certain sound qualities. In music, 'a light blue is like a flute, a darker blue a cello; a still darker a thunderous double bass; and the darkest blue of all – an organ'. Green is 'the placid, middle notes of a violin'. Both white and black are silences of different qualities. White silence is 'one pregnant with possibilities' whereas black silence is 'a silence with no possibilities'. Light warm red is 'a sound of trumpets, strong, harsh, and ringing'. Orange's note is 'that of the angelus, or of an old violin'. Violet, a 'cooled red', is pronounced rather 'sad and ailing' and is linked to 'an English horn, or the deep notes of wood instruments (e.g. a bassoon)' (Kandinsky 2008: 89). Some synaesthetes may vehemently disagree with Kandinsky's connections; others may find harmonies or resonances with their own experiences. To a non-synaesthete the connections appear arbitrary, perhaps in the same way that we believe, after Saussure, the word 'tree' or 'arbre' to be arbitrarily connected to the concept of 'tree' or the object of a tree itself. 'Imagine the whole of perception being like a crystal scultpure', writes Richard Cytowic in his book on synaesthesia.

> It breaks. The shards scatter. Think of each shard as a modality, an indivisible unit representing one aspect of perception. We are now free to reassemble the sculpture any way we like, but even if we tried to glue it back exactly the way it was, we would certainly stick together a few shards that previously didn't go together. This is how synaesthesia is. (Cytowic 2018: 4)

For the purposes of my argument in this chapter, this affirmation of connected modalities – various, multifarious connections that differ between individuals – is an exemplary process in resisting perceptual hierarchies such as ocularcentrism in favour of thinking perception differently.

Sensory categorisation is related to the form/matter distinction in complex ways, which is one of the reasons why this chapter explores the potential for reassembling the hierarchies of sensory perception in both human and non-human animals. A number of scholars have commented on the richness of this area in their surveys of the development of the field of new materialism. Kyla Tompkins points towards the new materialist encounters with the sensory as 'the most intellectually exciting reading of New Materialism's critical potential' (Tompkins 2016). Tompkins here cites Dana Luciano, who also states that it is the sensory dimension of new materialism which is the most compelling contribution. Luciano argues that 'first, the sensory has always played a part in the analytic, and second, that our languages for how that works need to be enlarged and refined. The critical move away from the human demands an anthro-decentric rethinking of the sensory, a revision of the divisions among the senses and of modern sensory hierarchies' (Luciano 2015: 2). This call to the sensory among new materialist scholarship is also echoed by Chad Shomura (2017) and Michelle N. Huang (2017). As a literary scholar, Huang's provocation is particularly interesting: 'What are the implications of New Materialism for literary analysis, a methodology so focused on the concretization of form?' (Huang 2017). Not only this, but Huang also echoes both Luciano and Tompkins in saying that 'we might root the experimental power of language in its challenge to our sensory-perceptual apparatus' (Huang 2017). The relationships between matter and form, language and the senses, and the varieties of variation clearly (or blurrily, depending on your choice of ocular focus) deserve some further investigation.

We will begin with Thomas Tomkis's seventeenth-century play *Lingua,* in which the conventionally categorised five senses are characterised and personified, and then a sixth is added.

> (COMMUNIS SENSUS) The number of the *Senses* in this little world is answerable to the first bodies in the great world: now since there be but five in the Universe, the four elements and the pure substance of the heavens, therefore there can be but five Senses in our *Microcosm*, correspondent to those, as the sight to the heavens, hearing to the air, touching to the earth, smelling to the fire, tasting to the water; by which five means only the understanding is able to apprehend the knowledge of all corporal substances: wherefore we judge you to be no *Sense* simply; onely thus much we from henceforth pronounce, that all

women for your sake, shall have six *Senses*, seeing, hearing, tasting, smelling, touching, and the last and feminine sense, the sense of speaking. (Tomkis 1607)

In the concluding lines to Tomkis's play, the character Communis Sensus grants the stock prating female character Lingua the 'sixth' sense of speaking. Lingua is then bound and held captive in a grotesque enactment of the admonition of talkative women and forced very literally to hold her tongue, which is synecdochically (and, arguably, mereotopologically), both her tongue and her entire being. The idea of a 'sixth' sense is a common one, though this is often considered as a more mystical or psychic internal sense linked to the 'inner' vision championed by philosophers such as Plato and Democritus, at the expense of external optical vision. We could see this as one attempt at a topological defamailiarisation of our conventional sensory segmentation.

How else might we *characterise* an additional sense beyond the regular five? In his book *The Five Senses* Michel Serres posits the idea of a sixth sense which corresponds to the enigma of the sixth tapestry of the Cluny series *The Lady and the Unicorn* (c.1500), titled 'Mon Seul Desir' and depicting the lady returning some jewels to a casket. 'Indeed a sixth sense is necessary, in which the subject turns in on itself and the body on the body' (Serres 2016: 54). In his description of the scene, Serres likens the skin of the body to the material of the tent in front of which the lady stands, and also the fabric of the tapestry itself. For Serres the internal sense is language, and language is the anaesthetic that dulls the senses. Strangely Serres's reading of the sixth internal sense as language entwines with Tomkis's play as quoted above. In the holding of the tongue *as tongue* as we see in Tomkis's *Lingua*, the tongue-being would have to undergo significant contortions – we might even say deformations. It would have to hold itself within itself, or beside itself while being both part and whole of itself, perhaps calling for mereotopology (which is concerned with part-whole structures: see Varzi 1998).

> The body is composed like a book: a topology of tailoring, the pieces are stitched together at first; a geometry of sounds, next, the first global synthesis through the medium of language; and once again a topology of mixtures, the cook makes refinements based on the vicinity of ingredients to one another. (Serres 2016: 228)

Serres's topological signature implicitly informs and inspires much of today's moves towards disciplinary interpenetrations and diffractions. The move towards inter- and transdisciplinarity is itself enmeshed with topology: the reorientations of proximities and distances that occur in the spatial deformations are precisely what occurs when one discipline touches or interpenetrates with another. Angus Fletcher sums this up in his book *The Topological Imagination* when he states that imagined links '*between seemingly disjunctive fields of thought* . . . are virtually all topological' (Fletcher 2016: 41). Serres brings together science, literature and mathematics in a way that is quite unlike any other thinker. The phenomenon of isomorphism necessary for topological figurings is precisely what Serres perceives across disciplines as well as being appropriate for our conceptions of time or the corporeal surface; it is thought itself that is topological. In his conversations with Latour, Serres asks us to imagine a handkerchief, first spread out and ironed, then crumpled and placed in a pocket. Once crumpled, folded, even torn, points previously spaced out may become proximate (Serres 2016: 60). While this conversation pertains to *time* as the topological thing (which Serres points out can get confused with the classical measurement of time, which is geometric, metrical and linear), in *The Five Senses* Serres turns his attention to the skin. In his elaboration of the concept of the sense of variation and through the description of the tapestry, Serres distinguishes between discrete and continuous variety, and then demonstrates how this distinction can be blurred. Discrete, as the colours and taxonomies of flora and fauna; continuous, as the pinkish hue of the woman's skin from the roses or the unicorn with a goat's beard. These are, in Serres's words, variations on the idea of variety, and the object most appropriate to illustrate this is the skin, which is both discrete *and* continuous. 'Our skin could be called variety, in a precise topological sense: a thin sheet with folds and plains, dotted with events and singularities and sensitive to proximities . . . The skin varies, discrete, continuous inexpertly sewn, horned. It varies: woven, historiated, tattooed and legendary' (Serres 2016: 60–1). If we think of the skin in this way, as *variety* as Serres does, perhaps we should think it both synchronically and diachronically: from synvariance to skinvariance.

Deforming Dimensions

> Topology is the geometry of distortion . . . Topology seems a queer subject; it delves into strange implausible shapes and its propositions are either childishly obvious (that is, until you try to prove them) or so difficult and abstract that not even a topologist can explain their intuitive meaning. But topology is no queerer than the physical world as we now interpret it.
> (James R. Newman, *The World of Mathematics*, Vol. 1 (1956), p. 70, quoted in Fletcher 2016: 14)

Within conventional geometry there are five Platonic solids which Euclid then wrote about in the *Elements*: tetrahedron, cube, octahedron, dodecahedron and icosahedron. Platonic solids are regular, convex polyhedrons constructed by faces which are polygons identical in shape, size and angle. Topologically, the dodecahedron (which has twelve faces and vertices) can be described as an approximation of the sphere and vice versa. The sphere is a *continuous* approximation of the dodecahdreon whereas the dodecahedron is a *discrete* approximation of the sphere. They are not the same geometrically, but topology is not about measurement. They are, however, homeomorphic. Logically this may not make sense, but intuitively it does.

Topology was born in 1735 in Königsberg, Prussia. Mathematician Leonhard Euler tried to find a way to walk through the city by crossing each of its bridges once and only once. He proved that it was not possible to do this by using topology. It was a rejection of geographical exteriority. In 1750 Euler developed a famous formula for a polyhedron:

$$v - e + f = 2$$

where v is the number of vertices of the polyhedron, e is the number of edges and f is the number of faces. This was revolutionary because it permits us to think of geometry without measurement.

Then in 1813 Antoine-Jean L'Huillier published a formula which developed Euler's. He noticed that Euler's formula was wrong for solids which had holes in them. If g is the number of holes a sold has, Lhuilier showed thus:

$$v - e + f = 2 - 2g$$

This formula was the first topological invariant.

Deformation is the spatiotemporal process to which topological shapes are subjected, and during which they their properties remain an invariant. Conventionally this deformation can take place in three ways while the properties of the shape remain identical: these are stretching, folding and bending. The most famous example is the torus (the doughnut) which can become a coffee cup if the skin of the torus is deformed. These two shapes are not the same geometrically, but they are homeomorphic: they share the same form, the same properties. Topological shapes retain their properties under continuous deformation. Even a topological shape can have a dimension added. In 1865 August Möbius published a description of the Möbius band. He described this as a non-orientable shape because it could not be filled with compatibly oriented triangles. A Klein bottle (first described by Felix Klein in 1882) is another non-orientable surface, meaning that one could traverse its surface all over and return to the point of origin having been flipped upside down.

In the Cartesian division of body and mind or soul, it would appear that the human body contains three-dimensional properties: size, weight, shape, colour and motion through space and time. Mental, emotional or spiritual properties would exist outside of this sphere: consciousness, intentionality. In the now widespread critique of Cartesian dualism which has especially proliferated since Immanuel Kant's reconfiguration of metaphysics, these very different systems are superimposed upon, within, through one another. Is it possible, then, to consider the self as topological? In terms of multiple systems working upon systems and the reliance of different kinds of perception and figuration, perhaps it does make sense to speak of a topological self beyond that of Lacanian discourse. Lacan's perception of the topological subject is a development of Freud's conception of the topographical psyche. According to Lacan, human subjectivity has the structure of a topological space. Extimacy (*extimité*): exteriority plus intimacy or what Lacan calls 'intimate exteriority' (Lacan 1997: 139). Strangely resonant with Karen Barad's description of exteriority within phenomena, this term for Lacan contains the inside and the outside; it is both exteriority within and interiority without. As with the example of 'boycunt' in Chapter 1, this term contains both oppositional terms within itself. The torus shape expresses this because its insides are its outsides. Similarly, the Möbius strip is simultaneously both inside and outside; there is no separation.

The link between psychoanalysis and topology is made explicit in Lacan's seminars, but is implicit in other thinkers such as R. D. Laing. In Laing's poem below from his collection *Knots* (1970), the geometrically impossible possibility of simultaneous devouring or consuming between two lovers is presented in terms of predation and prey, of desire as the desire to imbibe, and its opposite: the fear of being imbibed.

> She is devoured, by him being devoured
> by
>   her devouring desire to be devoured
> He is devoured by her being devoured
>   by him not devouring her
> He is being devoured
>   by his dread of being devoured

> She is being devoured
> > by her desire to be devoured
> His dread of being devoured
> arises from his dread of being devoured by
> his devouring
> Her desire to be devoured
> arises from her dread of her desire to
> devour
> > > > (Laing 1970: 18)

It would appear that the ultimate goal of the two lovers described in Laing's poem would indeed be a simultaneous devouring. Each lover would consume the other. The fact that optically we cannot perceive this and visually we might struggle to draw it doesn't mean we must reject it as a possibility. Topological objects rely on a general understanding that their rendering in 3D space will *always* be radically insufficient. It has been understood for a good number of decades that language contains more possibilities than drawing 3D images on a 2D piece of paper, though computer mappings offer more options with the addition of time giving the illusion that what we are seeing in a pixelated topological model on our screen is in fact a shape under continuous deformation.

More recently, the following line from Sofia Samatar's prose poem 'The Noble Torturer' also articulates topological stretchings, bendings and contortions:

> The Noble Torturer provides his own sunset. He rides into himself. (Samatar 2016)

This particular auto-helio-centricity is reminiscent of Kate Tempest's rewriting, refolding and refleshing of the 'Godcub' Tiresias in her poem 'The Boy Tiresias': Sun of himself. All things are his moons' (Tempest 2014: 41). There is an interesting synecdochic (or perhaps mereotopological, again) movement here, again reminiscent of the seventeenth-century character Lingua holding her tongue *as tongue*. To be the sun *of yourself* requires deformation beyond Euclidean geometry: the tautological self-centric self, which perhaps provides a useful physical demonstration of why topology has been conceived as a multifariously useful model for psychical spaces.

Going back to Samatar, her character is an amalgam of patriarchal brutality and its structures of protection. The violence evoked in the poem is calculated and nuanced.

> The Noble Torturer is working on an elevated level of manpain. It's far more sophisticated than, for example, Russell Crowe's character in that Gladiator movie.

In the description of the Noble Torturer doling out pain to the non-specified 'you' addressed in the poem, the concurrent and opposing movements of objectification and subjectification, mattering and meaning, are produced through the cutting of corporeal surfaces.

> When he cuts you, you only exist in the cut. You are all surface, all exterior, while his interior develops. He goes on the journey of pain with you, but as your pain makes you more emphatically a body, his pain gives him something resembling a soul. His personhood advances in direct proportion to your thingness. (Samatar 2016)

Corporeality is everything here: the violation of another person's corporeal surface causes this person to feel as though they are *all surface*. This is more extreme, more brutal than a process of objectification; it is a violent existential flattening, while the building up of the torturer's soul evokes a kind of simulacrum of the soul. The pain is felt, harnessed and channelled into the job at hand in this chilling depiction in which the torturer figure operates as a persona for any number of actual torturers operating in the world as we speak, and Samatar's piece constitutes a courageous attempt to both familiarise and defamiliarise our perception of this activity.

Aside from psychoanalysis and psychiatry, topological figurings have been employed for cultural theory (Lury et al. 2012), phenomenological literary analysis (Fletcher 2006) and science writing (Margulis and Sagan 2007). In their essay 'The Uncut Self' Lynn Margulis and Dorian Sagan talk of a self that is topological.

> This is not the classical Cartesian model of the self, with a vital ensouled *res cogitans* surrounded by that predictable world of Newtonian mechanisms of *res extensa*; it is closer to Maturana and Varela's conception of autopoiesis, a completely self-making, self-referring, tautologically delimited entity at the various levels of cell, organism, and cognition. (Margulis and Sagan 2007: 16)

The essay enacts its own autopoiesis, beginning *in medias res* with the second part of a sentence which begins at the end creating a cycle: 'full circle, not based on the rectilinear frame of reference of a painting, mirror, house, or book, and with neither "inside" nor "outside" but according to the single surface of a Möbius strip'. The last words of the essay complete the sentence: 'Topologically the self has no homuncular inner self but comes' (Margulis and Sagan 2007: 16, 25). The reader is then forced to conform to linearity of the essay form. It becomes an eternally self-devouring object.

Deforming Perception

In order to develop a multisensory perception of how language matters it is necessary to go beyond the two well-documented phenomena of the *sound* and *shape* of language. This requires an understanding of language that is both synaesthetic and, as I will argue, topological. If we are now convinced of the legitimacy of topological models for thinking about sensory systems, what then is required to think this? A sensory system would retain its properties regardless of deformation, but what would sensory deformation look, sound, smell, taste or feel like? One answer to this could be synaesthetic entanglements as the 'deformation' or defamiliarisation of sensory segmentation. In terms of the history of philosophy, even the five senses separated and segmented are looked upon with suspicion in favour of idealised internal perception, clear and distinct. Plato distrusted external vision in favour of the mind's eye. According to later doxographers Democritus was apparently so impressed by Plato's reasoning here that he blinded himself in order to 'see' better. The link between ocularcentrism and Enlightenment reasoning is clear even from the vision-based word 'enlightenment' itself.

So why has ocularcentrism prevailed? The distance required to focus and perceive visually arguably provides the basis of the subject-object dualism typical of western metaphysics. The result of this is that

> the eye is the hinge point between the subjective and the objective, the window to the world and the mirror of the soul. In this spectatorial epistemology, the ocular subject has become the ultimate source of all being, with 'the world' being seen, reflected in, represented by, objectified, and instrumentalized by the sovereign subjective self. (Kavanagh 2004: 449)

As well as a distancing function, the eye also distinguishes and separates, as Juhani Pallasmaa notes: 'The gradually growing hegemony of the eye seems to be parallel with the development of Western ego-consciousness and the gradually increasing separation of the self and the world; vision separates us from the world whereas the other senses unite us with it' (Pallasmaa 2012: 28). Renaissance metaphysical poetry would have it rather differently; the eyes of the lovers in Donne's poem 'The Exstasie' become like vines or tendrils which almost horrifically leap out of their sockets and twist around one another. 'Our eye-beames twisted, and did thred / Our eyes, upon one double string' (Donne 1994: 34). This both materialises and animates vision; vision is complexified.

Vision complexified: let's complexify it further. It is Haraway's famous 1988 article 'Situated Knowledge: The Science Question in Feminism and the Privilege of Partial Perspective' in which vision is discussed from a feminist new materialist perspective. The article discesses the problems of scientific objectivity in terms of the popular constructionist perspectives that had spread through the social sciences at the time of the article's writing in the late 1980s. In Haraway's words, even the narratives of objective science are reduced to narrative and rhetoric in the social constructionist perspective: 'History is a story Western culture buffs tell each other; science is a contestable text and a power field; the content is the form. Period.' (Haraway 1988: 577). Rather than discussing the primacy of vision as a problem, Haraway argues in this article for a particular type of vision which she calls partial perspective: 'particular and specific embodiment' rather than a false transcendence of vision. Partial perspective offers the potential for the rejection of the splitting of subjectivity and objectivity. It is the perspective from which we are attempting to see that Haraway believes requires attention: 'an optics is a politics of positioning' (Haraway 1988: 586).

The perception of a topological shape also arguably requires a more complex sensory mechanism than external vision. In his article on topology and culture Julian Henriques points out that a number of the great topologists were blind, thus displacing the ocularcentrism of the Western world.

> For philosophy, traditionally vision has been privileged as the most 'noble' of the senses – on the basis of the distance it gives from corporeal contamination, unlike touch for instance. But with topology the mind's eye loses its grip, it could be said, yielding to the possibility of auditory, gestural, kinetic and other forms of conceptualization ... The mathematical imagination leaps further than the places anyone can visualise. (Henriques 2012: 335)

Once the mind's eye loses its grip thus, further interdependent perceptual systems are possible, as we learn from non-human animals such as cephalopods, for whom perception is a complex matter. Didier Anzieu suggests in *The Skin Ego* that 'Thought may be as much an affair of the skin as of the brain' (Anzieu 1989: 9), and we can learn more about this from non-human animals such as cephalopods who absolutely do think with their skin.

If our eyes can be tentacles then can our tentacles be eyes? On octopus diffracts the haptic and the topic through its very being – through its tentacularity, as Haraway would call it (Haraway 2016). Peter Godfrey-Smith argues that the birth of social behaviour can be sourced in the phenomenon of *quorum sensing*, which happens at a bacterial level. This is the name for the process wherein a bacterium both produces and senses a chemical. In terms of natural history, this can be traced back to the Cambrian period and marks the beginning of the entanglement of one animal's life in another because it meant that the animal's mind evolved in response to other minds. In Godfrey-Smith's account of cephapolodic consciousness derived from biologist Detlev Arendt, two nervous systems – one on the surface and one on the inside – met in a jellyfishlike animal in the Cambrian period. He calls this the bilaterian body plan. The animal we know today as the octopus, however, according to Godfrey-Smith, has an entirely different sense of embodied sensory existence, living 'outside the usual brain/body divide (Godfrey-Smith 2016: 76). Not only this, but if an octopus or a cuttlefish senses or decides something, its colour changes in an instant. These animals display their mood and attitude towards other beings through the colour of their skin. The skin of an octopus contains specialised cells called chromatophores, which make colours more or less visible to the brain inside. The skin of an octopus also contains opsins, which are pigmented light-sensitive proteins in the eyes. Interestingly, as Godfrey-Smith observes, octopuses also go through elaborate displays of colour change when seemingly unobserved. So as well as this display of 'ongoing chromatic chatter', octopuses also see with their skin (Godfrey-Smith 2016: 128).

As well as cephalopods, we can also apprehend spiders as sensory virtuosi. Eva Hayward presents a comparative and compelling account of the optic/haptic world of the spider:

> These silken lines reference the skeletization of surface, the web is an extension of the surface affects of the spider; *it feels with its web*. Likewise, the human body is stretched topographically, places and bodies are put into process, or rather they emerge through a spatial, temporal, corporeal generativity. I am not suggesting that bodies are ruptured or burst open such that they are boundless, but instead, bodies and cities are inter- and intra-threadings, like so many sensuous vectors that run outward from the spider in the middle of its web. (Hayward 2010: 231)

The link between the spider and the city is that it creates its own environment, its own city, through its own sensory organs. 'The web emerges through the spider's sensuous milieu; it builds with the world through the aperture of its sensorium' (Hayward 2010: 232). Hayward here is discussing trans*-becoming in terms of environmental and intra-sensory entanglements; she weaves spiders, streets and transsexuals together. Hayward points out that some of the effects of the non-human hormonal drug Premarin affects one's proprioceptive sense just as much as one's external presentation: 'vision is distorted, one is disoriented by racking focus; haptic senses, to touch, are reworked making handled things feel like never before; sense of taste is refracted through hormonally changed buds; smells redefine space' (Hayward 2010: 229). There is the sense of an overspilling and consequent blurring between subject and environment in all these senses. Hayward links this blurring with Susan Stryker's account of transsexual BDSM practices which, in her words, enact a *poiesis* which collapses the boundary between 'the embodied self, its world and others' (Stryker 2008: 39). Stryker narrates a flogging scene at a San Francisco sex party and turns to Bergson's *Matter and Memory* wherein the stimulus/response system does not register the internal/external corporeal boundary but rather 'a continuous movement in which a force's vector is prolonged and deflected into the movements of living matter; it is a wave transmitting itself through various media' (Stryker 2008:41). The continuous movement is what is felt through and between and within both the spider and the web, 'an *optic skin*, a connective tissue, building a home that senses in order that the spider might feed, entrap, and make more of herself' (Hayward 2010: 243; my italicisation). The transposition from one sense to another – from optics to haptics, for example – is precisely what Hayward adumbrates with 'fingeryeyes', derived from observing cup corals at the Long Marine Laboratory. 'Crossing the animating impact of nerve organs, fingeryeyes diffract seeing through touching; optical grasping, or tactful eyes, haptically and visually orient the sensual body across mediums (Hayward 2010a: 581–2). The fingeryeyes splice haptic and optic perception; Hayward here learns from coralline sense. The cross-species mutation described in terms of the engagement between Hayward's fingeryeyes and the corals is itself a kind of synaesthesia, in terms of multiple sensory becomings.

INTERSTITIUM 1: The Surface, or Alice and the Hermunculus

We are the bearers of skewed, not quite flat, unreplicated surfaces, deserts over which consciousness passes fleetingly, leaving no memory.

(Serres 2016: 22)

The skin is nothing less than the shape of shape.

(Connor 2004: 36)

Alice progressively conquers surfaces. She rises or returns to the surface. She creates surfaces.

(Deleuze 1998: 21)

The quotation above is from Deleuze's very short essay on Lewis Carroll in *Essays Critical and Clinical*: Deleuze presents Alice as adolescent 'becoming' subject, climbing to the surface of sense and operating from this surface position armoured by the logics of Wittgensteinian language games, Victorian etiquette and Euclidean geometry, adapting quickly each time these logics are challenged but just about retaining her sense of propriety throughout. In his extended treatment of Carroll, *The Logic of Sense*, however, Deleuze creates Alice herself as a conceptual persona for his own surface of language or sense. Using Alice as a fictional persona who both embodies and expresses the paradoxical elements powering the system outlined in *The Logic of Sense*, Deleuze develops the links between language and corporeality already abounding in both *Alice's Adventures in Wonderland* and *Through the Looking-Glass, and What Alice Found There* (1865, 1871). This Interstitium allows the surface, as persona itself, to speak back.

The opposition between bodies and language, between 'word' and 'thing', is something Deleuze plays in between throughout *The Logic of Sense*. The surface inheres between oppositions and therefore problematises them. The tension between literality and figurality in language is very much highlighted in Carroll tales, but the use of Carroll to embody the development of poststructuralist linguistic theory from pre-Socratic to contemporary times is Deleuze's creation. While acknowledging Carroll's position as Victorian recreational mathematician, Deleuze alternatively presents Carroll interpenetrating with the Stoics as a hinge on which proto- and post-structuralism pivot, forcing the distinction drawn by Saussure between synchronic and diachronic linguistics into an interpenetrating n-dimensional spatiotemporality. 'Structuralism, whether consciously or not, celebrates new findings of a Stoic and Carrollian inspiration' (Deleuze 2004b: 83). Deleuze presents Carroll as a proto-poststructuralist and then uses Alice as a moveable lever who operates between both sides. She is, in fact, 'the frontier, the cutting edge, or the articulation of difference' (Deleuze 2004b: 35). This is Deleuze's description of sense, but in her movements and utterances throughout Wonderland Alice operates as a figure who embodies this frontier or articulation. A frontier or a surface presupposes two opposite facing sides. As Deleuze also explains, sense is the articulation of difference between bodies and propositions, between word and thing (see Palmer 2014). As Deleuze says in his essay on Carroll and drawing on Stoicism, 'Pure events escape from states of affairs' (Deleuze 1998: 21). The Stoics distinguish between pure events and their spatiotemporal actualisation in states of affairs. The distinction is therefore a binary opposition between corporeal and incorporeal. On one hand is the corporeal realm of bodies and states of affairs, and on the other is the incorporeal realm of time, place and sense. Events are the entities that complexify the opposition, as does language itself. They are not, however, identical to one another. Events are incorporeal transformations but they have corporeal effects. The articulation of difference is precisely this surface requiring both sides. As Deleuze points out here, the tension within language between these supposed oppositions is precisely what underpins structuralism and is apprehended by Carroll through the ludic.

Deleuze begins *The Logic of Sense* with Alice. 'It pertains to the essence of becoming to move and to pull in both directions at once: Alice does not grow without shrinking, and vice versa' (Deleuze 2004b: 3). Alice is the figure who embodies the pure event of sense, growing and shrinking at the same time. This 'becoming' eludes the present because 'it does not tolerate the separation or the distinction of before and after, or of past and future' (Deleuze 2004: 3). This is later described as the Aion or 'pure and empty form of time' (Deleuze 2004b: 108) outlined in both *Difference and Repetition* (2004a) and 'On Four Poetic Formulas that Might Summarize the Kantian Philosophy' in *Essays Critical and Clinical*. Because *The Logic of Sense* is predominantly about language, however, the pure and empty form of time becomes the pure infinitive verb. 'As it expresses all language events in one, the infinitive verb expresses the event of language – language being a unique event which merges now with that which renders it possible' (Deleuze 2004: 212). Alice-as-surface encapsulates the paradoxical coincidence of the literal and the figurative modes of language, expressed in the Stoic *lekton* (language as both word and thing) as well as the coincidence of *langue* and *parole* expressed within the infinitive verb. Deleuze's use of the infinitive verb, and its linking to both corporeality and psychoanalysis, draws on Irigaray's text 'On Phantasm and the Verb' in *To Speak Is Never Neutral*. One of the verbs Irigaray uses as an example is *to absorb*. The power relations inherent in this grammatical process are immediately apparent. 'To absorb implies that something in the world, exterior to the subject, is brought into its sphere, or its space. What was exterior and foreign becomes interior and part of the subject, assimilated by the subject' (Irigaray 2002: 56). The particularities of this verb in corporeal and alimentary terms are discussed further below, but for the purposes of discussions around becoming and Alice's growing/shrinking simultaneity, it is important to acknowledge Deleuze's argument that the infinitive form of the verb is the only form to uphold every potential materialisation at the same time, demonstrating the power of formal linguistic structures to affirm multiplicity and unity at the same time – or, as Deleuze and Guattari later put it, 'PLURALISM = MONISM' (Deleuze and Guattari 2004b: 23).

Striking the surface

It is interesting that Deleuze chooses Alice at this particular stage in his career, when his relationship to psychoanalysis was more complex than an outright rejection, and when in fact a good deal of *The Logic of Sense* is devoted to some interesting readings of Melanie Klein. Klein's world is particularly resonant for Carroll's Wonderland; in her work, infantile, latent and adolescent stages of childhood are all contingent upon this surface which not only permits both phantasy and reality, but actively blends the two. In Klein's violent world of object relations, children not only have sexual desires from infancy; they also have anxieties, neuroses and guilt (Klein 1997). Klein advocates the use of play-analysis to work through early infantile anxieties. The outcome of play analysis illustrates the Kleinian infant entering a chaotic world of part objects. The breast is such an object. The breast is the prototypical part object. It is both good and bad. The Kleinian world is one of aggression and violence from birth, and as Deleuze is well aware, very much like the violent and literalist Wonderland. Klein perceives infants to operate in the same way as adults suffering from psychoses. In Kleinian psychoanalysis, *all* aspects of mental life are tied to object relations. Noreen O'Connor asks what Klein's theories would have been like if she had *not* assumed a split between the inner and the outer worlds? She also importantly points out that the reduction of all human expression to a finite number of symbolic objects renders Klein's theory of language as one that separates out language and thought, or one in which meaning exists outside linguistic practices. According to O'Connor, this means that Klein's theory is in line with essentialist, universalist, foundational theories (see Ellis and O'Connor 2010).

According to Elizabeth Wilson, Klein perceives the child as 'war-torn and tyrannical' (Wilson 2015: 50), whereas D. W. Winnicott perceives the child in a more positive light and promotes the theory of the transitional object as the initial possession of the child that is 'not-me' (Winnicott 2005: 6). Deleuze continues along tyrannical lines, placing Klein along with Artaud in the thinking of depths, rather than Carroll, whom he aligns with the surface. The Kleinian nursing infant is, for Deleuze, 'stage, actor and drama at once' of what he describes as the Kleinian 'theatre of terror' (Deleuze 2004b: 215). The way in which Deleuze describes the Kleinian process of the splitting of the breast and body of the mother into partial objects is mirrored almost exactly with his description of Louis Wolfson's treatment of the 'mother tongue'. Wolfson felt the need to translate instantaneously from the mother tongue in order to protect himself from what he felt were physically damaging particles of language. The parallels with Kleinian partial objects are clear, and it is the materiality of the language that is being foregrounded here: the danger of the linguistic surface to cause physical harm. The threat of violence from word-objects is comparable to the Kleinian and the Carollian models on account of their literality. Wolfson's particular type of creative translation is not a straightforward one; he splits apart the offending word and locates a similar sounding word for each of its components in one of the four main languages he knows. Literality is of fundamental importance here, but the real crunch and bite occurs with the realisation that literality is multifarious too. 'You're nothing but a pack of cards!' Alice screams, negating in order to foreground the good literality, in order to separate phantasy from reality, although we know that just as in infancy, childhood and adolescence, our reliance on the permeability of this separation is as vital as oxygen for breathing.

Gendering the surface

> As a receptive surface, the body's boundaries and zones are constituted in conjunctions and through linkages with other surfaces and planes: the lips connected with the breast in orality, possibly accompanied by the hand in conjunction with an ear, each system in perpetual motion and interrelation with the other ... Libidinal intensifications of bodily parts are *surface effects*, interactions occurring on the surface of the skin and various organs. These effects, however, are not simply superficial, for they generate an interior, an underlying depth, individuality, or consciousness. This *depth* is one of the distinguishing features marking out the modern, Western capitalist body from other kinds. (Grosz 1995: 34)

The gendered nature of the challenge to Cartesian reason has been well mapped out by Elizabeth Grosz and described as 'the crisis of reason's *inability to know itself,* to enclose and know itself from the outside: the inadequation of the subject and knowledge' (Grosz 1995: 26). While *Alice in Wonderland* is classified as a book for children, the challenges faced by Alice in terms of extreme growing and shrinking, experimentation with substances, encountering unknown patterns of discourse and behaviour, environmental abnormalities and subversion of expectations, the fear of being rejected by peers and an overall suffusion of existential doubt are all themes common to adolescent life and literature as well as to philosophy. Alice's embodiment and animation of certain philosophical realms has been extremely well documented for many decades (see Gardner 1999 for the originary commentary on *Alice*, Lecercle 1994 for a helpful focus on nonsense and Davis 2010 for a more populist approach).

As well as a proto-structuralist, Carroll could equally be described as a proto-surrealist (see McAra 2011). The most obvious linking point, as Robert Belton outlines, is the perception of Alice as the traditional *femme-enfant*, or child-woman. This figure is conventionally 'a manipulable, fairylike muse, enchanting in her innocence, youth and purity' (Belton 1993: 65). This description is obviously worthy of a feminist rewriting from a fictive public of a thousand non-innocent Alice-personae, but in addition to this we can also go further in using Deleuze's embodiment of Alice in order to discern a newer, more grotesque, more adolescent Alice whose problematisation of spatiotemporal dimensions is more directly linked to power. While the hyphen conjoining *femme* and *enfant* arguably operates as a spatiotemporal shift resulting in a dynamic transition between two states, Deleuze's initial presentation of Alice as embodying 'the simultaneity of a becoming whose characteristic is to elude the present' (Deleuze 2004: 3) is a more radical challenge to any notion of staticity whatsoever.

Permeating the surface

The anthropomorphisation of food and its reverse, the rendering-edible of words, is a device found everywhere in the *Alice* books and I have discussed this elsewhere (Palmer 2014: 154). In his well-documented criticism of Carroll, Artaud describes Carroll's poem 'Jabberwocky' as 'the work of a man who ate well' (Artaud 1940: 448). This does not appear to have been the case according to Carroll's biographers.

> He himself ate very little: one meal a day, only. He was ram-rod straight to the end of his life, thin as a rail, and thought little of taking twenty-five mile walks . . . For a man who was so austere in his tastes, food held his interest and dominates the imagery of his jokes from his juvenilia onwards. (Warner 2003)

Virginia Woolf writes brilliantly about Carroll's own supposedly childlike state, characterising it very perceptively and empathetically in alimentary terms – or if not strictly alimentary, then very much in terms of a process of digestion or indigestion. If Carroll's supposedly trouble-free existence (according to him) was an 'untinted jelly', then contained within this jelly was a 'perfectly hard crystal'. This crystal, according to Woolf, is childhood.

> For some reason, we know not what, his childhood was sharply severed. It lodged in him whole and entire. He could not disperse it. And therefore as he grew older this impediment in the centre of his being, this hard block of pure childhood, starved the man of nourishment. (Woolf 1929, in Philips 1971: 48)

The crystal is a material impossible to absorb, and material absorption is evaded by remaining at the surface. Deleuze's comments on Alice's alimentary obsessions precisely articulate the fears thrown up by the depths of materiality. 'The ideal little girl, incorporeal and anorexic, and the ideal little boy, stuttering and left-handed, must disengage themselves from their real, voracious, gluttonous, or blundering images' (Deleuze 2004: 30). One of the points being made here is that the ingestion or absorption of food into the body is perceived by the anorexic as a threat to the body's ideality. The body as nothing *but* surface could maintain a semblance of immateriality, which is perhaps the desire of the anorexic that he refers to here. Deleuze suggests that Alice is 'overwhelmed by nightmares of absorbing and being absorbed' (Deleuze 2004: 29), because whichever way round the process happens, absorption requires depth and capacity.

Splitting the surface

Bivalency appears to structure the surfaces of both Platonic verticality and Stoic horiztonality. In Plato's *Symposium* Aristophanes gives the mythological account of the *androgunon*, which Stella Sandford discusses in *Plato and Sex* (2010). This was the third type of human being which contained both male and female genitalia. The male was born from the sun, the female from the moon and the third type that shared both male and female was born from the moon. These types of human had four legs, four arms and one head but with two faces, and two sets of genitals. As a punishment for making an attempt on the gods, says Aristophanes, Zeus cut each human in two, thus creating the account of desire that we can see in psychoanalysis: desire is lack (see Sandford 2010: 43).

In comparison to Platonic metaphysics, the Stoics were staunch materialists. Platonic Ideas are utterly rejected by the Stoics (see Sellars 2006). In Stoic ontology, both corporeals and incorporeals are real, but only corporeals exist. The only thing that exists for Stoics are bodies; there is no immaterial existence, in contrast to Platonic metaphysics. We also know that theirs is a flat ontology, also in opposition to Platonic metaphysics. As with Spinoza (and later Deleuze), only bodies can act and be acted upon. Incorporeals are not transcendental ideals but are what is beyond the body: they do not exist, but subsist.

In his discussion of Deleuze and the Stoics, Ryan Johnson compares two events: the death of the Stoic Seneca and the death of Gilles Deleuze. This dual death frames Johnson's discussion of the twofold nature of the event in Stoic philosophy and the paradoxical Stoic theory of incorporeals, which Deleuze reads in *The Logic of Sense*. So it is as though Stoic events are Janus-faced, or perhaps, as Johnson suggests, it can be encapsulated in a double-headed statue to be found in third-century Rome: one side with the face of Socrates; the other with the face of Seneca. 'Although they share one brain, they engage the world in opposite directions.' What exists between Socrates and Seneca? A shared brain, a 'crack without thickness' (Johnston 2017: 271). What figure does Johnon employ to enable us to think about the complexity of the Stoic surface? None other than the Möbius strip, which Johnson believes is useful for many Stoic inventions.

The Stoic flat surface contains some interesting qualities which Deleuze scrutinises and opens up throughout *The Logic of Sense*. The Deleuzian-Stoic surface is also a frontier. It is all edge. In Stoic thought, bodies are causes in relation to one another. Their effects are not bodies but events. So the meaning of these effects is in excess of the bodies themselves. These events, according to the Stoics, are excessive. They relate to the bodies that cause them but also to one another. This is a kind of quasi-causality. So events have a double relation: both from/to the bodies that produce them but also the relation to/from their effects/events.

The Stoic event would be therefore conceived as bivalent; in the manner of an edge. It is the dividing nature of this edge that leads to Deleuze's thinking of time as two opposing and yet simultaneous accounts of time: as Aion and Chronos. The verb 'to cleave' or noun 'cleavage' – which is used by Deleuze in *The Logic of Sense*, and then by Deleuze and Guattari in *Anti-Oedipus* and *A Thousand Plateaus* – has interested thinkers at various points due to the enigmatic appeal of its opposing and intertwining definitions – to simultaneously split asunder and to join together. This word constitutes a critique of bivalency which in Deleuze's *The Logic of Sense* is articulated in terms of Stoic causality.[6]

---

[6] See Palmer (2014) for an account of Aion and Chronos in relation to linguistic spatiotemporality, in particular for a reading of the line of Aion as operating analogously to the frontier-line of the avant-garde.

The Stoics were quite queer in terms of their theories about mixtures and bodies. The Stoics believed that bodies were mixed with one another without losing their essential essence, and give the famous example of a drop of wine in the ocean. This is from the writings of the Stoic Chrysippus, who says that a drop of wine pervades the whole ocean. This is their theory of total blending as opposed to particulate or fusion mixture (for example, different kinds of seeds would be a particulate mixture while bread would be a fusion mixture). Active and passive substances can occupy the space – they can be mutually co-extensive. So the soul, which is a body, and an active substance, called the pneuma, can pervade the body, which is passive matter. But size doesn't matter here, which is why the drop of wine is mutually co-extensive with the entire ocean. The rejection of what we see as conventional spatiality – you can see why Deleuze liked this and why he places the Stoics alongside Lewis Carroll in a forest of trees which are in an eternal state of greening. I have discussed these aspects of Deleuze's thought elsewhere (Palmer 2014); for now the focus is on cleavage as a splitting and simultaneous joining of spatiotemporality. Deleuze says at this point that in the Stoic thinking, time must be grasped twice: firstly in the corporeal sense of one body acting upon another, and secondly the incorporeal eternal attribute of being. All bodies are causes in Stoic thought, and they oppose bodies-causes to effects.

The skin is the interface, the bivalent edge. Among many functions it operates as the frontier touching both the interior and exterior of our bodies. Grosz highlights the importance of the skin in this function of 'double sensation', such as when the subject touches one part of itself with another.

> This is the twisting of the Möbius strip, the torsion or pivot around which the subject is generated. The double sensation creates a kind of *interface* of the inside and the outside, the pivotal point at which inside will become separated from outside and active will be converted into passive (a line of border which is not unlike the boundary established by the duplicating structure of the mirror, which similarly hangs on the pivotal plane represented by the tain of the mirror). (Grosz 1994: 35–6)

If we consider the skin as the surface that covers the body, the shedding and subsequent ingestion of this corporeal surface is symbolic in multiple ways. There is an interesting moment in Carrington's surrealist story 'The Debutante' (1939) [2017] when the protagonist, who is a hyena disguised as a human debutante and covered in the skin of the actual debutante's murdered maid, tears off its human-skin surface covering and eats it. This moment is interesting for a number of reasons. The literalised shedding of the 'mask' of feminine humanity and the beast underneath is starkly obvious, and Natalya Lusty has aligned Carrington's story with Joan Rivière's famous 1929 essay 'Womanliness as Masquerade' (Lusty 2007). In addition to this literalised symbolic shedding, the action of consuming one's own outer surface presents the limit as becoming one overall orifice-object, or perhaps, in the terms of Deleuze and Guattari (following Artaud again, of course), a body without organs.

Stretching the surface

> The child accepted the strawberry suspiciously for it was, although not large, the size of her head. She sniffed it, turned it round and round, and then essayed just one little bite out of it, leaving behind a tiny ring of white within the crimson flesh. Her teeth were perfect.
> At the first bite, she grew a little.
> Kelly continued to mumble: 'There must be some rational explanation.'
> The child took a second, less tentative bite, and grew a little more. The mandrakes in their white nightgowns woke up and began to mutter among themselves.
> (Carter 2002: 133)

Angela Carter's Alice in her story 'Alice in Prague, or The Curious Room' is described as 'alchemical homunculus' by Anna Kérchy (Kérchy 2016: 5). The homunculus has been historically understood as a miniature version of a man, created artificially by alchemical means. The homunculus is linked to the Jewish figure of a golem due to the symbolically similar processes of artificially breathing life into a diminutive body. The golem myth originates in Prague, home to the original legend of the Golem of Prague, created by a Cabbalist Rabbi Löw. Carter's Alice is transported to sixteenth-century Prague, home to Emperor Rudolf II, who was sometimes described as the 'mad alchemist'. Alice consumes, grows, shrinks, puzzles over logical conundrums in typical Alice fashion. More singular to Carter's tale, however, is the grotesque Arcimboldo-inspired fruit woman Summer, referred to mainly as 'it', created for the pleasure of the Archduke.

> The size and prominence of the secondary sexual characteristics indicate that this creature is, like the child, of the feminine gender. She lives in the fruit bowl ... her hair is largely composed of green muscat grapes, her nose a pear, eyes filbert nuts, cheeks russet apples somewhat wrinkled – never mind! ... But now, what devastation! Hair mashed, nose squashed, bosom pureed, belly juiced.
> (Carter 2002: 136–7)

It is easy to interpret this grotesque automaton as the abject inversion of the innocent-looking Alice. There is something even more sinister and grotesque, however, about the damage inflicted on this entity through the almost comical yet disturbing penetration she endures from the Archduke. Another female body reduced to an inventory of anatomical fragments, but this time the fragments are consumable and perishable in a very literal sense. This being is a gendered conflation of the eating/speaking duality outlined in *The Logic of Sense*. The medical-sounding language used here of 'size and prominence of secondary sexual characteristics' brings to mind outdated masculinist descriptions of a particular type of homunculus: the cortical homunculus (see Penfield 1950 and Gorman 1969).

Spinoza is one of Deleuze's primary influences in the thinking of corporeal organisation and politics, Deleuze seeing in Spinoza the vital challenge to the Cartesian substance dualism in favour of substance monism. In his 1882 novel *Spinoza*, Berthold Auerbach imagines the young Spinoza using the figure of the golem to challenge the Cartesian mind–body split.

> Once upon a time a great Cabbalist lived in Prague, called the Rabbi Löw; he made a human figure of clay, and left a small aperture in the lesser brain in which he laid a parchment with the unutterable name of God written on it. The clod immediately arose and was a man . . . The great Rabbi Löw certainly never thought of Descartes, and yet his Golem had as much life as any man, if we are to accept the new view, that the union between soul and body is so slight, that at any moment it can be disjointed, and again reunited. (Auerbach 1882: 269–70)

Within twentieth-century neuroscience we have an attempt at a direct visual mapping of the ways that the brain feels the body's sensations. The amount of cerebral cortex devoted to any given body region is proportional to how richly innervated that region is, rather than the physical size of that part of the body. Areas of the body with greater or more complex sensory or motor connections are represented as larger in the homunculus, those with fewer or less complex connections are represented as smaller. The resulting image we get is of a distorted body, with disproportionately huge hands, lips, and face. In a development (and feminist criticism) of Freud, Grosz looks to neurological theories of the early twentieth century – particularly the figure of the cortical homunculus. Grosz criticises twentieth-century neurologists such as Gorman for their 'manifest sexism', stating that there is no mention of a female homunculus, nor is there any suggestion that the homunculus figure might differ for women (Grosz 1994: 35). In order to address this in the twenty-first-century, a group of neuroscientists published an article entitled 'The *Her*munculus: What Is Known about the Representation of the Female Body in the Brain?' (di Noto et al. 2012). This article provides the beginnings of a sexually differentiated 'hermunculus' that would take into account both the different body surfaces and internal organs, as well as 'the plasticity that may well occur during different reproductive life stages, including pregnancy, menopause and the ovarian cycle (di Noto et al. 2012: 2). They conclude that both an updated male homunculus and a new, explicitly female hermunculus would be extremely beneficial for neuroscientific iconography and therapeutic resources.

The cortical sensory hermunculus provides us with an alternative type of proportionality which exists and need not be perceived as secondary to physical extension in space, and need not be subsumed under the universal masculine default either.

It occurs to me that the treatment Carroll's Alice is subjected to in *The Logic of Sense* amounts to a presentation of her as a kind of hermunculus. The polysemy of *le sens* cements this. The creation of a conceptual persona is a type of metonymy, but it is also a process of alchemy. Fictional characters are like golems: little beings who reduplicate themselves as they are rewritten and given life. To return to the quotation from Deleuze that we began this Interstitium with: 'She creates surfaces. Movements of penetration and burying give way to light lateral movements of sliding; the animals of the depths become figures on cards without thickness' (Deleuze 1998: 21). Alice and her fictional spawn help us to see that the multifarious surface and the organisational body it houses is gendered, it is dynamic, it is permeable and it does indeed have thickness.

Deforming Touches: Queer Haptics

Haptic thinking develops considerably through Maurice Merleau-Ponty's *Phenomenology of Perception* (1945). Merleau-Ponty's famous example of one hand touching an external object while the other hand touches the first hand demonstrates, for him, that the body cannot be entirely constituted by touch just as it cannot be by vision.

> ... if I can, with my left hand, feel my right hand as it touches an object, the right hand as an object is not the right hand as it touches: the first is a system of bones, muscles and flesh brought down at a point of space, the second shoots through space like a rocket to reveal the external object in its place. (Merleau-Ponty 1945: 105)

James Gibson's book *The Senses Considered as Perceptual Systems* (1966) also constitutes an important attempt to enumbrate the human haptic perceptual system. Gibson points out that rather than a passive organ receiving stimulus, the haptic system engages in what he calls active perception. This demonstrates a two-way relationship between the perceiver and the stimulus; active perception for Gibson requires 'not only stimulation from the environment but also stimulation from the attentive actions and reactions of the observer' (Gibson 1966: 32). Both of the terms Gibson uses for the haptic sensory elements of the 'input system' are active: receptors, while sounding inert and passive, are still active but are *immobile*, whereas organs are active and mobile. Gibson notes the insufficiency of the five senses and also the lack of direct correspondence between one sense and one sensory nerve. 'An organ of sensitivity is a structure containing many energy receptors and many receptive units . . . The sensory nerves are anatomical expedients; there is not a specific nerve for each sense despite a popular idea to the contrary' (Gibson 1966: 41). We will return to organs later in the chapter. For now, let us consider how sensory perception as outlined by Gibson relates to verbal meaning. Gibson believes that they are related, for the simple fact that to touch and grasp something means to simultaneously grasp its meaning. Gibson sketches out a three-way relationship within perceptual meaning which mirrors Ogden and Richards's (1923) three-way relationship of verbal meaning (consisting of the referent, the symbol or word and the thought). Mapped onto this is Gibson's perceptual tripartite relationship of the environmental source, the stimulus invariant and what he calls the percept (Gibson 1966: 244).

While Gibson himself does not use the concept of topology itself when describing perceptual systems, he does nevertheless use the vocabulary of topology as a vital part of his system. The haptic system according to Gibson demonstrates an important relationship to deformation. All living tissue is sensitive to deformation, which in Gibson's system is defined as 'a change of shape' or 'non-rigid motion' which may include 'stretching, bending, pulling, rubbing, and the like' (Gibson 1966: 106). These deformations are of course the types of deformations which topological shapes endure and under which they retain their properties. More recent work in this field which builds on Gibson's thought is more explicit in its engagement with haptic perception as a dynamic system, using the concept of the *phase space*, which is a multidimensional space in which any given point corresponds to a state of the system under investigation (see Carello and Turvey 2017). This is itself a topological construct. Through phenomenological understandings of touch as double touch, topological figurings would be required to think this.

The symbolisms of intimacy and touch have been well documented within queer literary theory. Eve Sedgwick notes the agential and spatiotemporal complexity of touch and consequently its superiority: 'the sense of touch makes nonsense out of any dualistic understanding of agency and passivity; to touch is always already to reach out, to fondle, to heft, to tap, or to enfold' (Sedgwick 2003: 14). Touch is always multiple; it is also always both intimate *and* strange. As Carolyn Dinshaw says in her queering of Chaucer's Pardoner's tale, 'The dissonant hand renders what it touches unnatural, makes it strange' (Dinshaw 1995: 76). The dissonant hand, then, is estranging with its proximity. It is estranging or defamiliarising by its touch. As a researcher you can estrange through your proximity to a particular culture or discipline. To queer a concept is to estrange it from itself, to defamiliarise it, which is exactly what Sara Ahmed has done with phenomenology. For Ahmed, queer proximity involves an encounter when two bodies who are meant to exist along parallel lines intersect. The example she gives is one of two racial lines which are perceived as parallel; the example is drawn from Countee Cullen's poem 'Tableau' (1925), of two boys, one black, one white, walking arm in arm.

> This is not just about any body, but specifically a black body and a white body. Two boys. It is the proximity of these bodies that produces a queer effect . . . The contact is bodily, and it unsettles the line that divides spaces as worlds, thereby creating other kinds of connections where unexpected things can happen. (Ahmed 2006: 169)

Here the process of queering the dividing line is narrated; this in itself is a moment of queer defamiliarisation. Queer effects for Ahmed are produced through proximity between subjects or objects which are supposed to exist on parallel lines; '*as points that should not meet*' (Ahmed 2006: 169). For Ahmed, a phenomenology of race and sex 'shows us how bodies become racialized and sexualized in how they "extend" into space: differences are shaped in how we take up space, or how we orient ourselves toward objects and others' (Ahmed 2006: 99).

Serres charts the ascendency of the haptic using a surprising conceptual persona: Cinderella. The erroneous translation of the particular material of Cineralla's 'glass' slipper is utilised here to present the triumph of haptics over optics. In his discussion of *Cinderella* and the 'vair' slipper (*vair* as homonymous with *verre* in French and translated as 'glass' in Charles Perrault's version of the fairy tale), Serres opts to foreground the flexible, varied and tactile nature of the vair (fur) slipper. Rather than the rigid and transparent glass we have the vair slipper: flexible, perfectly-fitting, perhaps even sentient itself. 'Recognition works by touch, not sight, by the stereospecificity of what which fits perfectly . . . The skin precedes the gaze in the act of knowing, vair wins a victory over glass' (Serres 2016: 64). In addition to this, Serres points out, it is sight which distinguishes and separates whereas touch tends towards mixture. Interestingly Serres points out that Leibniz was contemporaneous with Perrault, and would have been introducing his notion of the variable into mathematics at this time in the seventeenth century. 'Variation requires one to think both the stable and the unstable simultaneously, not pure instability, which is strictly speaking incomprehensible, but the invariant in the variation' (Serres 2016: 66). Through complex optical-haptical threadings and tattooings Serres posits the idea of variation itself as sense: 'Let us consider the *sense of variation*' (Serres 2016: 60; my italics). To consider sense itself as variation is to permit of not only the need for a plurality of sensory categories, but also that the categorisation of categories is unfinished. How is it possible to conceive of the sense of variation? Multisensory entanglement is one potential answer, as is a speculative approach to the notion of taxonomy itself, as the second Interstitium within this chapter documents.

For Karen Barad, touching is the primary concern of physics. Barad narrates the difference between the account of touch in classical physics, which is actually about electromagnetic repulsion, and the quantum theory of touching, which she describes as 'radically queer' (Barad 2012: 209). Quantum field theory, as Barad summarises in 'On Touching', is all about particles, the void and the field. Paradaoxes and infinities abound in this account. The simplest particle, the point particle, is an electron which emits a photon and exchanges it *with itself*. It is the *with itself* that Barad zooms in on: due to this self-engagement, or self-consummation, 'the very notion of "itself", of identity, is radically queered' (Barad 2012: 212). Not only that, but quantum field theory brings along with it the potential for touch to touch itself. Every level of touch brings with it an infinite set of new intra-actions; new touches. 'Hence, *self-touching is an encounter with the infinite alterity of the self. Matter is an enfolding, an involution, it cannot help touching itself*' (Barad 2012: 5). But if matter can not only touch itself but absorb itself or devour itself – as Richard Feynman discusses in the example in quantum field theory of the alternative way that an electron can go from place to place wherein it suddenly emits a photon only to absorb its own photon. Feynman calls this 'immoral' (Feynman 1995: 116); Barad calls this polymorphous perversity. In her poetic materialist examination of the philosophy and physics of touch, Barad draws attention to the 'infinite alterity' of the self, 'so that touching the other is touching all others, including the "self," and touching the "self" entails touching the strangers within' (Barad 2012: 7). The 'strangers within' the self expressed here demonstrate the perception of the body as a complex manifold that arguably constitutes what Barad would call exteriority within phenomena.

Interestingly, Barad directly equates infinity with perversity in her summarisation of quantum field theory. She writes about two types of perversity: one to do with self-touching and one to do with nakedness. What she calls 'renormalisation' is the production of a finite or 'normal' electron – what she calls the electron in drag – which is derived from the subtraction of different sized infinities. 'Perversion eliminating perversion' (Barad 2015: 400). This leads her to conclude that *every finite being is always already threaded through with an infinite alterity diffracted through being and time*' and 'Electrons are always already untimely. It is not that electrons sometimes engage in such perverse explorations: these experiments in intra-active trans*material performativity are what an electron is' (Barad 2015: 401). In this appealing account, the only question which strikes me is: how perverted are these examples? If self-touching and nakedness are perverted then we are all perverted. Eternally, constantly, thoroughly, inherently and infinitely, by Barad's account we are all both radically queer *and* perverted. Down to our smallest iotas, we cannot *not* touch ourselves.

INTERSTITIUM 2: *Speculative Taxonomies*

- **SPECUFABULA** – fabulating, ficting, conventional taxonomical division
- **SPECUPHYLA** – transversality, intersectionality, superdiversity
- **SPECULUDA** – zoology, cryptozoology, dendrology, oenology
- **SPECQUANTA** – afrofuturism, quantum reality
- **SPECULEXIA** – neology, gyne-cology, crone-ology, word webs
- **SPECTAXA** – eyes, hormones, vowels, interstices, spectra, streaks, exoskeleta, ridges, whorls

Specufabula

The context for this discussion is a speculative taxonomy itself. Spawned from the same weird SF taxonomy – speculative fabulation, speculative feminism, science fiction, speculative fiction, science fact, science fantasy, string figures – promulgated by Haraway (2013) and others, a speculative taxonomy of taxonomies must reject disciplinary segregation and conceptual termina. It must think transversally and toposophically, with a series (or taxonomy) of: alogisms, neologisms, fictemes, matterphors and pataphors.[7] A speculative taxonomy is not just autopoeitic but is also transversal as well as homeorrhetic. It is neological. It is a rhizome adrift in a river.

'Taxonomists often confuse the invention of a name with the solution of a problem' (Gould 1981: 188). Perhaps the invention of a name does not purport to be the solution of a problem but the creation of one. This is a problem in the Deleuzian sense, beyond the dualism of questions and answers or truth and falsehood: 'the affirmation of a problematic register' (Wasser 2017: 50). The need for new taxonomies is clear: the world is messy and complex. As Elizabeth Grosz says:

> A new humanities becomes possible once the human is placed in its properly inhuman context. And a humanities that remains connected not only to the open varieties of human life (open in terms of gender, sex, class, race, ethnicity, nationality, religion and so on) but also to the open varieties of life (its animal and plant forms) is needed, one that opens itself to ethologies and generates critical ecologies. (Grosz 2011: 21)

The speculative element is required because the operation of *ficting*, as we might want to classify it, requires the creation of other worlds, or a type of wording, worlding or wor(l)ding (see Haraway 2016; Le Guin 1989).[8] In terms of a taxonomy that is speculative, the juxtaposition of the unstable and sometimes ludic operation of *speculating* with the seemingly serious operation of *classifying* may appear incongruous, but the incongruity of taxonomy itself becomes clear as soon as historical examples are consulted.

---

[7] Matterphor is Fred Botting's term in a vampyric context, in a chapter called 'Dark Materialism: Object, Commodity, Thing' (Hogle and Miles 2019). For more on pataphors see Schie (2008); for more on alogisms see Firtich (2004).

[8] The operation of ficting and the unit of the ficteme will be found in Charlie Blake's forthcoming article 'Of Mirrors and Unicorns: Ficting in the *Lichtung* of Analytic Philosophies'.

Historically taxa may be organised in various shapes and forms: they may be arborescent, circular, cladistic, genealogical, mereological, rhizomatic, scalar, serial, tabular or a combination of these. The ways that these taxonomies could be classified through (but not limited by) the ways that the similarities relate to the differences; their relative mobility or staticity and consequently their relationship to time; their respective representations or articulations whether visual, linguistic or otherwise; or the geometric or alphanumeric systems used to express them. In Peter Burke's *Social History of Knowledge* (2000) a number of varying knowledge systems and distinctions are discussed: *scientia* and *ars*, public and private knowledge; legitimate and forbidden knowledge; higher and lower knowledge; liberal and useful knowledge; 'book-learning' and the 'knowledge of things'; quantitative and qualitative knowledge; assorted types of knowledge tree from Ramon Lull's *Arbor Scientiae* (*c*.1300), trees of logic (i.e. the 'Tree of Porphyry'), trees of consanguinity, trees of grammar, trees of love, trees of battles, even a tree of Jesuits; and then, as Burke points out, 350 years before Foucault, an archaeology of knowledge dreamed up by Johann Heinrich Alsted (Burke 2000: 87). Burke enumerates a historically tripartite system or 'tripod' of knowledge systems composed of three subsystems: curricula, libraries and encyclopaedias. The Renaissance curriculum subdivides into the *trivium* (grammar, logic and rhetoric) or the more advanced *quadrivium* (arithmetic, geometry, astronomy and music). This differs from the equivalent in Islam where the 'foreign sciences' of arithmetic and natural philosophy were distinguished from the 'Islamic sciences' of the Quran (*hadith*), Muslim law (*fiqh*), theology, poetry and the Arabic language (Burke 2000: 92). The cataloguing and classification of items in libraries is understood within the field as *bibliographic control* and its tools have three basic functions: identifying or finding items, collocating or gathering items, and evaluating or selecting items (Taylor 2000: 6–7). Encyclopaedias are generally alphabetically ordered lists giving information on subjects or aspects of subjects. It is interesting to note that traditionally the encyclopaedia does not distinguish between fiction and myth and contemporarily accepted facts. As Umberto Eco notes, through studying Pliny, '. . . *the encyclopedia does not claim to register what really exists but what people traditionally believe exists – and hence everything that an educated person should know, not simply to have knowledge of the world, but also to understand discourses about the world*' (Eco 2009: 26).

Specuphyla

The most often-cited historical taxonomies are Pliny's *Natural History* (*c*.1 AD) and Linnaeus' *Systema Naturae* (1735), both of which are often quoted nowadays as examples of paradoxical attempts to classify the unclassifiable (as in the Borges/Foucault example quoted later in this chapter). The main points to draw from these historical taxonomies are that they are conceived of as ahistorical, transcendental and static. Static categories cannot support or express difference, which presupposes the need for categorisation that is both multiple and dynamic.

The perception of insufficiency in existing classificatory systems to account for the complexity and plurality of becomings and doings is a problem that cuts across disciplines. We might perceive intersectionality and superdiversity as two systems of classifying social lived experience, and these could be opposed, diffracted or simultaneously affirmed. Elizabeth Grosz describes the process of identifying intersections as a classifying system thus: 'This merging and multiplication of forms of oppression is always understood as the accretion, accumulation, and complication of readily definable and separable processes of oppression' (Grosz 2011: 92). Grosz criticises the classificatory framework of intersectionality because it still has recourse to sameness. As she states, intersectionality

> actually attempts to generate forms of sameness, similar modes of access to social resources, through the compensation for socially specific modes of marginalization (for migrants, access to translation services; for battered wives, access to shelters, and so on) . . . No voice ever represents a group, category, or people without dissent; and no categories are so clear-cut and unambiguous that they can be applied willy-nilly, without respect for the specific objects of their investigation. (Grosz 2011: 94)

Not only is intersectionality too static in Grosz's summation, but it also forbids both fuzziness and movement within and between intersections. As discussed in Chapter 1, to perceive the intersection itself as event alongside Jasbir Puar (2012) is a way of mobilising that does not eschew the prior work done by feminists of colour to conceive of the framework, a concern voiced eloquently by Ahmed (2008).

To counter the risks of reterritorialisaton or essentialism a speculative taxonomy must be affirmative and transversal. What this means in terms of method, according to Braidotti, is to 'create transversal links between the categories, while facing the "ethical vertigo" that is the sign of change' (Braidotti 2006: 123). To speculate is always to create transversal links between categories. Van der Tuin and Dolphijn and affirm the transversality of new materialism, citing Braidotti who describes new materialism as 'creating the conditions for the implementation of transversality' (Dolphijn and van der Tuin 2010; Braidotti 2006: 213). The significance of transversality for new materialism has also recently been highlighted in the new materialism online almanac entry for the term. 'Just as the word itself signifies in terms of the type of line you might draw when writing by hand, transversality opposes both verticality (in the sense of hierarchies and leaders) and horizontality, the sense of groups of people organising themselves within a particular "section" or compartment' (Palmer and Panayotov 2016). It focuses on the production of the new as well as processes of becoming, cutting across both text and matter and undoing this polarity as well as dualisms such as social/biological. According to Colin Gardner and Patricia MacCormack, Guattarian transversality is vital in the challenging of universal truths in favour of diverse epistemes.

> The dissipation of a universal truth addressed and reified by diverse epistemes that aspire to confirm the same ideological goals is not a dissipation of lived reality but an address to the in-between and the ablated in history and contemporary life. It multiplies speakers and speech so the singular content is unsustainable and new spaces for speech are available, new modes of expression, new openings for liberty, rather than an alternate content which fits within accepted discourse and can thus be argued against or assimilated depending on the augmentive quality it offers to dominant paradigms. (Gardner and MacCormack 2018: 3)

The power of a transversal methodology for thought and activism is extremely palpable here. Gardner and MacCormack demonstrate that the oft-heard accusations of post-structuralism as being fire to the flame of the so-called 'post-truth' relativism of contemporary life relies on precisely the arboreal epistemic discretion that post-structuralism aims to dismantle.

Speculuda

In *The Celestial Emporium of Benevolent Knowledge*, the fictional Chinese encyclopaedia discussed in Jorge Luis Borges's text 'The Analytical Language of John Wilkins' and famously quoted in Michel Foucault's *The Order of Things*, animals are divided into the following: (a) belonging to the emperor, (b) embalmed, (c) tame, (d) suckling pigs, (e) sirens, (f) fabulous, (g) stray dogs, (h) included in the present classification, (i) frenzied, (j) innumerable, (k) drawn with a very fine camelhair brush, (l) et cetera, (m) having just broken the water pitcher, (n) that from a long way off look like flies (Borges 1975). This list has amused and inspired various readers in various ways, rightly resulting in a proliferation of new ludic taxa. For example, David Byrne's *Arboretum* (2006) is a series of assorted taxonomies, many of which are arborescent in shape, yet the nature of their linkages is speculative or at best irreverent. For example, his 'Möbius Structure of Relationships' depicts a cyclical series of 'doings' which follow the Möbius band: 'Disliking Ignoring Forgetting Discovering Meeting Approaching Liking Loving Devouring Ingesting Consuming Destroying Pitying Dismissing' and then back to 'Disliking'. Another example, Byrne's graph 'Gustatory Rainbow' makes use of a Cartesian coordinate system to depict a synaesthetic entanglement of tastes, temperatures and variables of light, wherein the vertical axis runs from 'Cool' (left) to 'Warm' (right) and from Light (down) to Dark (up). On the vertical axis are colours, objects, foods and liquids. The words that are plotted in each of the four sections of the graph vary in their levels of specificity, from 'Oil' (somewhere between 'Cool' and 'Light') and two different types of 'Puce' – one North American and one European – plotted at different places in the section between 'Warm' and 'Light'. The sense here is the absurd nature of using a universal type of classificatory diagram to map a singular worldview. Rather than the suggestion of a prescriptive taxonomy, Byrne's diagrams are clearly intended as one of an infinite number of taxonomies. Byrne is not stating that this topological shape is the definitive structure of human relationships; neither is he suggesting that the series of verbs constitute every relationship. It is rather the suggestion that through the presentation of one particular and perhaps arbitrary taxonomy, an infinite number of alternatives may be spawned.

There are far too many examples of speculative taxonomies engaging with the ludic in order to present alternative classificatory systems to mention any but one or two more very briefly. Alphabetisation is a common organising principle and lends a semblance of order which may not be reflected in its contents. Caspar Henderson's *Book of Barely Imagined Beings: A 21st Century Bestiary* (2013), again inspired by Borges, lists organisms alphabetically with the contents page listing thus: 'Axolotl, Barrel Sponge, Crown of Thorns Starfish, Dolphin, Eel,

Flatworm, Gonodactylus, Human, Iridogorgia, Japanese Macaque, Kìrìpʰáò, the Honey Badger, Leatherback, Mystaceus, Nautilus, Octopus, Pufferfish, Quetzalcoatlus, Right Whale, Sea Butterfly, Thorny Devil, 'Unicorn' – the Goblin Shark, Venus's Girdle, Waterbear, Xenoglaux, Xenophyophore, Yeti Crab, Zebra Fish'. The book's inspiration is derived from the author's feeling that 'many real animals are stranger than imaginary ones, and it is our knowledge and understanding that are too cramped and fragmentary to accommodate them' (Henderson 2013: x). Bestiaries are medieval concepts, and Henderson is keen to present a contemporary version of this. Inspiration is definitely derived from Pliny's *Natural History*, an originary taxonomy if ever there was one. In *Why Read the Classics?* Italo Calvino selects a section of Pliny's fish taxonomy which is at least as arbitrary as the Borges example: 'Fish that have a pebble in their heads; Fish that hide in winter; Fish that feel the influence of stars; Extraordinary prices paid for certain fish' (Pliny the Elder *c*.1 AD; cited in Calvino 2013: 37).

The proposition of absurdities in taxonomical division is often an attempt to highlight the absurdity of the divisions that exist and purport to be utterly logical. A *reductio* of taxonomical rigidity is a speculative taxonomy itself. For a veritably vinous example, Colin Gardner uses Deleuze and Guattari's transversal lines of flight to think about flights of wine, retaxononomising wine taxa in order to combat the strict rules of organisations responsible for the categorisation of wines such as France's AOC (*appellation d'origine contrôllée*).

> In many ways, attempting to keep varietals and terroir safely contained within Deleuze's metaphorical closed vessels is much like our childhood practice of making sure that each component of a meal is limited to a discrete geographical region of the dinner plate, lest, horror of horrors, the carrots might actually touch the peas and the potatoes come into contact with the meat.

Against this segregation Gardner champions certain French winemakers who have set up viticultural methodologies in California, where, free from the jurisdiction of the AOC 'winemakers are free to zig-zag transversally across and between these otherwise closed vessels of production and consumption to create hybrid assemblages that defy the laws of their habitual blending' (Gardner 2014: 146, 147). Whether this is speculative taxonomy, libatory hybridity, oenological whimsy or perhaps all three is another question, but the drive to upset the rigidity of classification in favour of dynamic assemblages of vintnery is in the same lib(er)atory spirit as the other examples included in the current speculative classification.

Specquanta

The creation of transversal links between different or previously opposing epistemological traditions is a powerful tool within a speculative taxonomy. In 2015 Rasheedah Phillips of the Black Quantum Futurism Collective produced a 'BQF Correspondence Chart' which maps certain quantum phenomena onto physical descriptions, African spiritual or religious pheneomena and then a real-world correspondence. Wave-particle dualism, superposition, wave-fuction collapse, non-locality and entanglement, time symmetry and retro-causality, Heisenberg Uncertainty Principle/quantum uncertainty are described in short paragraphs then mapped onto African spiritual or religious phenonema and then a taxonomy of assorted 'real-world' phenomena. For example, wave-particle dualism is mapped onto the Ancient Egyptian concept of the Tuat, Ka and Qeb, sourced from Nur A. Amen's work in texts such *The Ankh: African Origin of Electromagnetism* (1989). This is then mapped onto the following correspondences: optical illusions, mind–body duality, figure-background duality taking descriptions from David Grandy's *Everyday Quantum Reality* (2010), and double consciousness from W. E. B. Du Bois's *The Souls of Black Folk* [1903]. This particular linkage – between double consciousness and wave-particle dualism – highlights the inherently political project of linking up quantum theory, African lore, physical descriptions and sociological race theory. This (transversal) traversal of disciplines is obvious and performs a number of functions. It forces the reader to think of scientific theories, sociological theories and spiritual beliefs as qualitatively comparable entities, but rather than leading to a kind of relativistic torpor the newly coined speculative links raise each epistemological level to a new plane altogether. This new plane is derived from the affirmation of not only transhistorical but perhaps panchronous equivocation. The speculative nature of the quantum theories discussed is what makes them particularly applicable to the other 'narratives' included; it is the apprehension of scientific discovery as creation which allows for alternative futures and pasts to be welcomed. Phillips's visionary chart is part of a speculative collection of works with the aim of 'experiencing reality by way of the manipulation of space-time in order to see into possible futures, and/or collapse space/time into a desired future in order to bring about that future's reality' (Phillips 2015: back cover).

Speculexia

Linguists and lexicographers have much to say about classificatory systems and taxa, particularly about the blind spots and problems encountered with phenomena such as fuzzy sets and polysemy. One solution to these issues to create new speculative dictionaries or thesauri, which are paradigmatic linguistic taxonomies operating according to the creator's particular agenda or whim. Leaving aside the extremist and reactionary aspects of Daly's essentialist feminism (alongside Lorde's open letter to Mary Daly discussed in Chapter 2) (see Gatens 1991 for a pertinent critique of Daly's *Gyn/Ecology*), what is interesting for us here is Daly's *Wickedary* (1988), a speculative network of what she calls Word Webs. Words are twisted, reshuffled, reordered and respelled; they are endowed with new meanings, characters and narratives. This is of course part of a broader project of the feminist reappropriation of sexist terms, but the difference here is that Daly creates neologisms and rearranges spellings rather than just attributing a new sense to an old term.

Rather than following a scheme, the *Wickedary* follows a 'skein', which means both a loosely coiled length of yarn or thread but also a flock of certain birds in flight. The seemingly aleatory nature of the skein is celebrated: 'The labyrinthine design of the *Wickedary* may appear twisted and contorted to those accustomed only to linear patterns such as graphs and charts. In fact, its order is organic and purposeful, and it can be compared to a flock of Wild fowl in flight' (Daly 1987: xvi) The *Wickedary* is in fact organised by a series of interconnecting webs, which present with a seemingly logical order. The first preliminary webs cover technical aspects such as history, spelling, grammar and pronunciation; there are then Word-Webs (of Elemental Philosophical Words) and Appendicular Webs. The presentation follows the conventions of the regular dictionary but spellings and definitions are radically new. The capitalisation of common nouns is a deliberate act of linguistic deformation with an assortment of reasons, mainly denoting new meanings of pre-existing words. Other entries are neologisms or portmanteaus:

> ... *Gyn/Ecology* is created by a slash in the old word gyne-cology, an oppressive word used to designate a gynocidal branch of murderous modern medicine ... In a double sense, then, the use of the double ax to create this word wrenches back Weird Word-power to cast Spells on the malignant medicine men and polluters who prey upon women and nature. (Daly 1988: 14)

The splicing of words and the concept of the 'double ax' is quite reminiscent of the deconstructive terminology that flourished in the 1990s, and it is interesting that Daly's deployment of this idea comes earlier, as her *Gyn/Ecology* was published in 1978. This text cannot be separated from its elements of problematic essentialism, but as an example of speculexical taxonomy the *Wickedary* is an entertaining resource.

Spectaxa

First square: speculative taxonomy of eyes. The human optical system is thrice protected. Covering the eye is the sclera. Covering the sclera is the clear, delicate membrane of the conjunctiva. Covering the conjunctiva is the cornea. A list of eyes, compiled by a seven year old. Black crow eyes. Not black like the feathers of a crow, but beaky and beady and darty and shiny hard black like the eyes of a crow or a blackbird. Other eyes. Frightening pale blue eyes. Eyes of a farmer with a gun. Cold weak teacup eyes which could be evil but probably aren't. What else? Warm hazel flecked with orange. Rare and delicious. And? Sky eyes and sea eyes. Eyes that reflect whatever blue they are looking at. Liquid melty chocolate eyes. Startling green eyes. Eyes like pond fire. Eyes like the slates of a cottage roof. Eyes you couldn't tell. Violet eyes. Scented eyes. Hindsight eyes. Eyes that look to the corners of the room. Restless eyes. Eyes elsewhere. Eyes tinged. Adult eyes in child's face. Sad eyes. Junkie eyes. Alkie eyes. Galaxies. Holes.

Second square: hormone spectaxa /hormone symphony. Sense cocktails elicit dermatological recontourings. The bump of the goose. The dermis is a fibrous layer that supports and strengthens the epidermis. What makes the tick tick? Hormone symphony of orchestral synthesised sounds. Because hormones are vibrations and the breath that blows through us. Mellow mellifluous melatonin is a clarinet sound outpouring honeyed sound levels checked for depression and depletion and suppression. Adrenaline battle-shrill violin sound equals happiness equals flight minus fight plus love minus danger. Gastrin reedy human oboe to be tasted while it eats you from the inside out. Cortisol is a tuba flooding hairy jowels halfway between anger and fear. Serotonin drum machine beat you have become meaningless shorthand alphabetised thus: A for amphetamines B for benzodiazeprines C for citalopram D for diazepam E for ecstasy F for fluoxetine G for gabapentine H for halcion I for imapramine K for ketamine L for lithuim M for morphine

N for nortriptyline O for olanzapine P for prozac Q for quetiapine R for reboxetine S for sertraline T for tramadol U for ultracet V for valium W for wygesic X for xanax Y for yosprala Z for zopliclone. Imbibe and synthesise.

Third square: Ooooooooaaaaaaaeeeeeeeeeeiiiiiiii. The geometry and cartography of the vowel quadrilateral. Perfect vowels are points in a continuous space. Consider the absurd task of segmenting some of these liquid strands into five units. Five nuclei. Five arbitrary termina. Knee. Uke. Lee. Eye. Five because it is the arbitrary number of segments prescribed by the Phonetic Alphabet, and five because a young boy in France had a go in 1871 and you think you can do better. A E I O U. Vowels. A is a door into a bat-filled haunted house. E is a segmented swimming pool flowing out from the left to the right. I sings high and lonely on a precipice, only a goat up there and thin air. O cannot separate from orange the dusty burning flamelike simian bumpled waxy citrus orb. U a vessel catching lukewarm pools of yellow flooding over.

Fourth square: interstices. The variegated materiality of the bits that join. In regular brickwork the interstices are cement, a gritty churning sludge which hardens and becomes concrete. In dry stone walling the interstices are small chinks of air. Visually: flashes of field and sky. In the body, the interstitium can be found nearly everywhere, just under the skin's surface. Vinculum. In the Western Ionian scale, the interstices are the spaces between two notes. Intervals. Chorda: rope or string. It is not space but something stretched tightly. The major second is an almost-uncomfortable vibrating touch. It is so close and sensitive it hurts and twangs. It is the tight string or cleft of a sexual organ. It is a bilabial fricative sound. Two lips humming a vibration. Halfway between orgasm and pain. A major third is a church sound. Round and comfortable and conservative. Ho ho, O yes, it chortles, round and rotund and aproned and floury from an afternoon baking scones. A fourth is a stag leap. Angular. A series of them, skittering into the woods off the road in the dark. Uneasy. A fifth is detective-dangerous. Faraway unknowable unplaceable ungraspable. The semitone interval hurts even more than the second. Think about what touching is for a second. Touching too close is flaying. One note plucks and pulls and flays the other. Pitch proximity as abrasive texture: sandpaper against flesh. Impossible to exist within this space.

Fifth square: spectra. Colours invite you into their respective parlours. One for each hexagon of the honeycomb head. The impossible object. Clavecin oculaire. Red is overdetermined and hyperbolic. Yellow offers you bright porcelain in the creamy pool of morning. Green tiptoes through a delicate glade. Brown is rich and viscous composite. Black is textured and infinite. Orange is always elsewhere. Purple is haunted and scented. Blue is aeons of itself. Pink is sugared. The intact surface of human skin is pitted by the orifices of sweat glands and hair follicles, and is furrowed by intersecting lines that delineate their own idiosyncratic patterns. Reading the ridges and grooves of the palms and the sole, the stretches of sand. Grooves and ridges. Reading the hills and reading the palms.

Sixth square: streaks. If a trajectory can create a streak of energy, of colour, of sensation, that streak itself could also be a tendril or a tentacle. Tending, intending, tendrilling in order to grab or grasp. Vector lovers. Streaks are nothing but lines or marks differing in substance or colour from their surroundings. Streaking the surface whilst stroking the surface. Whilst tentacles usually operate as suckered limbs around the mouth of sea-borne invertebrates, tentacles on some carnivorous plants are complex, highly touch-sensitive glandular hairs which move towards prey in order to secrete digestive enzymes. Streaks of sensitivity just like our hormonal pathways. To streak: to move quickly in a specified direction, sometimes while naked. Streaks of life, streaks of sound, streaks of vomit, streaks of piss.

Seventh square: speculexoskeleta. Networks and fretworks. Spindlework on show. Pins out. The leg of a pier. Barnacle encrusted, rusted and old. Look across at the ridged sand. Individuation and dermatoglyphics. Reading the future through particles of the past. A dramatisation of the transition from duality to deliquescence via the vying arts of palmistry and dermatoglyphics. Crystalline hopings shored up. Whorls and geomorphology. Splicing between fingerprints and sandbanks. The ridge details thereon will present differently to any other ridge details in any other possible world.

Sirens and Organs
Or
A Dramatisation of the Transition
From
Duality to Deliquescence
Via
The Diffracted Systems
Of
Acousticks and Opticks
Or
If These Whorls Could Talk

Staged in Blackpool, in the North West of England,
Grid Reference
SD 30603 35926
Grid Reference (6 figure)

X (Easting):	Y (Northing):
330603	435926
Latitude:	Longitude:
53.814969	−3.0554974

Those are the whorls that were her eyes.

Aux campagnes du ciel oculaire harmonie,
Du concert des couleurs te montre le genie.
[In the meadows of the sky ocular harmony
Shows you the genius of the concert of colours.]
(Lemierre [1769], quoted in Franssen 1991: 47)

It was now 5.23 a.m.
As if understanding his signal perfectly, a single piccolo played a single note and off in the east a solitary shaft of cool lemon light flicked across the sky. Milo smiled happily and then cautiously crooked his finger again. This time two more piccolos and a flute joined in and three more rays of light danced lightly into view. Then with both hands he made a great circular sweep in the air and watched with delight as all the musicians began to play at once.

The cellos made the hills glow red, and the leaves and grass were tipped with a soft pale green as the violins began their song. Only the bass fiddles rested as the entire orchestra washed the forest in colour.

(Juster 2008: 129)

> Principal proposition. So the pleasure and displeasure of all our senses consists in the same sort of vibrations, that is, in vibrations in harmonic proportion.
> (Castel [1726], quoted in Franssen 1991: 22)

> Even the Rays of Light seem to be hard Bodies; for otherwise they would not retain different Properties in their different Sides. And therefore Hardness may be reckon'd the Property of all uncompounded Matter. At least, this seems to be as evident as the universal impenetrability of Matter.
> (Newton 1979: 389)

> *O I do like to be beside the seaside . . .*
> (Glover-Kind 2018 [1907]: 8)

Through multiple wanderings, thoughtings and fictings I have tried to synthesise synaesthesia, tried again, failed again, failed better, and along the way realised that my own neuropolysemic entanglements are perhaps of a different kind. In my hometown of Blackpool, Lancashire, a cacophony of multifarious sirens and organs can be heard, seen, felt or complexly perceived. Some bewilderingly assault the optical and aural systems simultaneously; some have a pulse; some you can touch; some touch you. Organs and sirens: polysemous and intrafigural symbols as manifold sense organs. To conclude this chapter I attempt to chart a journey or love note to synaesthesia which takes place in several times and places within and around the town, which in all of its excesses, hedonisms, ejections, emissions and propulsions is for me a hub of sensory clash and entanglement. Through the skin of buildings, through portals on stained wallpaper, through multisensory yearnings, and finally to the sea. To the Palace we go.

The World Famous Palace Discotheque can be found on Blackpool Promenade. Three concrete semicircular appendages stick out from the sea wall, their curved shelves jutting out and over what lies below: sometimes sea, sometimes sand.

Three layers of tissue constitute the structure of the skin: the epidermis, the dermis and the subcutis. Within these layers we have the interstitium: the web of the loom.

Three categories of large linear sand ridges can be distinguished: tidal ridges, shoreface-connected ridges and long bed waves.

Ridged, lined and whorled surfaces. The skin of a building. The body in the sand.

SENSORIUM 157

Figure 4.1 The art deco squares of the Palace Nightclub, Blackpool Promenade, 2008.

Organs: instruments, tools, tendrils, viscera, sensoria. Aesthesis was for Aristotle the faculty of sense, covering both perception and sensation. As Mark Paterson points out in his book on haptics, it is interesting in Aristotle's thought that whether it is interpreted as *paschein* (an ambiguity of feeling) or pathos (suffering, experience, emotion), *aesthesis* involves 'a form of change, a necessary (but not sufficient) condition of perception' (Paterson 2007: 19). Aesthesis as a change, or perhaps a rate of change. A scale. Every organ exhibits, plays, presents or demonstrates a scale. Organs presuppose scales which consist of measured segmentations of change: variations. Variations might be of pitch, volume, colour, tone colour, timbre or sensation. What if we were to think transversally about these segmentations, in terms of their difference of both degree and kind? A speculative taxonomy transmutes the segmentation into something different. It estranges; it queers. The only difference between the variations within the speculative taxonomy of organs is perhaps the anthropocentric notion of an operator: a musician, a player, a conductor. An orchestrator.

Whorls: from fingertips to shells and back again. Scaling the Palace. So we burrow and we mine in order to ascend. Up steps to thinner sweeter air, sand-grit-concrete; deep down into sand, wet-damp-scratch; deeper down into skin, soft-hard-soft: does it matter? A process of abstraction, extraction and rarefaction. The skin of a building. Surfaces are more permeable than they look. The World Famous Palace Discotheque, lurid in the afternoon light, its giant curved squares sitting atop the building, corners softened, dancing capital letters P A L A C E spiky and tropically coloured, is something from another planet. It is an octopus lair.

Organs. The High Tide Organ in Blackpool is played by the sea. Eight pipes are attached to the sea wall, which are connected to eighteen organ pipes within the tentacular sculpture housed on the promenade. At high tide, the swell of water causes air to flow up the pipes and causes them to sound. The pipes are pitched harmonically around B flat. Is this a sense organ or a musical instrument or a tool used by the sea, or perhaps all three? The word 'organ' is a fusion of the late Old English *organe* and Old French *orgene*, both meaning 'musical instrument', and both derived from the Greek *organon* meaning 'instrument or tool' and the Latin *organa*, plural of *organum*, meaning 'musical instrument'. Only in the late fourteenth-century did the medieval sense of the word *organum* come to mean a certain part of the body. Blackpool's High Tide is unmistakeably derived from sea life, particularly cephalopodic life, which gives a different, tentacular sense to the organ. So what does it mean if an organ is a tentacle, or a tentacle is an organ? A sensitive instrument: a limb, a tool. A tendril.

Sirens. Ineluctable diffractibility of the sensory manifold: dervished rubbishing child gull cries.

Signatures of all things I am here to taste: deepfried candyfloss narcotic vinegartang.

You tell me to analyse I'd rather synthesise. Blend and multiply the senses. Why? Because sirens do more than make sound. Sirens make plaits with long hair composed of three elastic elements: 1) feeling 2) time 3) space. So. Stretch it out and spool it like syrup. Tempo rubato. Pull it apart. Time honey or time dough. What the music does to you, line by heartfelt line, whizzing from fifteen to nineteen and back again because you never really went anywhere. Teetering is really falling, falling is really landing. Rushing through the depths, nineteen eighteen seventeen sixteen fifteen. What sound does the am-lance make. The knee and the gnaw. A wail awave upon the veil. Wassail. Ululate. Throatcroak. Heartrasp. Warning. Nineteen senses. The honeyed voices inside the tincture bottle denounce engraved numbers in favour of a viscosity sliding scale.

The Palace is unmistakeably art deco in design, and holds itself incongruously next to the multi-storey car park, the Hounds Hill Shopping Centre, the grotesquely oversized plasterboard frontispiece of Coral Island, the themed amusement arcade. The Palace from another world and time. Its blue, curved, hollow squares are from outer space. Each square is a different size. The main body of the club is attached to a similarly decorated footbridge over the busy A584, the main prom road. Elastin holds the skin together. The lines of the skin flow in the general direction of elastic tension. The traffic flows bi-directionally, both north and south. Countless numbers of lines, deep and shallow and whorled, together with the pores, give every region of the body its own topology. The only invariant is the multiplication of taxonomies.

Like the furrows and ridges on the sand over there across the road on the beach, the lines on the palms and soles are mostly established by genetics, or by the lunar tides, before conscious time begins. Climb into a square and meet its lines: expand and bend your curved self to fit its dimensions. An octopus can condense its mass to such an extent that it can squeeze through a space the size of its eye.

Sirens. The myriad skins, surfaces and selves donned by Jazz Age Siren, WWII Resistance fighter and civil rights activist Josephine Baker offer unique comments on early twentieth-century fetishisations of female racialised sexuality and exoticism and Baker's knowing appropriation of these. In a simultaneous act of construction and being constructed, the star of La Sirène des Tropiques *(1927) Baker became all manner of racist and sexist stereotypes for the delectation of the public: 'the savage dancer, the Black Venus, exotic Jazz Age star, the liberated new woman, and the gender-bending cross-dresser' (Jules-Rosette 2007: 128). Baker had a house designed especially for her which in its very dimensions and apertures operated as emblem of her own perceived and objectified presence. The house contains a swimming pool as a central focal point with a viewing platform on all sides. In her book* Second Skin: Josephine Baker and the Modern Surface *Anne Anlin Cheng argues that Baker's body, her wearing of her skin as cloth, 'rewrites both the regressive and progressive histories that encode black female skin' ... leading us 'not to the separation of* essence and appearance but to an animated relay between epidermal certitude and stylistic vicissitude in the making of racial legibility' (Cheng 2010: 172). Cheng narrates a meeting between the young and newly successful Baker and a middle-aged architect, Adolf Loos, who promptly designs a house for Baker. The house was never made but its design lives on, a curious exhibit of a public/private interface. 'Inside the Baker House, the inside is made outside, and the trope of the womb becomes hypostatised as the swimming pool is in the middle of the house . . . [the house] reproduces a downright peep show. This architectural vision may therefore be said to exemplify the racial and sexual fantasies of European, masculinist, and Primitivist desire' (Cheng 2010: 52). Baker's later construction of a theme park ensconced within a chateau in the French countryside and her acquisition of a 'Rainbow Tribe' of twelve adopted children from across the globe constitutes a unique and radical attempt to affirm racial diversity at a time when this was not done, and maintaining showbusiness throughout. She made her own house an exteriority within. Child poet Minou Drouet visited the theme park and recited the following lines which Josephine taught her adopted children:

> I asked my little finger
> To whisper to me why
> My apple tree
> Strokes fanlike
> At the pink cheek of the sky . . .
> 　　　　(Baker and Bouillon 1978: 206)

Organs, or one organ in particular, have played a significant part in Blackpool's history since the nineteenth-century. The Wurlitzer organ in Blackpool Tower Ballroom has been there since 1935 and was made famous by Reginald Dixon, who played it for forty years, and more recently Phil Kelsall who has also been playing the Wurlitzer for forty years and is still going.[9] Organs require the playing of three keyboards and the reading of three staves: three simultaneous lines. The human operator must, perhaps, think topologically, or toposophically. There is something agentially interesting about the concept of an instrument. An instrument, by its very nature, does not have agency. Who, therefore, has the agency when the sea organ plays its sounds? Sea organs, Aeolian harps and wind chimes operate without *further* human intervention;

---

[9] See the following short interview with Phil Kelsall: <http://www.bbc.co.uk/programmes/p055s5fq>

they are shaped thus in order to harness the power of the wind or the waves in order to create musical sounds.

Sirens. Don't even get me started on words. The liquid ones and the crunchy ones and the ones in between. Eating Crunchy Nut Clusters with a touch of honey bathed in a cold milk bath. A nut is the hard full atom of a consonant. A mouthful of throthful faithful forthflowing mirthful youth crunching away hamstercheeks with milkdripping chins. Lunch. We munch our lunch on t'bench outside Tescos. The impossibility of Crisps. What you got there. Just a packet o' Chris. Who's Chris? Clusterfucktastic. Cuntstruck: spluttering resplendent over splurges of spliced splendour full splitting to burst my edges. Feeling angsts a bazillion. A packet of angsts. Ich habe Angst. Sniffing a with snoopy snout, sniggering away snotgreen snapjaws snipping at yer heels. Snot good enough. Just let yerself wallow in the bath for one second. Coagulate. Between a liquid and a solid. Languishing in soupy soapy sounds. Solid love liquid hate. Aereous. Aorta. Aurora. Aureole. Aureoliae. The Sirens led the sailors to their deaths with their song. Nineteen eighteen seventeen, had we but world enough and time.

Organs. Luis Bertrand Castel in 1725 wondered whether 'sound and light do not equally consist in the insensible wigglings of the sonorous and luminous bodies, and of the media that transmit them to our ears (and to our eyes)?' (Castel 1725, quoted in Franssen 1991: 19). In order to explore this question, Castel envisioned the *clavecin pour les yeux* or the ocular harpsichord. This would be a regular harpsichord somehow transmuted so that the pressing of the keys would bring out colours and their combinations, which would add further dimensions of harmony to the music. In his desire to discover the harmonies between colour and tone and keen to counter Isaac Newton's theory of primary colours, Castel made the claim that there were twelve distinct colours which matched the number of semitones in the diatonic scale. Castel wanted an absolute tonic in both tone and colour, and argued that this was the standard C and the colour blue.

Sirens of the early-to-mid twentieth century: stylish, troubled, strong. Bernhardt, Piaf, Dietrich, Baker. Grubby prints of them on the walls. Pianorific teenage wonderment: learning about Cecile Chaminade and Scott Joplin. Chaminade is an unsung heroine of French romanticism. Her Étude Romantique: an impossible waterfall with infinite tributaries designed to trip the fingers. And Joplin. Ragtime: cake walks, gallumphing left hand octaves, faster and faster and faster – so much fun! A sack race of notes falling over themselves, racing wrongly towards the end.

Thump.

Done.

Yes done, but done <u>wrongly</u>. The Maple Leaf Rag should be played <u>slowly</u>. It's meant to be a <u>dance</u>. You'll have them all sweating! They'll get their beads all tangled up! They want to be stately when they dance! Slow it right down! I don't want to feel like I've just run a marathon! You're giving me palpitations!

Vaster than empires and more slow.

Focus.

Fifteen senses running fast to stay in the same place. Stuck fast. Move closer / Set my soul on fire. Teenage songs draw blood. A fierce fast rivulet of red. The ease of teenage bag-slinging wrist-slitting love. Compass and biro tattoos, 4 REAL I.D.S.T. Sixteen seventeen eighteen nineteen. The smashing of beer bottles and the complete lack of pain. Honeyed voices as worms just under the skin. Buckfast coagulates and accelerates simultaneously. Viscosity in the bloodstream and the raised worms of half-healed scars. Bloodwort tramlines up your arm. Do not listen to a word I say / Just listen to what I can keep silent. Those times when fifteen senses rang true. A new sensory autobahn added to the vermicelli junction. Leaning out of a window smoking a cigarette and feeling your skin prickle with the sentience of the very air around you. No she said no I will Never. The sentience of the air multiplied by the sentience of your prickling skin. Sentience squared equals an exponentially levitating bodymindfuck. Eliot multiplied by Donne equals thinking feeling a feeling thinking thinking feeling. Thoughts have thoughts. Feelings have feelings too. Deal with it. She said it was too much to kiss on the lips because she had too many sensory receptors clustered there. Way more than the usual number. Batter my heart. Donne Donne Donne because we are too menny. Ha. I know the secret about too many – it's nineteen nineteen nineteen squared I don't care about pathologies I've got some too. Love hones the senses. Seventeen eighteen nineteen blades. A mark is nothing but a pen knife ink blood scream. It barks at no one else but me / Like it's seen a ghost. People reverberate through you. And there is nothing yet on this earth that you have encountered more powerful than the afterclang of those reverberations. How you move / The way you bust the clouds it makes me want to try. Sticky as lips. Licky as trips. Never has there been a purer joy than one of the opening of a new internal cavern. Private mythology. Archivist of feeling, documentation of moments, pause play repeat. Stubborn mute rocks rolling around inside the gut. Orchestras of echoes.

Again.

Focus.

Organs: Leonhard Euler, mentioned earlier in chapter in relation to the early beginnings of topology, also wrote on the analogy between colour and sound a little later, in 1761.

> You will please to recollect that the sound of a string depends on three things – its length, its thickness, and the degree of tension; the more it is stretched the sharper its sound becomes; and as long as it preserves the same disposition, it emits the same sound; but that changes as soon as the other undergoes any variation.
> Let us apply this to bodies which are the objects of vision. The minuter particles which compose the tissue of their surface may be considered as strings distended, in as much as they are endowed with a certain degree of elasticity and bulk, so that, being struck, they acquire a motion of vibration, of which they will finish a certain number in a second; and on this number depends the colour which we ascribe to such body. It is red when the particles of its surface have such a degree of tension that, being agitated, they perform precisely so many vibrations in a second as are necessary to excite in us the sensation of that colour. A degree of tension which would produce vibrations more or less rapid would excite that of a different colour, and then the body would be yellow, green, or blue, &c. (Euler [1761] in Brewster 1840: 72)

While progressively losing his sight throughout his adult life and eventually being pronounced completely blind, Euler was simultaneously attempting to produce a scientific correlation between the particles that make up objects of vision, the vibrations which make up objects of sound and the variations of vibration which he saw as producing the colour spectrum. The harmonisation of scales and spectra, scales upon scales, simultaneity of variation.

Sirens. Where are we? The revolving dance floor upstairs at the Syndicate superclub, Blackpool. Isaac Newton pronounced that lights were hard bodies. In this club our own soft bodies are spliced, speared, penetrated by tight beams of green. A laser occurs when the electrons in atoms absorb energy from a current and become excited. Excited! What would Newton have made of the green lasers in here. Trance Thursdays. A diet of commercial trance and forever we will have acid green drops of laser in our blood. Silence by Delerium – an extended version of Tiesto's In Search of Sunrise remix, which is already 11 minutes 35 seconds long. A million tracks laid down in a simulation, a synthesis, of a kind of harmonic Nirvana. Repetitions of the bass note, four beats in a bar, simple. It's always a female vocal. Ethereal. A powerful voice lost in feminine ragged breath. More breath than sound. The three-step bass line, used scores and scores and scores of times, fourth-fifth-sixth and then back down again. Bodies swooning all around, waterfalls of bodies, muscles writhing and contorting, more tree than human, grins stretching across faces, arms stretching like branches to the sticky ceiling. Streams and ribbons, threads and layers of liquid gold surrounding us from every side until we are wading, bathing, then drowning in thick molasses of sound. In this white wave / In this silence I believe.

Organs. It is perhaps no coincidence that organs are the instruments dreamed up, invented or employed by various synaesthetes and their admirers in order to create transversal links across, between, through and among various scales or senses. Following in the footsteps of Newton and Castel, in the twentieth century Alexander Scriabin invented the clavier à lumières, colour organ or 'Chromola' in which a colour scale was equated with the musical scale. A follower of theosophy and the occult, Scriabin wanted to create new dimensions with his work and invented his colour organ specifically for his symphonic work *Prometheus: The Poem of Fire* (1910). The colour organ encountered challenges not unlike Castel's. It apparently did not work during the first performance of *Prometheus*, and when it did work, both the idea and the piece were met with criticism. Scores of critics pointed out the limitations of the colour-pitch analogy as well as the ultra-'modern' and dissonant nature of the piece. One review of a performance in Carnegie Hall from *The Nation*, 25 March 1915, made the following comments:

> Granting that it can hardly be said that he has made a convincing demonstration of the desirability of such an alliance [between colour and music], at least as presumed by him; for although he endeavoured to show that certain colours, singly or in contrast, will produce similar effects on the senses and emotions as certain musical tones or chords, he has failed to make such connection clear to the spectator and hearer ... His musical score, moreover, represents the very extremes of ultra-modern cacophony, all harmonic euphony being avoided with a zeal worthy of a better cause. To harmonise with such a score, the colours thrown on the screen should therefore be equally hideous, whereas they are really beautiful, though monotonous. (Anonymous reviewer [1915], quoted in Klein 1926 : 244)

It appears that speculating in order to produce synergies between taxonomies is often met with disdain or suspicion. The link between colour-tone harmony and occultist thinking is at its most obvious in Scriabin, who along with colour harmony thinker Rudolf Steiner was interested in theosophy (see Bramble 2015). Even theorising colours themselves is sometimes received with disdain as overly fanciful or lacking in rigour; Johann Wolfgang von Goethe in his *Farbenlehre* noted that 'A dread of, nay, a decided aversion for all theoretical views respecting colour and everything belonging to it, has been hitherto found to exist among painters . . .' (Goethe 1967 [1810]: 189).

Sirens. How to see Chaminade's waterfall of notes in her Étude Romantique. Listen to it and think of what it does to you. Fifteen sixteen seventeen senses. How things bind and blend together. And you? What do you do see when you hear those tinkling raining patterns in Chaminade? Do you see glass? Do you see stairs that light up as you step on them like they have in the bit of Grease *when the fairy godfather man is singing Beauty School Dropout to Frenchie in his shiny white Elvis suit? Do you see les étoiles, brighter, thinner, sharper in French than English, tiny teaspoons on glass? Tinkle tinkle chink chink. Letter K, voiceless velar plosive, bright sharp high, narrow vowel space, minimal oxygen. Thin air summit white precipiceness. Scales ascending keys bright light steps tiptapping lighting up each plink a plink K for kettle bright metal upscale scale descale. Ha. Special K. My baby does K all day. K is the opposite of sludge. Repeated tinkling. And you try, try, try to see something more beyond the feeling of the tinkling notes, and you can't. Where has Chaminade gone? Parametric versus segmentary analysis. Music is speech is flow is phrase is water not sand no matter how fine. Networks, fretworks, blend to mesh. Felt not felt. Fractal. Becoming Proustian, are we? Shut up shut up shut up. Don't give me that infinitesimal sensibility. I don't want to drown in congealing gloop. I cannot slow down. Ever.*

Organs. Has anyone attempted to create an 'instrument' which utilises the concept of scale or spectrum aligned with erotic pleasure – in other words, a musical organ directly linked to human sexual organs? In Roger Vadim's *Barbarella* (1968), scientist Durand Durand's Excessive Machine, or orgasmatron, is intended to kill its inhabitants by orgasm: the concept the little death is literalised and the excess of pleasure produced by the machine kills its inhabitant. The pleasure machine is, of course, another type of organ directly affecting the human sexual organs. While its actual mechanisms are not quite clear, the operator plays the keys and makes music while the captive inhabitant is trapped inside and forcibly administered erotic stimulation until their death. Yet the machine is very quickly exhausted and burnt out by Barbarella's seemingly inexhaustible appetite. 'What kind of girl are you?' demands the inventor. 'Have you no shame?'

Sirens. These notes don't take you anywhere other than towards their own sound, which can be translated to movement but only the movement of fingers and their delicate and precipitative movement on the keys. Think of it like stroking. It is stroking. The sense of variation, fifteen sixteen seventeen learning to lift your fingers clean away and feel that invisible elastic always pulling you back. Just in time. Tempo rubato. Cats crawling on a piano.

And still you're trying to think about those notes.

Try a different tack. Try thinking about the melody itself. A phrase, descending and cascading like a woman's hair down her back. Arpeggio braids. Yes. A series. Always you think about the series. Try again. Fail again. Resolution. It goes like this, the fourth, the fifth. No, don't go down that route. That way lies the danger. Seventeen eighteen nineteen, come on now.

What exactly are we trying to do here?

The fusion of the vibratory fields. The curve of a melody. Organs of aesthesis, furl unfurl to touch and feel, grasp the sense, bind and blend. You are a gnat. A fucking gnat, and nothing else. Snapjaw venus flytrap moment-catching. Out, flick tongue, no wait, that's not a gnat, that's a frog catching a gnat. Fucking hell, this is hard work. Metaphorical bunny hops. Lateral leaping. Fucking bars of signification everywhere. The Zen masters had it right. Go on then. Do it. Bang your head against the wall. Noise pain space bright light. Chink. You strain to see and hear the simplicity of the melody somewhere in the midst of these twinkling lights –

AHA!

There ye go. Claritas is quidditas. Twinkling instead of tinkling. Congratulations, you have successfully created the conditions of possibility to see a sound as if 'twere a sight. As if 'twere a light. From tinkling to twinkling in one fell swoop.
    Phew. Jobdone. Offhome.

Organs. While the mechanics of the polysensory Orgasmatron are laughable and her character objectified throughout the film, Barbarella is vindicated and triumphant through her destruction of the machine, her desire not only exceeding its confines but dissolving its very mechanisms in a blow to the patriarchal restriction of female pleasure.

Sirens. Much harder but not a million miles away from faking an orgasm to synthesise love you aim to synthesise the synaesthete's experience and the impossibility of a venture has never dissuaded you before and never will. A = black, E = white, I = red, U = green, O = blue: vowels. What about the days of the week? Try and fail again. Tuesday Thursday lilac pale yellow pastel; Monday Wednesday Friday strong triad of white red and navy blue. Lemon squeezy. Since each of us was several, we were already quite a crowd. A million black squid liquids pooling round some kind of universal soul crustacean. Just stop doing all of it and let your hair down. Unwind the plait and it all joins up anyway. Feeling divided by time divided by space equals one honeycomb head. Earplugs are redundant when the sirens are inside. Consider trepanning the skull and plugging each rattling hexagon with pink and white fluffy marshmallows. Lie down on psychedelic patterned pillows tired out from all the infighting yet forever in awe of every single speck of dirt and noise that flies into the perceptive field. The apples fermented / Inside the lamented. Eighteen nineteen nearly twenty and your edges are going to burst. Cider inside her insides. A dirty spin cycle yet full of wonderment. Love on a real train with mud blood guts and gore. Let it go. The lonesome organ grinder cries / The silver saxophones say I. Certain words gain new harmonics. Choking over the pronouncement of a name. My vegetable love. Vaster than empires. And more slow.

Just stop and slow it all right down.

You are nineteen point five heavy sacks of potatoes; nineteen point five rotating blades orthogonal to the plane of the flesh; nineteen point five perforated bivalent edges softening and browning and waiting for something you feel is not entirely unconnected to the procurement and extraction of a jam from a fruit you know not yet what.

So. Become infinitesimal and sand-surf, slip-slide, skin-ski, helter-skelter your way down, or down into, a slope of skin, of land, of body, of sand. Make a new furrow.

Listen: the sea organ is playing.

Concluding comments

Throughout this book, a shape has emerged and perhaps shown itself, but only as it changes. It may have hovered but not quite settled, then transformed, shifted, altered, become other than itself, reconfigured and moved on. Perhaps the shape has undergone continual transformation – that description we encountered in the Introductions, in the words of Ezra Furman describing queer identity. The shape has not been explicitly referred to, though as the writing in each chapter has proposed, expressed, deformed and defamiliarised itself, a shape of proportions inspired by the unmathematical topological imagination and undergoing continual deformation.

The *shape-shifting* nature of the material-discursive operations described in the preceding chapters are why perhaps the most apt figure to take up to embody or enflesh this shape-shifter is the trickster figure that Audre Lorde invokes through Afrekete. The rewriting, refolding and refleshing of the trickster figure, found in folklore from a multitude of cultures, is useful because of its inherent deviance and potential for *more* deviance: deviance squared. The trickster is conventionally male, but as Lorde and others have shown us, this need not be the case. The trickster is archetypal, but as we have seen, archetypes suggest the notion of universal norms which is precisely what this book seeks to disrupt. Universal norms do not precede difference, which is why we need to rewrite concepts such as the trickster figure to accommodate that which does not fit inside those mythical norms.

Through this book, the three processes outlined in the three introductions – the threefold analogical statement I proposed at the beginning 'defamiliarising can be queering can be mattering' and later on 'rewriting can be refolding can be refleshing' – have been explored through the writing process itself. I have examined examples of defamiliarising/queering/mattering in each chapter while subjecting my own writing to those very processes in different ways. In the positing of 'synvariance' in Chapter 1 I proposed various deformations of syntagmatic logic, suggesting (playfully) that the reader follow a rose-strewn path in order to perceive the ways that language, made strange, can matter and shift. Chapter 2 was populated by a defamiliarised public of fictive personae, both intimate and estranged; figures wrested from their web of familiar associations and shifted around, just as Shklovsky describes, as if they were logs in the fire. The listing of these figures at the culmination of this chapter is another synvariance: an interruption to syntactical flow and a deformation to the rational order of word-things. Chapter 3 narrates more splicing of worlds through words: alternative realities spring forth through fictive imaginings that both are and are not the same as their progenitors. Chapter 4 addresses spatial deformation directly: through a deformation of dimensions in topology and a simultaneous challenge to sensory categorisation and distribution, which again splices senses so that by the end it is unclear whether we are listening or seeing but the distinction itself is rendered immaterial because we know that we are feeling. One word which has entwined itself within the strands of each chapter is *splice*. To splice words is to create new worlds.

From Chapter 1 through to Chapter 4 there has been a sense of deformation enacted through the language itself. The writing has diffracted through itself and followed multiple entangled conceptual and narrative paths. My intention in presenting these chapters in this way has been to show through doing. Through writing I aim to show how a formalist preoccupation with linguistic functioning need not be a static system and can also be materialist in multiple senses of the word. In my reading and thinking around these areas it has felt impossible to do it any other way: for an investigation into the splicing of the material and the discursive, the very lines of enquiry – letters, words, conceptual trains, traces and trails – must be themselves subjected to the processes that they are investigating. The mode through which these queering-defamiliarising-mattering processes of writing have emerged has often been ludic: the foregrounding of the nonserious in order to make a point that is serious. One example of wordsplicing encapsulating the serious business of the ludic that sticks in my memory is from another arch-defamiliariser, James Joyce: 'jocoserious' (Joyce 1998: 629). Joyce has not really featured explicitly in these pages but he has haunted them, and me, so much so that it is Joyce who I use as a springboard to end this book. What Joyce's splicing of oppositions shows us is that to perform the process – to enact a wordsplicing – is not a new thing. The task now being carried out by the writers discussed in this book is to deform the canon itself, to *de*form the 'mythical norm' of linguistic jocoseriousness away from the European white male. As a European white male, Joyce creates a dazzling performance of the gradual evolution or 'making-strange' of the English language in his 'Oxen of the Sun' chapter of *Ulysses*, but in doing so he operates as a mouthpiece for solely white men. There are no female voices in the procession of voices that make up this chapter. This lacuna is what has led me to want to operate as an alternative kind of mouthpiece, my own gesture of giving voice to the silenced voices that inhere within that particular modernist tradition.

This book has, in a way, been all about rewritings of different kinds. In 2018 Chris McCabe published *Dedalus*, not so much a rewriting but an imagined sequel; the book is set the day *after* the day in which Joyce's *Ulysses* is set. The book is reimagined in the digital age, with text message speak and gentrified advertising and talk of data bundles. The same chapter sequence as Joyce's is used and the same voices resound in McCabe's richly seamed text, with some new additional voices added. McCabe's 'Oxen of the Sun' chapter mimics Joyce's in that he moves through a series of voices, albeit an updated one: Marcel Proust, Virginia Woolf, Margaret Mitchell, Vladimir Nabokov, William Burroughs, Sylvia Plath, Thomas Pynchon, Margaret Atwood, Anne Michaels, Cormac McCarthy and Eimear McBride. The male-only roll call that we perceive in Joyce's 'Oxen of the Sun' is somewhat redressed in this list, and McCabe channels these voices in his version.

What is interesting and perhaps disappointing from a feminist perspective is that McCabe's final 'Penelope' chapter (which is the only part of Joyce's text devoted to female narration) is given over to the character of Stephen Dedalus, which to me, after such an enjoyable journey through Joycean soundsplicings, felt like one more silencing of a female voice by a male one. This led me to imagine and rewrite another 'Oxen of the Sun', but in another place and several other times, this time somewhere familiar and yet totally defamiliarised: a tram ride along Blackpool promenade at sunset with a great many voices chattering, interspersing past with present.

Where are we? We're still in Blackpool, Lancashire. A few of the special trams that run along the seafront are decorated with lights in the shapes of trains or rockets: a feast for the senses and a pull for the tourists. The tram with the rocket lights becomes Old Norse Sun goddess Sol, riding her chariot of horses through the sky as the sun sets. What follows is a hymn to Sol and every other voice that joins. It is written to be read out loud.

Epilogue

A Hymn to Sol
or
She Rides the Tram in Different Voices
or
A Heliochronic Tram Journey along Blackpool Promenade at Sunset
or
Radio Blackpool

(voices, multiple)
(deities, multiple)

Mother of the vibratory field,

All-nourisher, all-giver, all-destroyer
Ma-ga
Gaia
Blessings to you
So mote it be.

The tram with the rocket lights goes all the way from Starr Gate to Fleetwood Ferry.
Sun goddess Sol rides a chariot of horses through the sky.

Come sea-wolf, swallow us whole.
Riding our tram chariot through the darkening sea / sky / sea / sky / sea as the sea wolf swallows the sun and carries it in her belly.

O Radiant Star, O Lady of the Evening. At your battlecry the lands bow low and the people sing your praises. The threshold of tears is opened and the people walk along the promenade of great lamentations. Those sleeping on the streets and those sleeping in the shelters and those sleeping in the B&Bs: the people all lift their eyes to you.

O rattling trams, O sun, Your radiant Chariot – whither goes it on its way? Who decks it for you, lambent neon rocket, borne hitherward through prayer unto the sacrifice? Where is your halting place amongst the briny offerings? Be near me: O unfocused colours: shine resplendent.

The pissbrown sea. The organgrinding sea. The slatecold sea. The tablecloth sea. The bonechina sea. The anticlimactic sea. The plasticlogged sea. And cradled in your sludgy gut the reddening ageing darkening sun.

Solis ocassus.
Amor
Amare
Sol
Solis.
So.
(To love is to touch the sun)
(To love is to touch the edge of the sun)
(To touch the edge of the sun is to love)

(all-consuming)
(all-absolving)
(all-swallowing)
(as we are)
(before the rays of the sun)

Reserve your right to eat, for even to eat wrongly is better than not to eat at all. Stop at the van next to Queens Promenade and buy a vanilla Mr Whippy Soft Scoop with a Cadburys Flake for 99p. Carefully and quickly scoop out a triangle-shaped section of delicious pale cream sweetness from one side of the cone with your tongue. The curve created if you draw a line from one edge of your triangle ice cream hole to the other is a hyperbola. The ice cream is so delicious that you cannot help but immediately repeat this action until a bigger section of the empty cone is exposed. Now the curve drawn from one point of the cone to the other is a parabola. Soon you will have consumed enough that all sides of your ice cream cone are visible, making what looks like an uneven circle. Excellent! You now have an ellipsis. Now to see the final conic section you have two choices dependent upon the levels of air temperature, proximity of remaining icecream to an incompressible fluid that conforms to the shape of its container but retains a (nearly) constant volume independent of pressure, and pain caused by sphenopalatine ganglioneuralgia. You can either sit tight and wait for the internal energy of the remaining ice cream to become sufficiently agitated for the phase transition from solid to liquid to occur, thereby causing the uneven surface to right itself and for the ellipsis to become a perfect circle. The correct conclusion to the procedure would then be to remove the bottom tip of the cone with the front top and bottom teeth, immediately clamping the lips round the small aperture, sucking out the remaining melted ice cream from the bottom and subsequently enjoying the concomitant moistening of the dustysweet soggening nonsacramental paperlight wafer. All formally dogmatic biscuits are fallacious and must never be accepted by self-respecting persons as final. By both historical accounts I was flayed to death by oystershells, the skin razed entirely from the body and the limbs burnt at the Christian altar for an argument I was but bystander of, through jealousy or perceived threat to masculine Reason.

Year by year, across the wet dunes,

I have often gathered plastic bottles
    intoxicated with their beauty
    fondling them impudently

    I get my jeans wet with their lucid tears.

This creature, being of years fifteen-and-some, walked across concrete path in battered trainers somedeal full of sand, turning her thoughts to the worshipful maiden inside the sick-house to her sinister side, was within short time fighting against the devils which made turns around in her breast. Anon turned the mind of this creature towards devils and dark spirits, for dread she had of damnation. And anon this creature was wonderly vexed, for at the mouth of the lapping sea she saw devils with breath of low fires, devils with eyes of snakes and spite, devils who bade her she should forsake her friends, her family, her maiden sister Teresa who said:

Let nothing disturb you on your windblown path
Let nothing make you afraid
There is nothing which puts devils to flight

better than the
Unholy water of the
Ironflat coldgrey seesighsea.

This Summer time, I summerless, and serviceless also, And subject unto Heartsickness, that abroad I could not go. The fate of the workingclass Pensioner. P.S. So bloomin' lonely. And so on North West Tonight, the annual Britain in Bloom competiton reaches the Fylde Coast. And here in the studio we have our very own Blackpool in Bloom finalist for the year 1575 Ms Isabella Whitney walking us through her unique creation A Sweet Nosegay: One Hundred Philosophical Flowers. Isabella, can you talk us through your creation? Yes good Sir, it would delight me much. This simple Nosegay matters but little except in the Sense that I, though whole in Body and in Mind but very weak in Purse doth hope to ameliorate through presenting this Arrangement of Stalk and Petal some steadfast-held Connexions regarding the nature, type and composition of the Relations between Flora and Idea. Good Gentles if you do find your Cheeks fat with Questions please do not disdain to hover over the mingled scents of my blooming Garden. Apprehend at once the buzzing Knots attracted to the rainbow Nectars many: Stoic Yellow, Platonic Purple; I urge you now to taste a Petal here and there; please take and eat the Fruit of this Tree; I believe you will find that Empiricism crunches a noisy Red. Next to my Sophistry Rockery behold a Plant uncategorisable so I am forced to make an Approximation not of our current Times: it doth befall me to call this Blue Raspberry Logic something of the Absurd.

Under a rickety Pier, made for Love
Silent as yielding Maids Consent
She with a charming Languishment
Permits his roving teenage hands to push up her dress
And stop, and say,
Fair lovely Maid, or if that Title be
Too binary for Nobler thee,
Permit a Pronoun worthy of Mercury:
And let me ascribe They to Thee.

Aurora hail, and all the thousand hues,
Which deck thy progress through satsuma blues:
The sun she dips, and wide extends her creamy glow,
On ev'ry ridge of sand the shadows flow –

EPILOGUE 175

I saw a Light –
It thrust its Beam
Across my Path –
My Path did swerve –
The Light did cut
Its way inside –
and cleft–
My blackened Heart –

Who that cares much to know the history of how woman, man (and those clever enough to have transcended gender) behave under the varying experiments of Time, has not dwelt, at least briefly, on the life of Saint Theresa, has not smiled with some gentleness at the thought of the little girl walking forth one morning hand-in-hand with her still smaller brother, to go and seek the brightly-coloured packets of milk-chocolate covered Penguins in the discount buckets by the tills in Iceland? Out they toddled from rugged Abingdon Street Market clutching white paper bags with a 20p mix, milk teeth engaged in masticating extra-large Jelly Strawberries, small tongues aching and fizzing from the skinrazing sour 5p Astro Belts. That child pilgrimage was a fit beginning. Theresa's socio-economic status demanded a downtrodden life: what were the heavy tomes of Victorian moralism to her? Her flame burned quietly, and, fed from within, never soared except for the times when she was able to internally reflect on the segmented world served up for her. She found her epos in the teenage friendships and breakups; the singing of pop songs and the serving of teas and coffees in the BHS cafe; and ultimately at the gates of motherhood, where she found herself before she was but four short of twenty.

And then, she thought, what an evening – unfresh as if issued to disenfranchised teenagers on a beach! This cooling viscous claret of an evening, thick with late summer melancholia, so different to the piping hot Saturdays she remembers from childhood. The tram shelters would be ringing with toddlers' shrieks and picnicking families would be chinking stubbies and passing round packets of No Frills sausage rolls and packets of Monster Munch and Space Invaders. Which ice-lolly from the ice cream van was the best? Fabs, Twisters, Calippos . . . O the acidic red strawberry casing of a Mivvi, contrasted with the pale cold cream inside! So quick to melt, such a risk of losing your last bite, the sinking sensation watching it falling straight off your wooden stick and onto the concrete – nooooo! – and yet now, entering the circular point with the emptying beach, the cafés closed, the tram shelters enshadowed with darkness, she fabulated and thus sprang forth the invisible and palimpsestic pinpoint marks of melted ice-lolly stains dotted all along the path. Imagine if they were all lit up as we stepped on them, like the Illuminations, just for a second, light-blobs on the concrete, just like illuminated splats of chewing gum on the pavement. There would be *thousands*.

A sea is to sky is to see is to sigh
To see is to sigh is to sea is to sky

So.

Green splinter peel painty bench. Piering. A cross. The moveable her eyes on.

Eye.
                    Wood eye.
Eye.
                    A wood.
Either gnaws.
                    The gnaws.
Its knot warm.
                    Yer knot wrong.
Either gnaws.
                    Eye.
Right enough.

Watch Trev and Ann eat sandwiches from foil drink coffee from flasks and we all watch the sun stoop low. A whole whale underground and a stoop to lift reach under it why never only ever do it when you really really need it through the whispered clouds what do we have? Only times of harsh clenching when this is not one of those and it is only when you are thrice times tired. Thrice times tired and full of rage.

    Twist your body in order to feel. Stretch your body in order to ground. Lift your body in order to love. Let it swell and overflow and oh. Interject if you must. Say the decent thing the decent thing say the decent thing. Interruptions and self-interceptions and self-thwarting. Never again never ever again. Going for people really going for people in the repetition you understand what I mean by really *going* for people it does not need to be hard it can be easy just put your head in the stream. And really in the tradition you know in the tradition you know normally in the tradition we go here then we put this here and normally when we go out we just head out and when you go for people I mean really *go* for people I was really going to go for them I mean really *go* for them all of them in one go one two three quick swallows down.

To suck in the stomach I mean *really* suck in the stomach on your tiptoes firming the calf and sitting down pulling up the quadriceps and feeling them taut and feeling your torsion now that is love. Squirling down in your seat screwdrivering down into one point underneath you on this wooden bench now that is love lifting yourself up by your arms now that is love. Lifting the bucket and lending the bucket and not minding the horrorstained bucket now that is love. Pegging out my smalls now that is. Sticks under the pier and being high and dropping things and stones being quicker. Grabbing on suddenly without deciding now that is love.

Whirl up sea –
Screw down sun –
Cover us with your pools of lemonblue –

The tram with the rocket lights
Strobing its colours
Shooting up a black vein
The Real Northern Line
Fluorescent sunflowers towering over
Tower incandescent with spectral lights
Dirty rainbows arch and sing all about us
Whirl us up connecting us
Digital orgasming synaesthesis
Connect the body to the wire in the wall
Turn, and run straight into me
Livestreaming plastic paradise
Bassline generators squelch through mossy depths
We are dinosaurs kneeling and kissing the foot of we know not what
At the shrine of your gleaming exoskeleton

If the world was an egg you'd be my everything. As it stands, however, the world is vast and multiple, and you, dear Humpty, are a numpty.

I danced to the tune of the rose's musk
And squeezed fat theory from a rhino's tusk

At the foot of the tower our own shadows disappear as the feet of
thousands for whom I cannot speak and yet for whom I must speak
rising like a sea mist
shouting and dancing
there will be fire.

Esta puente, mi estalda. Esta puente, mi estalda.
This. Bridge. Called. My. Back.

But.

To give voice is to take space. I just can't do it. I can't speak for her
but I did hear her speak to me and she said yes, keep going, you can
never know the edges of this but to imagine it, to put yourself there,
to keep saying and to think of who you allow to speak you, you are
doing some of the work. When you stand at the top of the tower and
you think of Afrekete, when you say these names, when you build the
programmes and burst open the canons and unsettle the categories,
when you splice subjects and voices and words together, when you
give space where there was none, voice where there is none, you are
doing some of the work and the work is nowhere near done so just
keep going.

Ok.

ENTER LUCE AND HÉLÈNE

LUCE:	I am a slab of raw fish recently skinned.
HÉLÈNE:	You are the empty cipher, the tool I use to carve myself out of myself.
LUCE:	The slab splits to a maw, hungry for a hurt, as nourishment, as punishment.
HÉLÈNE:	The maw grins wide and splits open, leading to a cavern leading to a tunnel leading to infinite caves.
LUCE:	The caves are only there for you, but you are nothing. You are infinitely replaceable.
HÉLÈNE:	All the maw seeks is a mirror of you, an echo of you, a gulp of you, a gust of you, to fill the sails, the wallpaper wettings of these insides.

LUCE: Maw, you were not me. Your unflappable flesh was solid with no windows. When I cut holes in myself, burned myself, ejected myself, sliced myself and spliced myself, your steady decibels dripped their pragmatism into my ear, forming a yellow pool in the centre.

HÉLÈNE: No longer young but still raw, now more of a puzzle, the gaping yawn from whence I came, now there I crane, eternal winged propulsion into you, not you, but my own uncertain shadow.

LUCE: Desire is the fierce pull of someone else's desire.

HÉLÈNE: The heart hits a complex echo internally, again, again.

LUCE: It has been stretched, but those who stretch it will never be its occupants.

HÉLÈNE: Each time it happens, a new cavern opens.

LUCE: Why does impossibility breed desire.

HÉLÈNE: Because it is safer. Because it is safer. I don't want to kiss you because I want to imagine forever what it is like to kiss you.

LUCE: When it hardens and when we harden. Does hardening preserve or kill.

HÉLÈNE: When I paint you onto my nails and it hardens. When I smear youshadow across my lids and it hardens.

LUCE: When I smear feelings across the wall and they harden. When water dilutes. When blood hardens.

HÉLÈNE: When precipices extend. When time hardens. When it plays itself out in seconds.

LUCE: When the first utterance betrays the painful end.

HÉLÈNE: When eyes turn to knives then burning bushes then cooling mosses. It softens and it hardens.

LUCE: We soften and we harden.

HÉLÈNE: When it is not clear that a feeling is a feeling or an echo of a feeling.

LUCE: A reeling.

HÉLÈNE: When the object is obscured from reach leaving a feeling. When sleep is obscured from reach leaving a shadow. When touch is obscured from reach leaving an imprint.

LUCE: When taste is untasted burning a hole where the tongue should be.

HÉLÈNE: When cans of worms are left unopened.

LUCE: When holes are drilled into cans to let the worms breathe.

ENTER JULIA

JULIA: When a body is a vector.
LUCE: When the vector is youwards.
HÉLÈNE: When darts hit fences.
LUCE: Darts and arrows hit fences purple juice spilling youwards.
JULIA: Purple blooming violet love juice dripping youwards.
HÉLÈNE: Youwards as the mobile real.
LUCE: Fences.
HÉLÈNE: Lust concrete.
JULIA: Stuck fast and close but apart.
HÉLÈNE: Close but apart.
LUCE: Trapped close not touching not quite touching but close not yet touching but close and apart.
JULIA: What is a gap.
HÉLÈNE: Agape.

ENTER KATHY

KATHY: Eyedrowning. It doesn't matter whether I was a student of Professor Jakobson or not. If I was teaching defamiliarisation this is what I would say.

To conjugate strangeness:
I bite.
The woman was bitten.
The man took.
The woman held.
It gleamed.
It bent down.
They shifted.
They knew.
They tried.
They want.
They purpled.
They dripped.
They are about to fuck.

EPILOGUE

EXEUNT KATHY STAGE RIGHT
EXEUNT LUCE, HÉLÈNE AND JULIA
STAGE LEFT,
SIXFOLD ARMSLINKED.
A KNOT.
TOGETHER THEY ALL GO AND GET TATTOOS
OF
A TRIFOLD ROSE WREATH:
INKSISTERS,
BLOODSISTERS,
SPAWN OF BORROMEA

Composed upon Westminster Bridge
[here we were kettled]
later--- London s'burning
from *feral* fires: mouth *feral*:: a word? really?
                                      shops / wounds / buses / shells
they/we are/burst through jagged entrance holes
                                      - bleeding Meccas glitter -
//flatscreen tellys rrrrripped//   off of off /
                      bookies walls /
      bloodspattered gleaming lifted NIKES
                                     footlockers new cut t t t teeth
ritual hysteria
(en)(over)genders division   splitapart headwoundz
                                  spilt civil bloodmoney
                                  spit civil mouths unclean

scum rot in hell

And have YOU catered for the end?

        O but for and from
        our trans*sisters
        a new trans*istor trans*mitter
        right here
        in the race
                for   t'top   of   t'Tower

V
e
r
t
i
g
o
It
hap-
pens
the first time
on
the
Pepsi Max
Big One chugging
up queasy from deep-fried
pier doughnut grease
high ponytail facelift
skull crisped by hairspray
doused head to toe
in Impulse Zen on
the human conveyor belt
strapped loosely in pairs by frayed black
straps next to Lee Jenkins six inches shorter
than you chugging and chinking slows and stops
one silent second and allllll is blue 360 blue lazy
susan whirligig blue blue dish blue plate sky blue
tablecloth sea blue crazy blue strings of streets splay
out veining the land rolling in an upside-down bucket
of blue unending horizonless and later this tropical
Blackpool blue will come back and flood you a gutful
of Irish Sea flatness all depth and no depth upturning your
insides holding your breath twelve floors upin a glass-fronted
library a bloat of concepts knifed through by the fear that the
words and the organs you are holding in will eject themselves
if you breathe out again
one second is enough to show that
one second is enough
    I open myself

                  Just one Apple-flavoured Cogito is enough to give
                  me the iBoke.
                          Astride Central Pier   O your crooked spine
            soft furnishings (your rotten gut)   woven by children
                  fibres on the lungs   this string
                  your faux brickies boots   spun in
                  Lancashire mills
built for American tourists (full working machinery)   all nice and ready
          (to sever a limb)
              Look look looksee we took the economy flight
        One million children into one fuckermouth HEX
                Our conferencecounselling consciencecancelling bosefones HEX
                            David Cameron
sunburnt and ticked off
                  in economy
no legroom here you see
They took the economy seats you see
      a gesture of deigning
red pigface shining   one million needles into your eardrums
one million screams to pierce as you turn up the volume
turn down the screaming masses
on the austerity flight

      She had me. We can all say. She had me. Monstrous birth. Except the
        first. To some. What is birthing. Birthing when tis wrong.
        No shapes left to fit. Other dimensions. A voice is birthing.
        Rendered material. Render it. Nothing but your own ragged
renderings. Your own shorn sharpenings. My voice as pencil.
Sharpened and the bits you discard. Voiced detritus. If 'tis a thing.
A thing 'tis. Prove through doing. Leave to rise. Leave to prove.
                Play to something.   Ragged reroutings.

Delivered

Fuck though it hurts so. Words can't get out. Knowing though
now somehow I will. Looking ahead knowing not knowing. Pre-
tending not knowing. Dumb words. Words like grunts is all. We
bond when we moan about shit. Shit stuff that's happened. stuff
to look forward. Stuff to hold like real stuff only in words. Only
good when there's stuff to hold onto. No good talking when
nothing. That empty feeling. Begin with a moan. Know where
you are with a moan. Fuck sake. Takin the fuckin piss. It's takin
the piss. Whatever it is it's takin. It always starts like that. Begin
with a no. not even a saying. Just shaking the head. Keeping
uptight. Don't be daft you've gone soft. Show
them who's boss. Whoever's boss it ain't me. That's
smart that. It were mega. But what did you feel like
when it were happenin? Nuffin. Nowt. I en't seen
nuffin muffin. See ye later. Big moment whatever.
Didn't even remember.

She clocks off at ten weary down to the core of her
everything sore in her wanting to find all the answer to
questions that fray at her headachey brain like:
is there a method in this madness?
That flame – don't stop it, don't let it go out,
as if you had a choice, hearing the squeak
in the rappers' voice on the radio, the hysteria
in times when those who think they are cleverest
are not the cleverest, the best lack all conviction,
the worst full of passionate intensity,
so real it hurts, and someone tells you
everything is true and you think you know
what they mean.

⊕

        dog-eat-dog logic don't seem so different
          and yet all these incendiary metaphors
           work both ways. In the small shards between
    hurts, queer nihilist and Christian conservative nod
      awkward streaks of understanding on a bench in
            a park amongst shrieks of youth.
                  Everything is true.

   I am red, I am white, I am dying, I am sick, I am fairer
    than thee, I am the shape of your argument, the stamen
      to penetrate, the pistil to protrude, the lips to linger,
figure for your form, emblem for your fulsome wantonness,
the red that stains, the sharp that pricks, the mouth that bites,
  the vulva that engorges, the petals that fall, the web of
   the loom, the clouds that bloom and burst above you,
           the fallen carpet beneath you

Little pistils of creativity. From nonsense to the proper name. Idea germination space. App incubator. Brandpod. Onwards and upwards. We counter austerity with growth. A little pruning never did any harm. What's in a name? The name of your university must be included in every paragraph of the handbook. Brands are propagated through repetition. As roses through watering. What's in a name? Institution is such a clinical word. We are merely vehicles. Fertilise them. Only fragments, no whole texts allowed. Plastic straws suck concepts and plaster them onto the surface of the world. This space is for marketable learning, not a factory for ideas. Roll out the astro turf and sprinkle your slug pellets. Semantics is nothing but a word, and words are things we stumble over. Try working to

⊕

ATMs on campus? Statistical correlations indicate the strength of the relationship between things, but there is an unequal distribution of power within each relationship.
Meet tower with tower.

Two towers,
both alike in geometry,
and in between,
a stretched and twittering net of puckered air.
The queerfeministwhitewesterner cannot sleep,
reads of Circe through the night,
and drifts to a greening glade.
Scotland or Surrey or Sussex or the South Downs,
no movement, just the hum of silence,
then just the tiniest twitter, tremble,
one, two, three leaves shiver
in a demonstration of agency.

This stillness has a quality
it drips and pours right into me
it filters, slanted, through the trees,
in lights and shadows, softly.
The fizz and zing of scalp and spine,
hurt of cold and bloom of blood,
and all along the senseless edge
our bones are singing, shrilly.
Always so bright, so bright and so wild.
She. Stills. Leaves.

Get Your Perfect Boy Brow With This Boy Brow Brush. Secure

Yeah but still now I would like to be able to say no ta thanks but no thanks no I would prefer not to actually not right now and also go back and say no to all the times back then no to all the times when I wanted to say no and couldn't

say it aged sixteen throwing up drunk locked in bathrooms with lads in party houses when mums and dads go out and lads somehow get hold of cases or Fosters and Carling and girls get bottles of Hooch or WKD or Bacardi Breezers

or we just all go for it with bottles of Glens vodka and bongs in the garden and dodgy white powders with Dreamscape rave compilations and CrazySexyCool and Spice Girls and Usher and Born Slippy over and over and over again lager

lager lager lager downing shots of vodka out the cap and things go faster and faster and faster like a merry-go-round reeling type feeling and I'm so invincible

I can do anything supercharged with booze and fags and drugs and oestrogen in my bloodstream hardens me like clear nail varnish I go outside to the skate park across the road with some of the lads and throw myself down the half pipe from top to bottom no skateboard just my rolling body because I can't feel any pain aged sixteen getting drunk and fucking and

getting knocked up by mistake

and even now aged nineteen not like that time Nicola Rogers in the changing rooms felt my gymnast biceps to see how hard they were and held on just a bit too long but I didn't stop her even though she had short spiky hair her jawline was so firm and her mouth so determined she didn't really have any friends but in that changing room after PE that time touching my arms and legs there was a weird spark like a weird twisty eye beam coming from her eyes and going right into me when she looked at me saying *you're hard as fuckin nails* and me just laughing gormlessly not knowing the right thing to say when the weird girl in your PE class touches your body and looks at you funny that was the only time I really felt the feeling like proper throbbing right in the centre of the clit where he never knows to touch

Bibliography

Acker, K. (1997) *Eurydice in the Underworld*. London: Arcadia.

Ahmed, S. (2000) *Strange Encounters: Embodied Others in Post-Coloniality*. Oxford: Routledge.

Ahmed, S. (2004) *The Cultural Politics of Emotion*, 2nd edn. Edinburgh: Edinburgh University Press.

Ahmed, S. (2006) *Queer Phenomenology*. Durham, NC and London: Duke University Press.

Ahmed, S. (2008) 'Imaginary prohibitions: some preliminary remarks on the founding gestures of the "New Materialism"', *European Journal of Women's Studies*, 15 (1): 23–39.

Ahmed, S. (2010) *The Promise of Happiness*. Durham, NC and London: Duke University Press.

Alabanza, T. (2017) *Before I Step Outside (You Love Me)*, Chapbook. Available at <www.travisalabanza.co.uk>

Alabanza, T. (2018) *Burgerz*. London: Oberon.

Alaimo, S. (2010) *Bodily Natures: Science, Environment and the Material Self*. Bloomington and Indianapolis: Indiana University Press.

Alaimo, S. and Hekman, S. (eds) (2008) *Material Feminisms*. Bloomington and Indianapolis: Indiana University Press.

Amen, N. A. (1989) *The Ankh: African Origin of Electromagnetism*. Brooklyn: A&B.

Anzieu, D. (1989) *The Skin-Ego*. London and New York: Routledge

Artaud, A. (1988) [1940] Incomplete letter to Henri Parisot, in *Selected Writings*, ed. and trans. S. Sontag. Berkeley: University of California Press, p. 448.

Artaud, A. (1988) *Selected Writings*, ed. and trans. S. Sontag. Berkeley: University of California Press.

Askin, R. (2016) *Narrative and Becoming*. Edinburgh: Edinburgh University Press.

Askin, R., Beckman, F. and Rudrum, D. (eds) (2019) *New Directions in Philosophy and Literature*. Edinburgh: Edinburgh University Press.

Atwood, M. (1974) *You Are Happy*. Oxford: Oxford University Press.

Atwood, M. (2005) *The Penelopiad*. Edinburgh: Canongate.

Atwood, M. (2011) *In Other Worlds: SF and the Human Imagination*. London: Virago.
Auerbach, B. (1882) *Spinoza*, trans. E. Nicholson. New York: Henry Holt.
Austin, J. L. (1962) *How to Do Things with Words*. Oxford: Clarendon Press.
Avenassian, A. and Hennig, A. (2015) *Present Tense: A Poetics*, trans. Nils F. Schott with Daniel Hendrickson. London: Bloomsbury.
Avenassian, A. and Hennig, A. (2018) *Metanoia: A Speculative Ontology of Language, Thinking and the Brain*, trans. Nils. F. Schott. London: Bloomsbury.
Ayache, E. (2010) *The Blank Swan: The End of Probability*. Chichester: Wiley.
Ayache, E., Negarestani, R., Pool, M., Abreu, M. and Lyall, S. (2011) *The Medium of Contingency*. Falmouth: Urbanomic.
Babcock-Abrahams, B. (1975) '"A tolerated margin of mess": the trickster and his tales reconsidered', *Journal of the Folklore Institute*, 11 (3): 147–86.
Badiou, A. (2005) [1998] *Handbook of Inaesthetics*, trans. A. Toscano. Stanford: Stanford University Press.
Bahktin, M. (1990) [1924] *Art and Answerability: Early Philosophical Essays by M. M. Bakhtin*, ed. M. Holquist and V. Liapunov, trans. V. Liapunov and K. Brostrom. Austin: University of Texas Press.
Baker, J. and Bouillon, J. (1978) *Josephine*. London: W. H. Allen.
Ball, M. C. (2001) 'Old magic and new fury: the theaphony of Afrekete in Audre Lorde's "Tar Beach"', *NWSA Journal*, 13 (1): 61–85.
Barad, K. (2001) 'Re(con)figuring space, time, and matter', *Feminist Locations: Global and Local, Theory and Practice*, ed. M. DeKoven. New Brunswick, NJ: Rutgers University Press, pp. 75–109.
Barad, K. (2003) 'Posthumanist performativity: toward an understanding of how matter comes to matter', *Signs: Journal of Women in Culture and Society*, 28 (3): 801–31.
Barad, K. (2007) *Meeting the Universe Halfway: Quantum Physics and the Entanglement of Matter and Meaning*. Durham, NC and London: Duke University Press.
Barad, K. (2012) 'On touching – the inhuman that therefore I am' (v. 1.1), revision of article in *differences*, 23 (3): 206–23.
Barad, K. (2014) 'Diffracting diffraction: cutting together-apart', *Parallax*, 20 (3): 16–87.
Barad, K. (2015) 'Transmaterialities: trans*/matter/realities and queer political imaginings', *GLQ: A Journal of Lesbian and Gay Studies*, 21 (2–3): 388–422
Bataille, G. (1985) [1929] *Visions of Excess: Selected Writings 1927–1939*, trans. A. Stoekl with C. Lovitt and D. Leslie Jr. Minneapolis: University of Minnesota Press.

Bate, J., Levenson, J. L. and Mehl, D. (eds) (1996) *Shakespeare and the Twentieth Century: The Selected Proceedings of the International Shakespeare Association World Congress*. London: Associated University Presses.

Bauer, D. (2019) 'Alienation, freedom and the synthetic how', *Angelaki*, 24 (1): 106–17.

Beckett, S. (2001) [1929] 'Dante . . . Bruno . . . Vico . . . Joyce', in *Disjecta: Miscellaneous Writings and a Dramatic Fragment*, ed. R. Cohn. London: Calder, pp. 19–33.

Beckham, B. (1972) *Garvey Lives!* Providence: Brown University.

Beckman, Frida (ed.) (2011) *Deleuze and Sex*. Edinburgh: Edinburgh University Press.

Belton, Robert J. (1993) 'Androgyny: interview with Meret Oppenheim', in Mary Ann Caws, Rudolf Kuenzli and Gwen Raaberg (eds), *Surrealism and Women*. Cambridge, MA and London: MIT Press, pp. 64–76.

Benias, P. et al. (2018) 'Structure and distribution of an unrecognised interstitium in human tissues', *Scientific Reports*, 8: 49–7.

Benjamin, A. (2016) *Towards a Relational Ontology: Philosophy's Other Possibiliy*. New York: SUNY.

Bennett, T. (1989) [1972] *Formalism and Marxism*. London and New York: Routledge.

Bergson, H. (1974) [1932] *Two Sources of Morality and Religion*, trans. R. Audra, C. Brereton and W. Carter. Westport, CT: Greenwood Press.

Bergson, H. (2001) [1889] *Time and Free Will: An Essay on the Immediate Data of Consciousness*, trans. F. L. Pogson. Mineola, NY: Dover.

Bergson, H. (2002) *Key Writings*, ed. K. A. Pearson and J. Mullarkey. London and New York: Continuum.

Berlant, L. and M. Warner, M. (1998), 'Sex in public', *Critical Inquiry*, 24 (2), special issue *Intimacy*, pp. 547–66.

Binet, L. (2017) [2015] *The Seventh Function of Language*, trans. S. Taylor. London: Vintage.

Blake, C. (2017) 'Of Mirrors and Unicorns: Ficting in the *Lichtung* of Analytic Philosophies'. Forthcoming.

Blake, C. (2018) 'Orpheus and the vanishing note', *Angelaki*, 23 (3): 178–93.

Blanchot, M. (1981) *The Gaze of Orpheus and Other Literary Essays*, ed. P. Adams Sitney, trans. Lydia Davis. Barrytown, NY: Station Hill, pp. 99–104.

Blanchot, M. (1995) *The Work of Fire*, trans. C. Mendell. Stanford: Stanford University Press.

Bleich, D. (2013) *The Materiality of Language: Gender, Politics and the University*. Bloomington: Indiana University Press.

Bohr, N. (1958) *Atomic Physics and Human Knowledge*. New York: Wiley.

Borges, J. L. (1962) [1939] *Ficciones*. New York: Grove Press.

Borges, J. L. (1975) [1952] *Other Inquisitions, 1937–1952*. Austin: University of Texas Press.

Botting, F. (2019) 'Dark materialism: object, commodity, thing', in J. Hogle and R. Miles (eds), *The Gothic and Theory*. Edinburgh: Edinburgh University Press.

Bowers, S. R. (1990) 'Medusa and the female gaze', *National Women's Studies Association Journal*, 2 (2): 217–35 <http://www.jstor.org/stable/4316018> (last accessed 15 April 2019).

Brah, A. and Phoenix, A. (2004) 'Ain't I a woman? Revisiting intersectionality', *Journal of International Women's Studies*, 5 (3): Feminist Challenges: Crossing Boundaries, 75–86, available at <http://vc.bridgew.edu/jiws/vol5/iss3/8> (last accessed 30 October 2018).

Braidotti, R. (2002) *Metamorphoses: Towards a Materialist Theory of Becoming*. Cambridge: Polity.

Braidotti, R. (2006) *Transpositions: On Nomadic Ethics*. Cambridge: Polity.

Braidotti, R. (2013) *The Posthuman*. Cambridge: Polity.

Braidotti, R. and Bignall, S. (eds) (2019) *Posthuman Ecologies: Complexity and Process after Deleuze*. London and New York: Rowman & Littlefield.

Braidotti, R. and Hlavajova, M. (eds) (2018) *Posthuman Glossary*. London and New York: Bloomsbury.

Braidotti, R. and Regan, L. (2017) 'Our times are always out of joint: feminist relational ethics in and of the world today: an interview with Rosi Braidotti', *Women: A Cultural Review*, 28 (3): 171–92.

Bramble, J. (2015) *Modernism and the Occult*. New York: Palgrave Macmillan.

Brecht, B. and Bentley, E. (1961) 'On Chinese acting', *Tulane Drama Review*, 6 (7): 130–6.

Brewster, D. (ed.) (1840) *Letters of Euler on Different Subjects in Natural Philosophy*, Vol. II. New York: Harper & Brothers.

Bruzelius, M. (1998) 'H.D. and Eurydice', *Twentieth Century Literature*, 44 (4): 447–63.

Bühlmann, V. (2018) 'Invariance', in R. Braidotti and M. Hlavajova (eds), *Posthuman Glossary*. London and New York: Bloomsbury, pp. 212–16.

Bühlmann, V., Colman, F. and van der Tuin, I. (2017) 'Introduction to New Materialist genealogies', *Minnesota Review*, 88: Special Focus: New Materialist Genealogies, pp. 47–58.

Burke, P. (2000) *A Social History of Knowledge: From Gutenberg to Diderot*. Cambridge: Polity.

Butler, J. (1993) *Bodies that Matter: On the Discursive Limits of 'Sex'*. London and New York: Routledge.

Butler, J. (1997) *Excitable Speech: A Politics of the Performative*. New York and London: Routledge.

Butler, O. (1998) 'An alternative universe', interview in *LA Times*, October 1998. Available at <http://articles.latimes.com/1998/oct/18/magazine/tm-33581> (last accessed 28 May 2018).

Byrne, Charlotte (ed.) (1998) *Lewis Carroll*. London: British Council.

Byrne, D. (2006) *Arboretum*. San Francisco: McSweeney's.

CCRU (2001) 'Lemurian Time War', in D. Schniederman and P. Walsh (eds), *Retaking the Universe: William S. Burroughs in the Age of Globalization*. London: Pluto, pp. 274–91.

Calvino, I. (2013) [1991] *Why Read the Classics?* trans. Martin McLaughlin. London: Penguin.

Carello, C. and Turvey, M. T. (2017) 'Useful dimensions of haptic perception: 50 years after *The Senses Considered as Perceptual Systems*', *Ecological Psychology*, 29 (2): 95–121.

Carrington, L. (1975) *The Oval Lady, Other Stories: Six Surreal Stories*. Santa Barbara: Capra.

Carrington, L. (1939) [2017] 'The Debutante', in *The Oval Lady, Other Stories: Six Surreal Stories*. Santa Barbara: Capra, pp. 21–6.

Carroll, L. (2001) [1865, 1871] *Alice's Adventures in Wonderland and Through the Looking-Glass*. Ware: Wordsworth.

Carter, A. (2002) *American Ghosts and Old World Wonders*. New York: Vintage.

Cavarero, A. (1995) *In Spite of Plato: A Feminist Rewriting of Ancient Philosophy*, trans. S. Anderlini-D'Onofrio and Á. O'Healy. Oxford: Blackwell.

Caws, M., Kuenzli, R. and Raaberg, G. (eds) (1993) *Surrealism and Women*. Cambridge, MA and London: MIT Press.

Césaire, A. (1986) [1949] *Lost Body (Corps Perdu)*, trans. C. Eshleman and A. Smith. New York: George Brazilier.

Chen, M. Y. (2012) *Animacies: Biopolitics, Racial Mattering, and Queer Affect*. Durham, NC and London: Duke University Press.

Cheng, A. (2010) *Second Skin: Josephine Baker and the Modern Surface*. Oxford: Oxford University Press.

Chomsky, N. (1957) *Syntactic Structures*. The Hague: Mouton.

Cixous, H. (1975) 'At Circe's, or the self-opener', trans. Carol Bové, *boundary*, 3 (2): 387–97.

Cixous, H. (1976) 'The Laugh of the Medusa', trans. Keith Cohen and Paula Cohen, *Signs*, 1 (4): 875–93.

Clarke, A. (2016) *Author of the BLANK Swan*. London: Banner Repeater.

Coase, H. (2018) *Callisto: A Queer Epic*. London: Oberon.

Colebrook, C. (2008) 'On not becoming man: the materialist politics of unactualised potential', in S. Alaimo and S. Hekman (eds), *Material Feminisms*. Bloomington and Indianapolis: Indiana University Press, pp. 52–84.

Colebrook, C. (2011) 'Matter without Bodies', *Derrida Today*, 4 (1): 1–20.
Connor, R. et al. (1997) *Cassell's Encyclopedia of Queer Myth, Symbol and Spirit*. London and New York: Cassell.
Connor, S. (2004) *The Book of Skin*. London: Reaktion Books.
Cook, E. (2001) *Achilles*. New York: Picador.
Crenshaw, K. (1989) 'Demarginalizing the intersection of race and sex: a black feminist critique of antidiscrimination doctrine, feminist theory and antiracist politics', *University of Chicago Legal Forum*, 1 (8): 139–67.
Cuboniks, L. (2018) *The Xenofeminist Manifesto: A Politics for Alienation*. London: Verso.
Curtis, J. (1976) 'Bergson and Russian formalism', *Comparative Literature*, 28 (2): 109–21.
Cytowic, R. (2018) *Synaesthesia*. Cambridge, MA: MIT Press.
Daly, M. (1979) [1978] *Gyn/Ecology: The Metaethics of Radical Feminism*. London: Women's Press.
Daly, M. and Caputi, J. (1988) [1987] *Websters' First New Intergalactic Wickedary of the English Language*. London: Women's Press.
Davis, Richard Brian (ed.) (2010) *Alice and Wonderland and Philosophy: Curiouser and Curiouse*. Hoboken, NJ: Wiley.
de Freitas, E. (2017) 'The laboratory of speculative sociology', in V. Bühlmann, F. Colman and I. van der Tuin (eds), *Minnesota Review NM Special Focus: Introduction to New Materialist Genealogies: New Materialisms, Novel Mentalities, Quantum Literacy*, 88: 116–26.
de Freitas, E. (2019) 'Love of learning', in R. Braidotti and S. Bignall (eds), *Posthuman Ecologies: Complexity and Process after Deleuze*. London and New York: Rowman & Littlefield.
DeKoven, M. (ed.) (2001) *Feminist Locations: Global and Local, Theory and Practice*. New Brunswick, NJ: Rutgers University Press.
Deleuze, G. (1998) [1993] *Essays Critical and Clinical*, trans. D. Smith and M. Greco. London and New York: Verso.
Deleuze, G. (2004a) [1968] *Difference and Repetition*, trans. P. Patton. London and New York: Continuum.
Deleuze, G. (2004b) [1969] *The Logic of Sense*, trans. M. Lester and C. Stivale, ed. C. Boundas. London and New York: Continuum.
Deleuze, G. (2006) [1988] *The Fold: Leibniz and the Baroque*, trans. T. Conley. London: Continuum.
Deleuze, G. (2010) [1962] *Nietsche and Philosophy*, trans. H. Tomlinson. London: Continuum.
Deleuze, G. and Guattari, F. (1986) *Nomadology: The War Machine*, trans. B. Massumi. New York: Columbia University Press.

Deleuze, G. and Guattari, F. (1994) [1991] *What Is Philosophy?* trans. G. Burchell and H. Tomlinson. London and New York: Verso.

Deleuze, G. and Guattari, F. (2004a) [1972] *Anti-Oedipus*, trans. R. Hurley, M. Seem and H. Lane. London and New York: Continuum.

Deleuze, G. and Guattari, F. (2004b) [1980] *A Thousand Plateaus: Capitalism and Schizophrenia*, trans. B. Massumi. London and New York: Continuum.

Derrida, J. (1997) *Of Grammatology*, trans. G. C. Spivak. Baltimore and London: Johns Hopkins University Press.

di Noto, P. M., Newman, L., Wall, S. and Einstein, G. (2012) 'The *hermun*culus: what is known about the representation of the female body in the brain?' *Cerebral Cortex* (April). DOI: 10.1093/cercor/bhs005.

Dickinson, E. (2009) [1868] *The Pocket Emily Dickinson*, ed. Brenda Hillman. Boston and London: Shambhala.

Dinshaw, C. (1995) 'Chaucer's queer touches / a queer touches Chaucer', *Exemplaria*, 7 (1): 75–92. DOI: 10.1179/exm.1995.7.1.75 (last accessed 15 April 2019).

Dolphijn, R. (ed.) (2018) *Michel Serres and the Crisis of the Contemporary*. London: Bloomsbury.

Dolphijn, R. and I van der Tuin (eds) (2012) *New Materialism: Interviews and Cartographies*. London: Open Humanities Press.

Donne, J. (1994) *The Collected Poems*, ed. Roy Booth. Ware: Wordsworth.

Doolittle, H. (H.D.) (1988) *Selected Poems*, ed. Louis H. Martz. New York: New Directions.

Dosse, F. (1997) [1991] *History of Structuralism. Vol. 1: The Rising Sign 1945–1966*, trans. D. Glassman. Minneapolis and London: University of Minnesota Press.

Driscoll, C., Garland, C. and Hickey-Moody, A. (2011) '(Hetero)sexing the child: Hans, Alice and the repressive hypothesis', in F. Beckman (ed.), *Deleuze and Sex*. Edinburgh: Edinburgh University Press, pp. 117–34.

Du Bois, W. E. B. (2007) [1903] *The Souls of Black Folk*. Oxford: Oxford University Press.

Eades, Q. (2017) *Rallying*. Perth: UWA Publishing.

Eco, U. (2009) [1988] *The Infinity of Lists*, trans. Alastair McEwen. London: MacLehose Press.

Ehrmann, J. (1971) 'The death of literature', trans. A. James Arnold. *New Literary History*, 3 (1): Modernism and Postmodernism: Inquiries, Reflections and Speculations, pp. 31–47.

Ellis, M. and N. O'Connor (2010) *Questioning Identities: Philosophy in Psychoanalytic Practice*. London: Karnac.

Emirbayer, Mustafa (1997) 'Manifesto for a relational sociology', *American Journal of Sociology*, 103 (2): 281–317 <http://www.jstor.org/stable/10.1086/231209> (last accessed 21 January 2017).

Eshun, K. (1998) *More Brilliant than the Sun: Adventures in Sonic Fiction*. London: Quartet Books.

Eshun, K. (2003) 'Further considerations on Afrofuturism', *CR: The New Centennial Review*, 3 (2): 287–302.

Fernandes, L. (1997) *Producing Workers: The Politics of Gender, Class, and Culture in the Calcutta Jute Mills*. Philadelphia: University of Pennsylvania Press.

Feuerbach, L. (2008) [1841] *Essence of Christianity*, trans. G. Eliot. Walnut: MSAC Philosophy Group.

Feynman, R. (1995) *QED: The Strange Theory of Light and Matter*. Princeton: Princeton University Press.

Firtich, N. (2004) 'Worldbackwards: Lewis Carroll, Aleksei Kruchenykh and Russian Alogism', *Slavic and East European Journal*, 48 (4): 593–606 <https://www.jstor.stable/3648814> (last accessed 6 June 2018).

Fletcher, A. (2016) *The Topological Imagination: Spheres, Edges, and Islands*. Cambridge, MA: Harvard University Press.

Foley, J. (2017) 'Word the World Better', postcard, part of *Engineering Fictions* box set of scores. Dublin: CONNECT <www.engineeringfictions.wordpress.com>

Forslid, T. and Ohlsson, A. (2010) 'Introduction: literary public spheres', *Culture Unbound*, 2: 431–4. Linköping: Linköping University Electronic Press <http://www.cultureunbound.ep.liu.se> (last accessed 21 March 2018).

Foucault, M. (1988) [1984] *The History of Sexuality, Vol. 3: The Care of the Self*, trans. Robert Hurley. New York: Vintage Books.

Foucault, M. (2005) [1966] *The Order of Things: An Archaeology of the Human Sciences*. London and New York: Routledge.

Franssen, M. (1991) 'The ocular harpsichord of Louis-Bertrand Castel: the science and aesthetics of an eighteenth-century cause-célèbre', *Tractrix*, 3: 15–77.

Fraser, N. (1990) 'Rethinking the public sphere: a contribution to the critique of actually existing democracy', *Social Text*, 25/26: 56–80.

Freeland, C. (1994) 'Nourishing speculation: a feminist reading of Aristotelian science', in B. On (ed.), *Engendering Origins: Critical Feminist Readings in Plato and Aristotle*. Albany: SUNY Press.

Freeland, C. (ed.) (1998) *Feminist Interpretations of Aristotle*. State College: Pennsylvania State University Press.

Furman, E. (2018) *Lou Reed's Transformer (33 1/3)*. London: Bloomsbury.

Gardner, C. (2014) 'Transversality, deterritorialization, and the A.O.C. – constructing lines of flight from flights of wine', *Contemporary French and Francophone Studies*, 18 (2): 142–9. DOI: 10.1080/17409292.2014.900923 (last accessed 5 June 2018).

Gardner, C. and P. MacCormack (eds) (2018) *Ecosophical Aesthetics*. London and New York: Bloomsbury.

Gardner, M. (1999) *The Annotated Alice: The Definitive Edition*. New York and London: Norton.

Gass, W. H. (1979) *The World with the Word*. New York: Alfred A. Knopf.

Gatens, M. (1991) *Feminism and Philosophy: Perspectives on Difference and Equality*. Bloomington and Indianapolis: Indiana University Press.

Gatens, M. (2009) 'The art and philosophy of George Eliot', *Philosophy and Literature*, 33 (1): 73–80. DOI: 10.1353/phl.0.0037 (last accessed 21 February 2019).

Gatens, M. (2013) 'Cloud-borne angels, prophets and the old woman's flowerpot: reading George Eliot's realism alongside Spinoza's beings of the imagination', *Australian Literary Studies*, 28 (3): 1–14. DOI: 10.20314/als.a38bcb13ed (last accessed 25 January 2017).

Gatens, M. and Douglas, S. (2011) 'Revisiting the continental shelf: Moira Gatens on law, religion, and human rights in Eliot, Feuerbach, and Spinoza', *Feminist Legal Studies*, 19 (1): 75–82. DOI: 10.1007/s10691-011-9167-4 (last accessed 21 February 2019).

Geerts, E. et al. (2018) 'Superdiversity: a critical intersectional investigation', *Tijdschrift voor Genderstudies*, 21 (1): 1–5. DOI: 10.5117/TVGN2018.1.GEER (last accessed 7 July 2018).

Germanà, M. and Horton, E. (eds) (2013) *Ali Smith: Contemporary Critical Perspectives*. London: Bloomsbury

Gibbens, S. (2018) 'New human "organ" was hiding in plain sight', *National Geographic* <http://news.nationalgeographic.com/2018/03/interstitium-fluid-cells-organ-found-cancer-spd/> (last accessed 9 April 2019).

Gibson, J. (1966) *The Senses Considered as Perceptual Systems*. Boston, MA: Houghton Mifflin.

Glover-Kind, J. (2018) [1907] 'Oh I do like to be beside the seaside', in *Poems by the Sea*, ed. B. Moses. New York: Windmill Books.

Godfrey-Smith, P. (2016) *Other Minds: The Octopus, the Sea, and the Deep Origins of Consciousness*. New York: Farrar, Strauss & Giroux.

Goethe, J. W. von (1967) [1810] *Theory of Colours*, trans. C. Eastlake. London: Frank Cass.

Gorman, W. (1969) *Body Image and the Image of the Brain*. St Louis: W. H. Green.

Gould, S. J. (2006) [1981] *The Mismeasure of Man*. New York and London: Norton.

Grandy, D. (2010) *Everyday Quantum Reality*. Bloomington: Indiana University Press.

Greenstine, A. and Johnson, R. (eds) (2017) *Contemporary Encounters with Ancient Metaphysics*. Edinburgh: Edinburgh University Press.

Griffin, C. (2017) 'George Eliot's Feuerbach: senses, sympathy, omniscience, and secularism', *ELH*, 84 (2): 475–502. DOI:1353/elh.2017.0019 (last accessed 10 March 2020).

Grosz, E. (1994) *Volatile Bodies: Towards a Corporeal Feminism*. Bloomington and Indianapolis: Indiana University Press.

Grosz, E. (1995) *Space, Time and Perversion: Essays in the Politics of Bodies*. New York and London: Routledge.

Grosz, E. (2005) *Time Travels: Feminism, Nature, Power*. Durham, NC: Duke University Press.

Grosz, E. (2011) *Becoming Undone: Darwinian Reflections on Life, Politics, and Art*. Durham, NC and London: Duke University Press.

Guarino, N. (ed.) (1998) *Formal Ontology in Information Systems*. Amsterdam: IOS Press.

Gunkel, H., Hameed, A. and O'Sullivan, S. (eds) (2017) *Futures and Fictions*. London: Repeater.

Halberstam, J. (2018) *Trans*: A Quick and Quirky Account of Gender Variance*. Oakland: University of California Press.

Haraway, D. (1988) 'Situated knowledges: the science question in feminism and the privilege of partial perspective', *Feminist Studies*, 14 (3): 575–99.

Haraway, D. (1992) 'The Promises of Monsters: A Regenerative Politics for Inappropriate/d Others', in D. Haraway (2004) *The Haraway Reader*. London and New York: Routledge, pp. 63–124.

Haraway, D. (2003) *The Companion Species Manifesto: Dogs, People, and Significant Otherness*. Chicago: Prickly Paradigm Press.

Haraway, D. (2004), *The Haraway Reader*, London and New York: Routledge.

Haraway, D. (2013) 'S.F. science fiction, speculative fabulation, string figures, so far', *Ada: A Journal of Gender, New Media, and Technology*, 3. DOI:10:7264/N3KH0K81 (last accessed 23 June 2018).

Haraway, D. (2016) *Staying with the Trouble: Making Kin in the Chthulucene*. Durham, NC and London: Duke University Press.

Hayward, E. (2010a) 'Spider city sex', *Women & Performance: A Journal of Feminist Theory*, 20 (3): 225–51. DOI: 10.1080/0740770X.2010.529244 (last accessed 14 August 2018).

Hayward, E. (2010b) 'Fingeryeyes: impressions of cup corals', *Cultural Anthropology*, 25 (4): 577–99 (last accessed 8 August 2018).

Heidegger, M. (1967) *What Is a Thing?* trans. W. B. Barton and V. Deutsch. Chicago: Gateway.

Heidegger, M. (1971a) 'The Origin of the Work of Art', in M. Heidegger, *Poetry, Language, Thought*, trans. A. Hofstader. New York: Harper & Row, pp. 15–87.

Heidegger, M. (1971b) *Poetry, Language, Thought*, trans. A. Hofstader. New York: Harper & Row.

Henderson, C. (2013) *The Book of Barely Imagined Beings: A 21st Century Bestiary*. Chicago and London: University of Chicago Press.

Henriques, J. (2012) 'Hearing things and dancing numbers: embodying transformation, topology at Tate Modern', *Theory, Culture and Society*, 29 (45): 334–42. DOI: 10.1177/0263276412450468 (last accessed 2 November 2019).

Hogle, J. and Miles, R. (eds) (forthcoming) *Gothic and Theory*. Edinburgh: Edinburgh University Press.

hooks, b. (2015) [1981] *Black Women and Feminism*. London and New York: Routledge.

Huang, M. (2017) 'Rematerializations of race', *Lateral: Journal of the Cultural Studies Association*, 6 (1). DOI: 10.25158/L6.1.11 (last accessed 8 April 2019).

Hughes, C. (2011) 'Salivary identities: the matter of affect', *Subjectivity*, 4 (4): 413–33. DOI: 10.1057/sub.2011.17 (last accessed 28 February 2019).

Irigaray, L. (2002) [1985] *To Speak Is Never Neutral*, trans. G. Schwab. London and New York: Continuum.

Jacques, J. (2014) 'Juliet Jacques on Hélène Cixous: the Medusa gets the last laugh', *New Statesman*, 13 May <http://www.newstatesman.com/juliet-jacques/2014/05/juliet-jacques-h-l-ne-cixous-medusa-gets-last-laugh> (last accessed 23 January 2017).

Jakobson, R. (1971) *Selected Writings II: Word and Language*. The Hague: Mouton.

Jakobson, R. (1981) *Selected Writings III: Poetry of Grammar and Grammar of Poetry*. The Hague: Mouton.

Jakobson, R. (1985a) *Selected Writings VII: Contributions to Comparative Mythology. Studies in Linguistics and Philology, 1972–1982*. The Hague: Mouton.

Jakobson, R. (1985b) *Verbal Art, Verbal Sign, Verbal Time*, ed. K. Pomorska and S. Rudy. Oxford: Blackwell.

Jakobson, R. (1997) *My Futurist Years*, ed. B. Jangfeldt, trans. S. Rudy. Cambridge, MA and London: Harvard University Press.

Jakobson, R. and Waugh, L. (2002) [1979] *The Sound Shape of Language*. Berlin and New York: Mouton de Gruyter.

Jameson, F. (1972) *The Prison-House of Language: A Critical Account of Structuralism and Russian Formalism*. Princeton and Chichester: Princeton University Press.

Jameson, F. (1998) *Brecht and Method*. London: Verso.

Jeppesen, T. (2019) 'Queer abstraction (or how to be a pervert with no body): some notes toward a probability', *Mousse Magazine* <moussemagazine.it/queer-abstraction-travis-jeppesen-2019> (last accessed 8 February 2019).

Johnson, R. (2017) 'On the surface: the Deleuze-Stoicism encounter', in A. Greenstine and R. Johnson (eds), *Contemporary Encounters with Ancient Metaphysics*. Edinburgh: Edinburgh University Press, pp. 270–88.

Joyce, J. (1998) [1922] *Ulysses*. Oxford: World's Classics.

Joyce, J. (2002) [1939] *Finnegans Wake*. London: Penguin.

Jules-Rosette, B. (2007) *Josephine Baker, Art and Life*. Urbana: University of Illinois Press.

Juster, N. (2008) [1961] *The Phantom Tollbooth*. New York: Harper Collins.

Kandinsky, W. (2008) [1911] *Concerning the Spiritual in Art*, trans. M. Sadler. Portland: Floating Press.

Kant, I. (1987) [1790] *Critique of Judgement*, trans. W. Pluhar. Indianapolis: Hackett.

Kavanagh, D. (2004) 'Ocularcentrism and its others: a framework for metatheoretical analysis', *Organization Studies*, 25 (3): 445–64 <www.egosnet.org/os> (last accessed 2 October 2018).

Keeling, K. (2019) *Queer Times, Black Futures*. New York: NYU Press.

Kérchy, A. (2016) *Alice in Transmedia Wonderland: Curiouser and Curiouser New Forms of a Children's Classic*. Jefferson, NC: McFarland.

Khazaei, F. (2018) 'Grounds for dialogue: intersectionality and superdiversity', *Tijdschrift voor Genderstudies*, 21 (1): 1–5. DOI: 10.5117/TVGN2018.1.GEER, pp. 7–25 (last accessed 7 July 2018).

Kirby, V. (1997) *Telling Flesh: The Substance of the Corporeal*. London and New York: Routledge.

Kirby, V. (2011) *Quantum Anthropologies*. Durham, NC and London: Duke University Press.

Kirby, V. (2017) *What If Culture Was Nature All Along?* Edinburgh: Edinburgh University Press.

Klein, A.B. (1926) *Colour-Music: The Art of Light*. London: Lockwood & Son.

Klein, M. (1997) [1932] *The Psychoanalysis of Children*, trans. A. Strachey and H. A. Thorner. London: Vintage.

Kristeva, J. (1987) *Desire in Language: A Semiotic Approach to Literature and Art*, ed. Leon S. Roudiez, trans. Thomas Gora, Alice Jardine and Leon S. Roudiez. Oxford: Blackwell.

Kristeva, J. (1989) *Language: The Unknown*, trans. A. M. Menke. Hemel Hempstead: Harvester Wheatsheaf.

Lacan, J. (1997) [1986] *The Ethics of Psychoanalysis: The Seminar of Jacques Lacan, Book VII*, trans. D. Porter. London and New York: Norton.

Laing, R. D. (2005) [1970] *Knots*. New York: Routledge.
Latifić, A. (2018) 'The *Kino-Eye* Montage Procedure', *AM Journal*, 15: 23–33. DOI: 10.25038/am.v0i15.227 (last accessed 15 April 2019).
Le Guin, U. (1989) *Dancing at the Edge of the World: Thoughts on Words, Women, Places*. London: Victor Gollancz.
Le Guin, U. (2008) *Lavinia*. New York: Mariner.
Lecercle, J. and Riley, D. (2005) *The Force of Language*. Basingstoke: Palgrave Macmillan.
Lecercle, Jean-Jacques (1994) *Philosophy of Nonsense: The Intuitions of Victorian Nonsense Literature*. London: Routledge.
Levy, A. (1999) *Fruit of the Lemon*. London: Headline.
Lewis, M. J. (2012) 'Contingency, narrative, fiction: Vogler, Brenkman, Poe', *SubStance*, 41 (2): 99–118.
Liburd, T. (2016) 'Contemplation', *Cascadia Subduction Zone*, 6 (3) <http://www.thecsz.com/past-issues/csz-v6-n3-2016.pdf> (last accessed 15 April 2019).
Linnaeus, C. (1964) [1735] *Systema Naturae*. Nieuwkoop: B. de Graaf.
Lock, G. (1999) *Blutopia: Visions of the Future and Revisions of the Past in the Work of Sun Ra, Duke Ellington, and Anthony Braxton*. Durham, NC: Duke University Press.
Lorde, A. (1982) *Zami: A New Spelling of My Name*. Watertown, MA: Persephone Press.
Lorde, A. (1984) *Sister Outsider: Essays and Speeches*. Berkeley: Crossing Press.
Lorraine, T. (2011) *Deleuze and Guattari's Immanent Ethics*. New York: SUNY Press.
Luciano, D. and Roudeau, C. (2015) 'How the Earth feels: a conversation with Dana Luciano', *Transatlantica*, 1 (last accessed 22 May 2016).
Lury, C., Parisi, L. and Terranova, T. (2012) 'Introduction: the becoming-topological of culture, *Theory, Culture and Society*, 29 (4/5): 3–35. DOI: 10.1177/0263276412454552 (last accessed 31 October 2019).
Lusty, Natalya (2007) *Surrealism, Feminism, Psychoanalysis*. Aldershot and Burlington: Ashgate.
Lyotard, J.-F. (2011) [1971] *Discourse, Figure*, trans. A. Hudek and A. Lydon. Minneapolis: University of Minnesota Press.
McAra, C. (2011) 'Surrealism's curiosity: Lewis Carroll and the *femme-enfant*', *Papers of Surrealism*, 9 <http://www.surrealismcentre.ac.uk/papersofsurrealism/journal9/index.htm> (last accessed 7 February 2019).
McCabe, C. (2018) *Dedalus*. London: Henningham Family Press.
Mackay, R. (2011a) 'Introduction: three figures of contingency', in R. Mackay (ed.), *The Medium of Contingency*. Falmouth: Urbanomic.
Mackay, R. (ed.) (2011b) *The Medium of Contingency*. Falmouth: Urbanomic.

Malaspina, C. (2018) 'Transposition', in M. Schwab (ed.), *Transpositions: Aesthetico-Epistemic Operators in Artistic Research*. Leuven: Leuven University Press, pp. 225–44.

Margulis, L. and Sagan, D. (2007) *Dazzle Gradually: Reflections on the Nature of Nature*. White River Junction, VT: Chelsea Green.

Marx, K. (1970) [1932], *Economic and Philosophic Manuscripts of 1844*, trans. M. Milligan. London: Lawrence & Wishart.

Matějka, L. and K. Pomorska (eds) (1971) *Readings in Russian Poetics: Formalist and Structuralist Views*. Cambridge, MA and London: MIT Press.

Meillassoux, Q. (2006) *After Finitude: An Essay on the Necessity of Contingency*, trans. R. Brassier. London and New York: Continuum.

Merleau-Ponty, M. (2002) [1945] *Phenomenology of Perception*, trans. C. Smith. London and New York: Routledge.

Miller, J. H. (1992) *Ariadne's Thread: Story Lines*. New Haven: Yale University Press.

Miller, M. (2018) *Circe*. London: Bloomsbury.

Miller, N. K. (ed.) (1986b) *The Poetics of Gender*. New York: Columbia University Press

Miller, N. K. (1986a) 'Arachnologies: the woman, the text, and the critic', in N. K. Miller (ed.), *The Poetics of Gender*. New York: Columbia University Press, pp. 270–95.

Minh-ha, T. (1988) 'Not you/like you: post-colonial women and the interlocking question of identity and difference', *Inscriptions*, Special Issue 'Feminism and the Critique of Colonial Discourse', 34 <http://culturalstudies.ucsc.edu/inscriptions/volume-34/trinh-t-minh-ha> (last accessed 4 November 2018).

Mitchell, K. (2013) 'Queer metamorphoses: *girl meets boy* and the futures of queer fiction', in M. Germanà and E. Horton (eds), *Ali Smith: Contemporary Critical Perspectives*. London: Bloomsbury, pp. 61–74.

Mitchell, S. (2000) *Relationality: From Attachment to Intersubjectivity*. Burlingame, CA: Analytic Press.

Monae, J. (2015) Interview with *Blues and Soul*. Available at <http://www.bluesandsoul.com/feature/554/janelle_monae_funky_sensation/> (last accessed 15 April 2019).

Monod, J. (1972) *Chance and Necessity: An Essay on the Natural Philosophy of Modern Biology*, trans. A. Wainhouse. New York: Vintage.

Moses, B. (ed.) (2018) *Poems by the Sea*. New York: Windmill Books.

Muecke, S. (2002) 'The Fall: Fictocritical Writing', *Parallax*, 8 (4): 108–12.

Naiman, E. (1998) Shklovsky's dog and Mulvey's pleasure: the secret life of defamiliarization', *Comparative Literature*, 50 (4): 345–50. DOI: 10.2307/1771528 (last accessed 15 April 2019).

Newton, I. (1979) [1730] *Opticks: A Treatise of the Reflections, Refractions, Inflections and Colours of Light*. New York: Dover.

Nocek, S. M. (2016) '"Dangerously small things": response to Iris van der Tuin', *Australian Feminist Studies*, 31 (89): 267–75. DOI: 1080/08164649.2016.125439 (last accessed 20 August 2019).

O'Brien, F. (1993) [1967] *The Third Policeman*. London: Flamingo.

O'Sullivan, S. (2014) 'Art practice as fictioning (or, myth-science)', *diakron* <https://www.simonosullivan.net/articles/art-practice-as-fictioning-or-myth-science.pdf> (last accessed 1 April 2020).

O'Sullivan, S. (2016), 'Myth-science and the fictioning of reality', *Paragrana*, 25 (2): 80–93.

Ogden, C. K. and Richards. I. A. (2001) [1923] *The Meaning of Meaning*. Abingdon and New York: Routledge.

On, B. (1994) *Engendering Origins: Critical Feminist Readings in Plato and Aristotle*. Albany: SUNY Press.

Ovid (2008) [8 AD], *Metamorphoses*, trans. A. Melville. Oxford: Oxford University Press.

Pallasmaa, J. (2012) *The Eyes of the Skin: Architecture and the Senses*. Chichester: Wiley.

Palmer, H. (2014) *Deleuze and Futurism: A Manifesto for Nonsense*. London: Bloomsbury.

Palmer, H. and Panayotov, S. (2016) 'Transversality', *New Materialism Almanac* <https://newmaterialism.eu/almanac/t/transversality.html> (last accessed 1 April 2020).

Parisi, L. (2017) 'Automate sex: xenofeminism, hyperstition and alienation', in H. Gunkel, A. Hameed and S. O'Sullivan (eds), *Futures and Fictions*. London: Repeater, pp. 213–29.

Paterson, M. (2007) *The Senses of Touch: Haptics, Affects and Technologies*. Oxford and New York: Berg.

Penfield, Wilder (1950) *The Cerebral Cortex of Man: A Clinical Study of Localization of Function*. New York: Macmillan.

Pessoa, F. (2002) *The Selected Prose of Fernando Pessoa*, ed. and trans. R. Zenith. New York: Grove Press.

Philips, R. (ed.) (2015) *Black Quantum Futurism: Theory and Practice*, Philadelphia: Afrofuturist Affair/Future Sciences Books.

Philips, Robert (ed.) (1971) *Aspects of Alice: Lewis Carroll's Dreamchild as seen through the Critics' Looking Glasses 1865–1971*. New York: Vanguard Press.

Pliny the Elder (2004) [c.1 AD], *Natural History*, trans. John F. Healy. London: Penguin.

Pogoza, M. (photography) and Jennings, H. (words) (2016) 'Uchronia'. Available at <http://nataal.com/uchronia/> (last accessed 27 May 2018).

Pogoza, M. and Kirkley, C. (2015) 'Uchronia: imagining an alternate history where a Malian emperor discovered America', *Vice*, September, available at <https://www.vice.com/en_uk/article/zng5be/uchronia-0000744-v22n9> (last accessed 28 May 2018).

Probyn, E. (1993) *Sexing the Self: Gendered Positions in Cultural Studies*. London: Routledge.

Provost, K. (1995) 'Becoming Afrekete: the trickster in the work of Audre Lorde', *MELIUS*, 20 (4): 45–59. DOI: https://www.jstor.org/stable/467889 (last accessed 31 October 2019).

Puar, J. (2007) *Terrorist Assemblages: Homonationalism in Queer Times*. Durham, NC and London: Duke University Press.

Puar, J. (2012) '"I would rather be a cyborg than a goddess": becoming-intersectional in assembage theory', *philoSOPHIA*, 2 (1): 49–66. DOI: muse.jhu.edu/article/486621 (last accessed 20 September 2018).

Ra, S. (2005) *The Immeasurable Equation: The Collected Poetry and Prose*, ed. J. L. Wolf and H. Geerken. Stuttgart: Waitawhile.

Raha, N. (2015) 'The limits of trans liberalism', *versobooks.com* (blog) <www.versobooks.com/blogs/2245-the-limits-of-trans-liberalism-by-nat-raha> (last accessed 19 February 2019).

Raha, N. (2017) 'Against the day: transfeminine brokenness, radical transfeminism', *South Atlantic Quarterly*, 116 (3): 632–46. DOI: 10.1215/00382876-3961754 (last accessed 19 February 2019).

Raha, N. (2018) 'De/composition', in I. Waidner (ed.), *Liberating the Canon: An Anthology of Innovative Literature*. London: Dostoevsky Wannabe, pp. 198–202.

Ramirez, M. D. and Oakley, T. H. (2015) 'Eye-independent, light-activated chromatophore expansion (LACE) and expression of phototransduction genes in the skin of *Octopus bimaculoides*', *Journal of Experimental Biology*. DOI: 10.1242/jeb.110908 (last accessed 3 January 2018).

Rawlings, L. (2007) *Mutha' Is Half A Word: Intersections of Folklore, Vernacular, Myth, and Queerness in Black Female Culture*. Columbus: Ohio State University Press.

Renouvier, C. (2018) [1876] *Uchronie (l'Utopie dans l'histoire: esquisse historique apocryphe du développement de la civilisation européene tel qu'il n'a pas été tel qu'il aurait pu être)*. Sacramento: Creative Media Partners.

Rich, A. (1972) 'When we dead awaken: writing as re-vision', *College English*, 34 (1): 18–30. DOI: http://www.jstor.org/stable/375215 (last accessed 14 January 2018).

Riley, D. (2005) *Impersonal Passion: Language as Affect*. Durham, NC and London: Duke University Press.

Rimbaud, A. (1966) [1871] *Complete Works, Selected Letters*, trans. W. Fowlie. Chicago and London: University of Chicago Press.

Robinson, D. (2008) *Estrangement and the Somatics of Literature: Tolstoy, Shklovsky, Brecht*. Baltimore: Johns Hopkins University Press.

Rogowska-Stangret, M. (2017) 'Corpor(e)al cartographies of new materialism: meeting the elsewhere halfway', *Minnesota Review*, 88: Special Focus: New Materialist Genealogies. DOI: 10.1215/00265667-3786707.

Ryan, D. (2013) *Virginia Woolf and the Materiality of Theory: Sex, Animal, Life*. Edinburgh: Edinburgh University Press.

Samatar, S. (2015) 'The Noble Torturer', Bluestockings Magazine, available at <http://bluestockingsmag.com/2015/07/28/the-noble-torturer> (last accessed 15 April 2019).

Samatar, S. (2016) 'Notes toward a theory of quantum blackness', *Strange Horizons*, available at <http://strangehorizons.com/poetry/notes-toward-a-theory-of-quantum-blackness/> (last accessed 14 April 2019).

Sandford, S. (2010) *Plato and Sex*. Malden, MA and Cambridge: Polity.

Saussure, F. de (2011) [1916] *Course in General Linguistics*, trans. W. Baskin, ed. P. Meisel and H. Saussy. Chichester: Columbia University Press.

Schapiro, B. A. (1994) *Literature and the Relational Self*. London and New York: New York University Press.

Schie, H. V. (2008) *Pataphor*. Rotterdam: Veenman.

Schwab, M. (ed.) (2018) *Transpositions: Aesthetico-Epistemic Operators in Artistic Research*. Leuven: Leuven University Press.

Sedgwick, E. (2003) *Touching Feeling: Affect, Pedagogy, Performativity*. Durham, NC and London: Duke University Press.

Sellars, J. (2006) *Stoicism*. Chesham: Acumen.

Serres, M. (1982) *Hermes: Literature, Science, Philosophy*, ed. J. V. Harari and D. F. Bell. Baltimore: Johns Hopkins University Press.

Serres, M. (2016) [1985] *The Five Senses: A Philosophy of Mingled Bodies*, trans. M. Sankey and P. Cowley. London and New York: Bloomsbury.

Serres, M. with Latour, B. (1995) [1990] *Conversations on Science, Culture, and Time*, trans. R. Lapidus. Ann Arbor: University of Michigan Press.

Shawl, N. (2016) *Everfair*. New York: Tor.

Shklovsky, V. (1983) [1925] *O teorii prozy*. Moscow: Sovetskii Pisatel'.

Shklovsky, V. (1998) [1925] *Theory of Prose*, trans. B. Sher. Normal: Dalkey Archive Press.

Shklovsky, V. (2005) [1923] *Knight's Move*, trans. R. Sheldon. Normal and London: Dalkey Archive Press.

Shklovsky, V. (2017) *Viktor Shklovsky: A Reader*, trans. and ed. A. Berlina. London and New York: Bloomsbury.

Shomura, C. (2017) 'Exploring the promise of new materialisms', *Lateral: Journal of the Cultural Studies Association*, 6 (1). DOI: 10.25158/L6.1.10 (last accessed 8 April 2019).

Simpkins, R. (2016) 'Trans*feminist Intersections', *TSQ*, 3 (1–2): 228–34. DOI: 10.1215/23289252-3334427 (last accessed 11 February 2019).

Sinclair, J. (2010) 'It knocks on everybody's door', in J. Sinclair (ed.), *Sun Ra: Interviews and Essays*. London: Headpress, pp. 19–30.

Sinclair, J. (ed.) (2010) *Sun Ra: Interviews and Essays*. London: Headpress.

Sissel Hoel, A. and van der Tuin, I. (2013) 'The ontological force of technicity: reading Cassirer and Simondon diffractively', *Philosophy and Technology*, 26: 187–202. DOI 10.1007/s13347-012-0092-5 (last accessed 14 January 2017).

Smith, A. (2007) *Girl Meets Boy*. Edinburgh: Canongate.

Spillers, H. (1982) 'Formalism comes to Harlem', *Black American Literature Forum*, 16 (2): 58–63.

Spillers, H. (1985) 'Interstices: a drama of small words', in *Pleasure and Danger: Exploring Female Sexuality*, ed. C. Vance. Boston and London: Routledge & Kegan Paul, pp. 73–100.

Stein, G. (1922) *Geography and Plays*. Boston: Four Seas.

Stein, G. (1969) [1947] *Four in America*. New York: Books for Libraries Press.

Stein, G. (2004) [1926] *Look at me now and here I am: Selected Works 1911–1945*. London and Chester Springs: Peter Owen

Steinbock, E., Szczygielska, M. and Wagner, A. (2017) 'Thinking linking', *Angelaki*, 22 (2): 1–10. DOI: 10.1080/0969725X.2017.1322801 (last accessed 11 February 2019).

Steingraber, S. (2001) *Having Faith: An Ecologist's Journey to Motherhood*. Cambridge: Perseus.

Stockton, K. B. (2015) 'Reading as kissing, sex with ideas: "Lesbian barebacking"?' *LA Review of Books* <https://v2.lareviewofbooks.org/article/reading-kissing-sex-ideas-lesbian-barebacking/> (last accessed 8 April 2019).

Stockton, K. B. (2019) *Avidly Reads Making Out*. New York: NYU Press.

Stryker, S. (2008) 'Dungeon intimacies: the poetics of transsexual sadomasochism', *Parallax*, 14 (1): 36–47. DOI: 10.1080/13534640701781362 (last accessed 12 November 2018).

Stubbs, P. (2014) 'Art project at East London train station tweets speculative headlines to affect stock market algorithms. No, really', available at <https://www.artslant.com/lon/articles/show/40931> (last accessed 28 May 2018).

Taleb, N. N. (2007) *The Black Swan: The Impact of the Highly Improbable*. New York: Random House.

Tamboukou, M. (2010) *In the Fold between Power and Desire: Women Artists' Narratives*. Newcastle: Cambridge Scholars.

Tempest, K. (2014) *Hold Your Own*. London: Picador.

Theory, F. (2016) 'The ass menagerie: the oinking, yipping, sniffing Noah's Ark of gay New York', *The Voice*, 22 June <https://www.villagevoice.

com/2016/06/22/the-ass-menagerie-the-oinking-yipping-sniffing-noahs-ark-of-gay-new-york/> (last accessed 6 April 2019).

Thomson, R. G. (2017) [1997] *Extraordinary Bodies: Figuring Physical Disability in American Culture and Literature*, 20th edn. New York: Columbia University Press.

Tomkis, T. [1604–15] *Lingua, or, The combat of the tongue, and the five senses for superiority*. London: George Eld.

Tompkins, K. (2016) 'On the limits and promise of new materialist philosophy', *Lateral: Journal of the Cultural Studies Association*, 5 (1). DOI: 10.25158/L5.1.8 (last accessed 15 April 2019).

Tompkins, K. (2017) 'Crude matter, queer form', *ASAP/Journal*, 2 (2): 264–8. DOI: <https://doi.org/10.1353/asa.2017.0042> (last accessed 19 February 2019).

Trotsky, L. (2005) [1924] *Literature and Revolution*, ed. W. Keach, trans. R. Strunsky. Chicago: Haymarket Books.

Valéry, P. (1980) 'Remarks on poetry', in *Symbolism: An Anthology*, ed. T. G. West. London: Methuen, pp. 50–2.

van der Tuin, I. (2011) '"A different starting point, a different metaphysics": Reading Bergson and Barad diffractively'. *Hypatia: A Journal of Feminist Philosophy*, 26 (1): 22–42. DOI: 10.1111/j.1527-2001.2010.01114.x (last accessed 14 April 2019).

van der Tuin, I. (2014a) '"Without an analytical divorce from the total environment": advancing a philosophy of the humanities by reading Snow and Whitehead diffractively', *Humanities*, 3: 244–63. DOI: 10.3390/h3020244 (last accessed 15 April 2019).

van der Tuin, I. (2014b) 'Diffraction as a methology for feminist onto-epistemology: on encountering Chantal Chawaf and posthuman interpellation', *Parallax Special Issue 'Diffracted Worlds – Diffractive Readings': Onto-Epistemologies and the Critical Humanities*, ed. Birgit M. Kaiser and Kathrin Thriele, 20 (3): 231–44. DOI: 10.1080/13534645.2014.927631 (last accessed 15 April 2019).

van der Tuin, I. (2015) *Generational Feminism*. Lanham, MD: Lexington.

van der Tuin, I. and Dolphijn, R. (2010) 'The Transversality of New Materialism', *Women: A Cultural Review*.

Van Herk, A. (1986) *No Fixed Address: An Amorous Journey*. London: Virago.

van Midde, M., Virtù, L. V. and Cielemęcka, O. (2018) 'Editorial – trans materialities', *Graduate Journal of Social Science Studies*, 14 (2): 4–9.

Vance, C. (ed.) (1985) *Pleasure and Danger: Exploring Female Sexuality*. Boston: Routledge & Kegan Paul.

Vanderbeke, D. (1998) 'Man into woman into swine: transformations in Joyce's *Ulysses* and the *Odyssey*', *Papers on Joyce*, 4: 61–6 (last accessed 15 April 2019).

Varzi, A. (1998) 'Basic Problems of Meterotopology', in N. Guarino (ed.), *Formal Ontology in Information Systems*. Amsterdam: IOS Press, pp. 29–38.

Venn, C. (2010) 'Individuation, relationality, affect: rethinking the human in relation to the living', *Body & Society*, 16 (1): 129–61.

Vertovec, S. (2007) 'Super-diversity and its implications', *Ethnic and Racial Studies*, 30 (6): 1024–54. DOI: 10.1080/01419870701599465 (last accessed 23 January 2019).

Waidner, I. (2017) *Gaudy Bauble*. London: Dostoevsky Wannabe.

Waidner, I. (ed.) (2018) *Liberating the Canon: An Anthology of Innovative Literature*. London: Dostoevsky Wannabe.

Warner, M. (2002) 'Publics and counterpublics', *Quarterly Journal of Speech*, 88 (4): 413–25. DOI: muse.jhu.edu/article/26277 (last accessed 14 April 2019).

Warner, M. (2003) *Signs and Wonders: Essays on Literature and Culture*. London: Chatto & Windus.

Wasser, A. (2017) 'How do we recognise problems?' *Deleuze Studies*, 11 (1): 48–67. DOI: 10.3366/dls.2017.0251 (last accessed 23 July 2018).

Waugh, L. (1976) *Roman Jakobson's Science of Language*. Lisse: Peter de Ridder Press.

Waugh, L. (1980) 'The poetic function in the theory of Roman Jakobson', *Poetics Today*, 2:1a, Roman Jakobson: Language and Poetry, pp. 57–82. DOI: 10.2307/1772352 (last accessed 30 October 2018).

West, T. G. (ed.) (1980) *Symbolism: An Anthology*. London: Methuen.

Williams, J. (2015) *A Process Philosophy of Signs*. Edinburgh: Edinburgh University Press.

Wilson, E. (2015) *Gut Feminism*. Durham, NC and London: Duke University Press.

Winnicott, D. W. (2005) *Playing and Reality*. London and New York: Routledge.

Winterson, J. (1997) *Gut Symmetries*. New York: Albert Knopf.

Winterson, J. (2014) [1992] *Written on the Body*. London: Vintage.

Witt, C. (1998) 'Form, normativity, and gender in Aristotle: a feminist perspective', in *Feminist Interpretations of Aristotle*, ed. C. A. Freeland. State College: Pennsylvania State University Press, pp. 118–37.

Wittgenstein, L. (1980) *Culture and Value*, trans. P. Winch. Oxford: Blackwell.

Wittig, M. (1985) [1969] *Les Guérillères*, trans. D. le Vay. Boston: Beacon Press.

Womack, Y. L. (2013) *Afrofuturism: The World of Black Sci-Fi and Fantasy Culture*. Chicago: Lawrence Hill Books.

Woolf, V. [1929] 'Lewis Carroll', in R. Philips (ed.), *Aspects of Alice: Lewis Carroll's Dreamchild as seen through the Critics' Looking Glasses 1865–1971*. New York: Vanguard Press, pp. 47–9.

Yarnall, J. (1994) *Transformations of Circe*. Urbana and Chicago: University of Illinois Press.

Yeats, W. B. (1963) [1923] *Selected Poetry*, ed. A. Norman Jeffares. London: Macmillan.

Zajko, W. and Leonard, M. (eds) (2006) *Laughing with Medusa: Classical Myth and Feminist Thought*. Oxford: Oxford University Press.

Filmography

Barbarella, film, directed by Roger Vadim. USA: Dino de Laurentiis Cinematografica, Marianne Productions, 1968.

Black Panther, film, directed by Ryan Coogler. USA: Marvel Studios, 2018.

La Sirène des Tropiques, film, directed by Mario Nalpas and Henri Étiévant. France, 1927.

Mothership Connection, film, directed by John Akomfrah. London: BFI, 1995.

Space Is the Place, film, directed by John Coney. Berkeley: North American Star System, 1974.

Discography

Chaminade, C. *Étude romantique*, Op. 132 (1909)

Joplin, S. *Maple Leaf Rag* (1899)

Scriabin, A. *Prometheus: The Poem of Fire*, Op. 60 (1910)

Lineography

(line fragments from *Sirens* section in Chapter 4)

A wail awave upon the veil – James Joyce, *Ulysses* (1922)

Had we but world enough and time; Vaster than empires and more slow; My vegetable love – Andrew Marvell, 'To His Coy Mistress' (1681)

Move closer / Set my soul on fire – Ash, 'Goldfinger', *1977* (1996)

Do not listen to a word I say / Just listen to what I can keep silent – Manic Street Preachers, 'Motorcycle Emptiness', *Generation Terrorists* (1992)

Since each of us was several, we were already quite a crowd – Gilles Deleuze and Félix Guattari, *A Thousand Plateaus* (1980)

Batter my heart – John Donne, 'Holy Sonnet 14', *Holy Sonnets* (1633)

Done because we are too menny – Thomas Hardy, *Jude the Obscure* (1895)

It barks at no one else but me / Like it's seen a ghost – Radiohead, 'The Tourist', *OK Computer* (1997)

How you move / The way you bust the clouds; Sticky as lips / licky as trips – The Cure, 'High', *Wish* (1992)

In this white wave / In this silence I believe – Delerium, 'Silence', *Poem* (2000)

How things bind and blend together – John Ruskin, *Praeterita* (1885)

My baby does K all day – Benoit & Sergio, Walk & Talk (2011)

Claritas is quidditas – James Joyce, *Stephen Hero* (1944)

The apples fermented / Inside the lamented / Cider inside her insides – Cider limerick, anon.

The lonesome organ grinder cries / The silver saxophones say I – Bob Dylan, 'I Want You', *Blonde on Blonde* (1966)

Index

ability
  dis/ability, 19
  disability, 21
  as identity category, 3, 80
accelerationism, 7, 8
Acker, Kathy, 1, 32, 42–3, 77–9, 180–1
aesthesis, 7, 157, 166
Afrekete, 32, 68, 85–7, 90, 168, 178
Afrofuturism, 96, 100–5, 143
Ahmed, Sara, 3, 14–18, 31, 47, 87, 141, 146
Alabanza, Travis, 3, 13, 18–19, 32, 45–7, 182
Alice (in Wonderland), 116, 128–39
alienation, 7–9, 29
Anzaldúa, Gloria, 59–60, 178
Arachne, 32, 68, 70–2, 90
Ariadne, 32, 68, 70–1, 90
assemblage, 55, 58, 64, 149
Atwood, Margaret, 32, 72–4, 75, 80, 100–1, 170
Avenassian, Armen, 32, 43, 53–5
axis, axes, 21–2, 32–3, 35–64, 76, 148

Baker, Josephine, 159–61
Barad, Karen, 21–6, 38, 41, 50, 58–62, 87, 89, 99, 101, 110, 112, 122, 142–3
Bataille, Georges, 30, 70
Black Quantum Futurism Collective (BQFC), 3, 104, 150
Blackpool, 33–4, 155–67, 171–87

Bohr, Niels, 50, 60, 99
boycunt *see* cunt
Braidotti, Rosi, 5–6, 10, 17, 20, 22–3, 51–2, 57, 68–70, 72, 89, 98, 146–7
Bühlmann, Vera, 22, 50–1

Callisto, 68, 82–4, 90
Carroll, Lewis, 92, 116, 129–39
Carter, Angela, 137–8
cephalopods, 126–7, 158
Chen, Mel Y, 16–24
Circe, 32, 43, 68, 80–2, 90, 186
Cixous, Hélène, 23, 27, 32, 43, 65, 80, 82, 87–8
class, 15, 19, 61–2, 73, 80, 144, 174
Colebrook, Claire, 23, 26–7, 41
contingency, 77, 105, 108–11
crip, 21
cunt
  Bloom as, 82
  boycunt, 62–4, 81, 122
  cuntpart, 64
  cuntstruck, 161
  rose as, 43
  sowcunt, 81

Daly, Mary, 85, 151–2
de Freitas, Elizabeth, 10, 108
defamiliarisation, 1–18, 23, 26–7, 31, 35–6, 42, 46–7, 55–6, 64, 66–9, 77–8, 88–90, 96, 116, 124–5, 141, 168–70

deform, 32, 35, 52, 66–7, 73, 78, 116, 120–2, 139, 168–9
deformalism *see* formalism
deformation, 33, 66–8, 115, 119–25, 140, 151, 168–9
Deleuze, Gilles, 5, 12, 21, 32, 55–60, 63, 69–70, 76, 88, 107, 128–39, 144, 149
Derrida, Jacques, 6, 16, 25–6, 36, 41, 59
diachrony, 12, 41, 44–7, 54–5, 120, 129
dildo, 95–6
disability *see* ability
doily, 40, 42–3, 51
Donne, John, 47, 95, 125, 162
dualism, 10, 12, 20, 22, 36, 38, 50, 53, 88, 104, 122, 125, 138, 144, 147, 150
dystopia, 13, 93–5, 98, 100–1

Eades, Quinn, 3, 32, 64
Eliot, George, 8–11, 74
Eliot, T. S., 111, 162
enstrangement, 4, 7
Eshun, Kodwo, 108, 112–14
estrangement, 4–10, 13–16, 67, 87, 96, 141, 157, 169
Euler, Leonhard, 121, 163
Eurydice, 32, 42–3, 68, 76–8, 90

feminism, 1–34, 35–9, 48, 56–62, 65–91, 97, 100, 106, 125, 133, 138, 144, 146, 151, 170, 186
fictioning, 98, 106–8
fictocriticism, 92–4
Field, The, 33, 91–2, 98, 107–8, 114
formalism
  and deformalism, 27–31, 52, 66
  and retroformalism, 6
  Russian formalism, 5–13, 15, 17–18, 24, 29, 36, 44, 49, 66

Furman, Ezra, 13, 48, 168
Futurrhythmachinic Discontinuum, 108, 114

Gatens, Moira, 10–11, 151
golem, 137–9
Grosz, Elizabeth, 33, 61, 132, 136–8, 144, 146
Guattari, Félix, 12, 14, 20, 29, 32, 55–9, 69–70, 107, 131–9, 147, 149

haptics, 2, 108, 116, 126–8, 139–42
Haraway, Donna, 10, 33, 59, 94, 96–101, 105–6, 112–14, 125–7, 144
Hayward, Eva, 21, 70, 116, 127–8
H.D., 32, 43, 65, 75–7
Hennig, Anke, 32, 43, 52–5
hermunculus, 128, 139
heteronym, 33, 72, 91–114
homeomorphism, 22
homeorrhesis, 49, 51
homonym, 26–7, 33, 62, 71, 74, 91–114, 142
homunculus, 33, 137–9
hylomorphism, 28

intersectionality, 1, 20, 22, 35–9, 49, 57–62, 85–6, 91, 143, 146
intersex, 47, 60
interstitium, 33, 86, 115–16, 128–9, 139, 142–3, 153, 156
intra-activity, 22, 58–62, 99, 142–3
intra-sectionality, 58–62
intra-sensory, 33, 127
invariance, 30, 35–7, 41, 44, 49–52, 55, 83
invariant, 12, 28–9, 37, 41, 49, 55, 110, 121, 140, 142, 159

Irigaray, Luce, 130, 178–80
isomorphism, 22, 25, 120

Joyce, James, 30, 34, 81–2, 169, 170

Kandinsky, Wassily, 117
Kirby, Vicki, 6, 23–5, 36–7, 41–2
Kirkley, Christopher, 102
Klein, Melanie, 131–2
Klein bottle, 122
Kristeva, Julia, 23, 25, 39, 180

Laboratory of Speculative Sociology, 108
Laboria Cuboniks, 8, 106
Lacan, Jacques, 33, 48, 116, 122
Laing, R. D., 122–3
Lavinia, 32, 68, 79–80, 89–90
Le Guin, Ursula, 32, 79–80, 91, 111–13, 144
Lingua, 118–19, 123
logic
  of the 'as', 62–4
  of the doily, 43, 51
  of penetrating/penetrated, 75
Lorde, Audre, 2–3, 11, 28–9, 38, 85–7, 151, 168

Marxism, 4, 7, 29
materiality
  of language, 24–5, 95
  material-discursive, 1, 35, 59–62, 98, 169
  material-semiotic, 1, 59, 96–7, 105–10
matter
  halfsmatterings, 114
  matter-realisation, 18, 33, 98
  as a noun, 1, 14, 19–28, 30, 35, 41–2, 50, 59, 62, 77–8, 89, 91–2, 99

spacetimemattering, 100
  as a verb, 1, 2, 21–7, 36, 41, 50, 58, 68, 91–2, 95–6, 99, 109, 112
MawuLisa, 85
Medusa, 32, 68, 80, 88, 90
Merleau-Ponty, Maurice, 139
Minh-Ha, Trinh, 59–60, 97
Möbius strip, 33, 121–4, 135–6, 148
Monáe, Janelle, 105
Muecke, Steven, 33, 43, 67, 92–3

non-binary, 47–8

O'Brien, Flann, 105, 107–8
octopus, 98, 116, 126–7, 149, 158–9
ocularcentrism, 118, 128, 125–6
omnium, 105, 107
organ grinder, 167
organgrinding, 172
organism, 28, 47, 51, 100, 124, 148
organs
  body without, 137
  of the body, 115, 132, 139
  as musical instruments, 33, 116–17, 155–67
  perception as, 6
  of perception, 15, 33, 127–8, 140
  of the sea, 167
  sexual organ, 153
orgasm, 153, 167, 177
Orgasmatron, 167
O'Sullivan, Simon, 33, 69, 106

Palmer, Helen, 5, 20–1, 29, 32, 41, 44–5, 56, 63, 69, 129, 133, 135–6, 147
paradigm, 22–3, 35–45, 55–6, 63, 65, 91, 147, 151

Penelope, 32, 65–6, 68, 71, 72–4, 170
perception
  organ of *see* organs
  shift in, 1–2, 14–17
personae, 32–3, 66–70
phenomenology, 3, 15–18, 139–41
Phillips, Rasheedah, 104, 150
Pogoza, Maciek, 102
posthuman, 5–6, 10, 23, 26, 50, 58–9, 84, 89, 99
poststructuralism, 36
psychoanalysis, 87, 122, 124, 130–9
publics, 32–3, 67–70, 72, 87–90

quantum
  anthropologies, 6, 36
  blackness, 103–5
  event, 108
  field theory, 142–3
  mechanics, 37–8, 104, 110
  physics, 50, 150
  reality, 143, 150
  theory of touching, 142
queer, 1–9, 13–19, 21–6, 30–5, 38–42, 46–50, 57, 60–70, 75–6, 78, 82–3, 88–91, 96, 116, 120, 136, 139, 141–3, 157, 168–9, 186

Ra, Sun, 103, 112
race, 3, 14–15, 19, 36, 38, 61, 87, 107, 141, 144, 150
Raha, Nat, 3, 19
retroformalism *see* formalism
roses, 39, 42–3, 47, 51–5, 65, 92, 117, 120, 168

Samatar, Sofia, 3, 103–4, 123–4
Saussure, Ferdinand de, 12, 25, 36–52, 117, 129
science fiction, 101

senses, 7, 9–10, 18, 21, 74, 115–28, 140, 156, 158–70
sensorium, 33, 115, 127
sensory
  entanglement, 142, 156
  manifold, 158
  multi-, 125, 142, 156
  poly-, 113, 142, 167
  significance of, 1, 7, 9, 33, 115–19, 125–8, 138–40, 162, 169
Serres, Michel, 22, 32–3, 43, 49–52, 116, 119–20, 128, 141–2
Shawl, Nisi, 104–5
sirens, 32, 116, 148, 155–67
skin, 2, 102, 115, 119–28, 132, 136, 142, 153–67
Smith, Ali, 32, 74–6, 113
sowcunt *see* cunt
speculative fabulation, 33, 39, 63, 87, 92–3, 98–100, 106, 108
speculative ontology of language, 54
speculative process philosophy, 52
speculative sign-making, 54
speculative spectrum, 100
speculative taxonomies, 30, 33, 116–17, 143–54, 157
speculative topoi, 100–1, 109
speculative vitalism, 107
Spinoza, Benedict de, 10–11, 135, 138
spit, 30–1, 70, 181
Stein, Gertrude, 32, 38, 42–3, 51, 54, 62–4
Stockton, Kathryn Bond, 95–6
Stoics, 27, 57, 129–36, 174
superdiversity, 61, 143, 146
surface, 5, 33, 53, 96, 102, 115–43, 153–67, 173, 185
sympoiesis, 10
synaesthesia, 33, 115–20, 128, 156

synaesthesis, 177
synchrony, 12, 37, 41, 44–7, 52–5, 120, 129
syntagm, 35–44, 56, 63, 76, 168
syntax, 27
synvariance, 32–3, 35–64, 69, 76, 90, 120, 168–9

taxonomy
  alternative, 30
  arbitrary, 148
  bestial, 149
  of colours, 54
  defamiliarisation of, 116
  detaxonomy, 30
  of flora and fauna, 54, 120, 149
  historical, 146, 149
  linguistic, 151
  of SF, 144
  shapes of, 145
  speculative *see* speculative
  speculexical, 152
  of taxonomies, 144
  of wine, 149
Tempest, Kate, 123
Terrapolis, 96–100, 112–14
Tomkis, Thomas, 118–19
Tompkins, Kyla Wazana, 30, 31, 118

topology, 20, 22, 33, 49–54, 61–2, 67, 70, 78, 99, 115–67
toposophy, 144, 160
torus, 121–2
trans*, 18–20, 48, 78, 80, 127, 143, 181
transfeminism, 19
transmaterialities, 143, 160
transposition, 128
tranversality, 6, 10, 20, 29, 93, 143–50, 157, 164

uchronia, 33, 87, 93, 98–102
utopia, 13, 33, 48, 67, 93, 98–109

van der Tuin, Iris, 8, 20–3, 59, 147
variance, 12, 15, 18–20, 28, 44, 49–52, 83
Verfremdung, 7–8

whorls, 143, 154–9
woke, 11–12
Woolf, Virginia, 38, 70–1, 87, 133–4, 170
wor(l)ding, 33, 91–114, 144

xenofeminism, 8, 106

Zami, 85–7

EU representative:
Easy Access System Europe
Mustamäe tee 50, 10621 Tallinn, Estonia
Gpsr.requests@easproject.com

www.ingramcontent.com/pod-product-compliance
Lightning Source LLC
Chambersburg PA
CBHW082141230426

43672CB00016B/2931